Doklam Standoff Implications for India, China and Bhutan

Doklam Standoff Implications for India, China and Bhutan

Dr. S. Chandra

PRASHANT PUBLISHING HOUSE
DELHI-110094

Published by :
PRASHANT PUBLISHING HOUSE
C-34, 28 Foota Road, Gali-3,
West Karwal Nagar, Delhi-110094
Phone : 011-22963970, Mob. : 9810396373, 8826258746
e-mail.: prashantpublishinghouse@gmail.com

Doklam Standoff Implications for India, China and Bhutan

First Published 2020

ISBN : 978-93-88526-25-8

PRINTED IN INDIA
Published by Mr. R.K. Jha M/s Prashant Publishing House and Published at H.S. Offset House Press, Delhi.

Preface

The Current Doklam crisis between India and China could be perceived as a Geopolitical theatre between India and China, embodying severe security implications on India, and a threat to Eurasian stability.

Whatever the logic for Doklam, that confrontation has exacerbated Thimphu's concerns about getting sucked into a Sino-Indian conflict. Bhutanese elites, and increasingly the public, believe they should settle their border with China, not tack a settlement onto India's more intractable dispute. Beijing has offered Thimphu a strategic swap, in which China would concede to Bhutan disputed territory in the north, in exchange for Doklam. New Delhi, however, firmly discourages conceding Doklam to China.

India has discouraged Bhutan from opening diplomatic relations with other countries, particularly China, encouraging it instead to conduct diplomatic relations through its embassy in New Delhi. But now, with China outpacing India economically and militarily and showing its power through incidents like Doklam, Bhutan's old elites and new, populist politicians increasingly worry about having hitched their wagon to the wrong horse. There is also a popular aspiration across Bhutan to emerge from India's shadow and assert sovereignty more tangibly. New Delhi has not handled this aspiration with sophistication and sensitivity.

India's concerns emanated from Chinese action to change the status quo on the ground by building a road in violation of China's existing understanding with both India and Bhutan. This had implications for the determination of the tri-junction point demarcating India, China and Bhutan — India says it is at Batang la while Chinese claim it to be at Gymochen — and the alignment of the India-China boundary in the Sikkim sector. India was working in close coordination with Bhutan at various levels, and was equally concerned about the violation of its 1988 and 1998 agreements with China; these do not allow any change in status quo while boundary negotiations were in progress.

China has been getting away for far too long. Its bullying of smaller neighbors, in this case Bhutan, must be leveraged politically to showcase China's bullying tactics. India cannot and should not keep silent on this issue. The issue resonates favorably in most parts of the globe and there is no reason why India and Bhutan cannot call for a security council meeting, where the issue will not get resolved tactically but can have major repercussions on world politics. So far, the Indian military has been categorical in highlighting the threat to the Siliguri corridor and it was its logical base for the action taken to stop road building earlier. So if considered militarily necessary, India and Bhutan should make additional provisions for defending the Jhampheri ridge. Only a calculation based on the dynamics of domestic politics can yield a suggestion to keep quiet. But this is about a major national interests issue that begs India to act and shine the light on China and its predations.

This is a reference book. All the matter is just compiled and edited in nature, taken from the various sources which are in public domain.

This book Doklam standoff to signify the magnanimity and gravity of the current crisis. At the end, the author recommends that Assertive Diplomacy at the Regional level for instance, India-ASEAN is the way ahead for India to counter China's belligerent expansionist policy of One China.

—*Editor*

Contents

1

Introduction

BACKGROUND

Doklam is an area disputed between China and Bhutan located near their tri-junction with India. Unlike China and Bhutan, India does not claim Doklam but supports Bhutan's claim. China's claim on Doklam is based on the 1890 Convention of Calcutta between China and Britain, which states in Article I:

The boundary of Sikkim and Tibet shall be the crest of the mountain range separating the waters flowing into the Sikkim Teesta and its affluents from the waters flowing into the Tibetan Mochu and northwards into other Rivers of Tibet. The line commences at Mount Gipmochi on the Bhutan frontier, and follows the above-mentioned water-parting to the point where it meets Nipal territory.

China asserts that by this Convention, the starting point of the Sikkim-Tibet border is "Mount Gipmochi on the Bhutan frontier" and that this clearly defines the tri-junction point. As per Chinese claims, Doklam is located in the Xigaze area of Tibet, bordering the state of Sikkim. However Bhutan was not a party to the Convention.

In 1949, Bhutan signed a treaty with India giving allowance to India to guide its diplomatic and defense affairs. In 2007, the treaty was superseded by a new Friendship Treaty that replaced the provision that made it mandatory for Bhutan to take India's guidance on foreign policy, provided broader sovereignty but also stated in its Article 2:

In keeping with the abiding ties of close friendship and cooperation between Bhutan and India, the Government of the Kingdom of Bhutan and the Government of the Republic of India shall cooperate closely with each other on issues relating to their national interests. From 1958, Chinese maps started showing large parts of Bhutanese territory as part of China. Localized tensions arose in the 1960s but in the 1970s negotiations between China and Bhutan, with India sometimes playing a supporting role, failed to create a consensus on the status of the Doklam plateau. Bhutan and China have held 24 rounds of boundary talks since they began in 1984, with notable agreements reached in 1988 and 1998, the latter also prohibiting the use of force and encouraging both parties to strictly adhere to peaceful means.

In the early 2000s, China built a road up the Sinchela pass (in undisputed territory) and then over the plateau (in disputed territory), leading up to the Doka La pass, until reaching within 68 metres distance to the Indian border post on the Sikkim border. Here, they constructed a turn-around facilitating vehicles to turn back. This road has been in existence at least since 2005. It is the southward extension of this road that has sparked the 2017 standoff.

Events

On 16 June 2017 Chinese troops with construction vehicles and road-building equipment began extending an existing road southward on the Doklam plateau.

On 18 June 2017, around 270 Indian troops, with weapons and two bulldozers, entered Doklam to stop the Chinese troops from constructing the road.

On 29 June 2017, Bhutan protested to China against the construction of a road in the disputed territory. According to the Bhutanese government, China attempted to extend a road that previously terminated at Doka La towards the Bhutan Army camp at Zornpelri near the Jampheri Ridge 2 km to the south; that ridge, viewed as the border by China but as wholly within Bhutan by both Bhutan and India, extends eastward approaching India's highly-strategic Siliguri Corridor. The Bhutanese border was reportedly put on high alert and border security was tightened as a result of the growing tensions.

On the same day, China Foreign Ministry released a map depicting Doklam as part of China. Using the map as illustration, China's Spokesperson Lu Kang read Article I of the 1890 Convention of Calcutta and asserted that it proved that the Donglang (Doklam) area, a territory North East of Gipmochi as shown on the map, belongs to China.

On 30 June, Ministry of External Affairs of India released the statement entitled *Recent Developments in Doklam Area* stating its official position. It charges China of changing status quo in violation of a 2012 understanding between the two governments regarding finalizing the tri-junction boundary points and causing security concerns, widely understood as at its strategic Siliguri Corridor. It says that "Indian personnel" at Doka La coordinated with Bhutan and "approached the Chinese construction party and urged them to desist from changing the status quo."

On 30 June, answering a question about Bhutan's protest, China's Spokesperson Lu Kang made the following statement about Doklam's history after asserting that the area where the construction activities are underway is totally under the jurisdiction of China because it is completely located on the Chinese side of the China-Bhutan traditional customary line:

Before the 1960s, if border inhabitants of Bhutan wanted to herd in Doklam, they needed the consent of the Chinese side and had to pay the grass tax to China. Nowadays the Xi Zang Tibet Archives still retain some receipts of the grass tax.

On 3 July 2017, China Foreign Ministry Spokesperson Geng Shuang stated that former Indian prime minister Jawaharlal Nehru accepted the 1890 Britain–China treaty:

On September 26 of the same year, when writing back to Premier Zhou Enlai, Prime Minister Nehru unequivocally stated "the boundary between Sikkim and Xi Zang, China was defined by the 1890 Convention. This boundary was demarcated in 1895. There is no dispute over the boundary between Sikkim and Xi Zang (Tibet), China". Indian media reported that Nehru's 26 September 1959 letter to Zhou, cited by China, was in fact a point-by-point refutation of the claims made by the Zhou on 8 September 1959. In the letter, which was accessed by Indian press albeit not published in its entirety, Nehru wrote: This Convention of 1890 also defined the boundary between Sikkim and Tibet; and the boundary was later, in 1895, demarcated. There is thus no dispute regarding the boundary of Sikkim with the Tibet region.

China Foreign Ministry Spokesperson Geng Shuang replied to India media's question about disputed tri-junction with the following comment:

The so-called tri-junction, as the name suggests, is a point. It is not a line, much less an area. India misinterprets tri-junction point as an area, from ulterior motives. This time, the trespassing point of Indian army, is on the Sikkim-China border, which is 2000 metres away from the tri-junction point, Mount Gipmochi, by the 1890 Treaty.

On 5 July 2017, the Chinese government said that it had for the past 24 months a basic consensus with Bhutan that Doklam belongs to China, and there was no dispute between the two countries. On 19 July 2017, China renewed its call for India to withdraw its troops from Doklam.

On 24 July 2017, Chinese Foreign Minister Wang Yi told reporters that it is very clear who is right and who is wrong in the standoff in Doklam, and that even senior Indian officials have publicly said that Chinese troops have not intruded into Indian territory. "In other words, India admitted that it has entered Chinese territory. The solution to this issue is simple, which is that they behave themselves and withdraw," Wang said.

On 2 August 2017, the Chinese foreign ministry released a 15-page official position statement *The Facts and China's Position Concerning the Indian Border Troops' Crossing of the China-India Boundary in the Sikkim Sector into the Chinese Territory*. According to this document, there were still over 40 Indian troops and one bulldozer in Doklam (Donglang) region. Beijing accused India of using Bhutan as "a pretext" to interfere and impede the boundary talks between China and Bhutan. The report referred to India's "trespassing" into Doklam as a violation of the territorial sovereignty of China as well as a challenge to the sovereignty and independence of Bhutan. China says in the 15-page document that it notified India regarding its plan to construct road "in advance in full reflection of China's goodwill".

On 3 August 2017, China charged with four reasons that "India is certainly not for peace" though it always puts peace on its lips.

On 4 August 2017, The Ministry of External Affairs of India refused to confirm or deny when asked why, if India received notification from China in advance on its plan to construct road, it had not used diplomatic channels before sending its troops across the border since it was asking for diplomatic solution.

On 8 August 2017, Chinese diplomat Wang Wenli claimed that Bhutan had conveyed to China through diplomatic channels that the area of the standoff is not its territory, saying, "After the incident, the Bhutanese made it very clear to us that the place where the trespassing happened is not Bhutan's territory." On the next day, the Bhutanese government denied this, saying over the phone "Our position on the border issue of Doklam is very clear" and referring to the governments 29 June statement.

On 15 August 2017, several Indian and Chinese soldiers were alleged to have been injured after a melee broke out between them when a group of Chinese soldiers were alleged to have attempted to infiltrate across the border near Pangong Lake into Indian controlled territory in Ladakh. An Indian intelligence officer said the confrontation occurred after Indian soldiers intercepted a Chinese patrol that veered into Indian-held territory after losing its way apparently due to bad weather.

On 16 August 2017, the state run news agency released a segment of its show "The Spark" on Twitter racially attacking India, the video named the "Seven Sins of India" portrayed a stereotypical Indian with a turban and beard and a typical Indian accent, the segment spoke of Indians having "thick skin" and "pretending to sleep" on the matter of the border standoff between the two countries. The video went on to claim India was physically threatening Bhutan, and compared India to a "robber who breaks into a house and does not leave". The content of the video were factually incorrect. The video has received strong backlash on Twitter as well as from the international media.

On 9 October 2017 China announced that it is ready to maintain peace at frontiers with India reacting to Indian Defence Minister Nirmala Sitharaman's visit to Nathu La.

BHUTAN'S HISTORY

As in other Asian cultures, historical facts as the West understands, and myths and legends are inseparably interwoven. Demons and saints were often, in the perception of the Bhutanese, actors more important than the worldly rulers and the lamas. Since the 16th /17th centuries, the country's history is better documented although unfortunately, many records, guarded for hundreds of years in the monastery-castles called Dzongs, built mainly of wood, were destroyed in fierce fires in the 19th and 20th centuries. Much of the early history relies on reports of British explorers who visited the country in the 18th to 20th centuries, on legend and folklore, and on the few written records surviving in dzongs, monasteries and temples.

One of the most important events in Bhutanese history was the arrival of the holy Tibetan lama Padmasambhava (the Lotus Born), also named Guru Rimpoche, in the 8th century. He was the founder of the Ningma-pa monastic order. He made the Tantric Mahayana Buddhism popular in Bhutan, superimposing the ancient Bon religion which was the main religion throughout the Himalayas before the advent of Buddhism. In the 13th century, Phajo Druk-Gom Shigpo, a lama from Ralung monastery in Tibet, introduced the Druk-pa Kagyu school in Bhutan. Its founder, Yeshey Dorji, had chosen Druk = the dragon, for his new monastic order when he saw these mystic animals fly in the sky while consecrating an important monastery. Soon Druk-pa Kagyu became the predominant school in Bhutan, and Druk, the Dragon was adopted as auspicious into the titles of the country, the people, the King, and even today, of the Bhutanese Airline, Druk Air. Until the change from the 16th to the 17th century, Bhutan was an unorganised conglomerate of numerous small principalities, practically one in each major valley of the mountainous land. Their chieftains spent much of their energy and means warring between themselves and with Tibetan warlords. Numerous monasteries were competing, more often than not without spiritual refinery, for superiority and thus, influence on and income from the peasants.

This scene changed drastically in 1616 with the arrival of another lama form Ralung monastery in Tibet: Ngawang Namgyal, who lived from 1594 to 1651. He was a descendant of the founder of Ralung, andrecognized as re-incarnation of Pema Karpo, the holy ruler-abbot of Ralung. But Ngawang's position as the new abbot of Ralung was successfully challenged by a ruler-abbot of the new order of the Yellow Hats, the Gelug-pa with the Dalai Lama at its head.

Many Druk-pa lamas fled the martial attacks of their rivals. Ngawang was just 23 years old when the powerful deity Mahakala, or Yeshey Goenpo, appeared to him in form of a Raven and sent him to Bhutan with the instruction to teach Buddhism there. Thus the Raven became a sacred symbol to be integrated into the crown of the rulers of Bhutan, the Raven Crown.

While teaching untiringly in every possibly dzong and village in Western Bhutan, Ngawang grew in spiritual and political power. Once he had secured the support of most of the important aristocratic families, Ngawang started organizing the power structure of the country: with overwhelming energy he proceeded to construct a chain of large dzongs, the monastery-castles, in the main valleys of Western Bhutan as centres of the religious and civil authority. But he had rivals. One of them called the King of Tsang in Tibet with his troops to help oust the newcomer. In 1639 Ngawang crushed the challenger and his Tibetan allies. After this great victory he assumed the impressive title of "Shabdrung", meaning "Precious Jewel at whose feet one prostrates" and opened the lineage of Shabdrungs in Bhutan. From now on, he was the religious and temporal ruler of Bhutan. While remaining the supreme power, he introduced a dual theocratic system of government: a Head Abbot, the Je Kempo, administered the religious institutions, a high officer with the title Druk Desi or, as the British travellers translated, Deb Raja was vested with the civil powers. He divided the country in administrative regions, headed by a Penlop (Prince-Governor), while at local level Dzongpons executed the authority, delegated from the centre. For the first time, a comprehensive system of laws was codified. Invasions by Tibetan-Mongolian troops in 1644 and 1647 were successfully repulsed and served to further unite the Bhutanese. When the Shabdrung died in 1651, the major part of Bhutan was united under his authority; five years later, also Eastern Bhutan was under full control of the central government.

In an intricate power game, the Shabdrung's death was kept a state secret for more than 50 years because the temporal and religious rulers could not agree on a successor. The moment the death of the Shabdrung was made public in 1705, civil wars broke out, spurred by rival claims to the office of the Shabdrung. The unity of the country was eroded, the regional princes, the Penlops, could rule with increasing autonomy, warring against each other. This situation prevailed until the early years of the 20th century.

The decline of Moghul India at the end of the 18th century allowed Bhutan to gain almost total control of the Indian principality of Cooch Behar, its direct neighbour in the south. Bhutan had annexed and fortified the 11 duars or gateways including the adjacent agricultural land, at its border with the plains of Bengal. The clash with the British East India Company was pre-programmed. Soon enough, the pretender to the throne of Cooch Behar (Khagenda Narayan), sought British help to oust the Bhutanese. A small British force was dispatched in December 1772 to the area and, despite heavy losses, uprooted the Bhutanese contingent from Cooch and captured 2 Bhutanese forts in the foothills 1. Alarmed by this unexpected defeat, the Deb Raja of Bhutan (Tshenlop Kunga Rinchen) called upon the Panchen Lama of Tibet to intercede with the Governor General Warren Hastings. The result was a peace treaty concluded between India and Bhutan in 1774 (25.4.) in Calcutta. More important, Hastings took, from now on, a serious interest in extending the British connexion beyond Bhutan to Tibet and to the fabled land of China which had remained, for all their efforts, beyond the Western reach. Hastings lost little time in sending the first British mission to Tibet: In May 1774 George Bogle, officer in the Bengal Civil Service, spend many weeks in Thimphu negotiating the passage to Tibet. His official report, mentioning, as a footnote, the use of tea in Bhutan as universal beverage, induced, to a great extent, the establishment of tea plantations in Northern India. The next missions to Bhutan were lead by Alexander Hamilton (1776 and 1777) and Captain Samuel Turner (1783), all aimed at improving trade between Bengal and Bhutan as well as Tibet, at the same token dealing with border disputes. Then, for a good 50 years, the British-Bhutanese contacts were dormant.

In the mean time, the Bhutanese had turned their attention to Assam, which bordered the Eastern half of Bhutan. Wile the Kingdom of Ahom in Assam was falling apart, Bhutan had annexed the 7 duars to the plains of the Brahmaputra. On the other hand, the British, as result of the Burmese war 1825/26, gained control of Assam. The duars with their fertile soil were of high British interest specially for the young tea planting industry. In a number of battles the British annexed, in the years until 1841, all the Assam duars, but eventually agreed to pay to Bhutan an annual compensation of 10.000 Rupees for its losses.

Despite this agreement, intermittent clashes at the border were notorious in the following 20 years, culminating in the 2. Anglo-Bhutanese war: from November 1864 British forces swept through the Bhutanese strongholds in the Bengal duars and were firmly in control in March 1865. In the Treaty of Sinchula (11.11.1865) Bhutan gave up any claims to the 18 duars to Bengal and Assam against an annual compensation of 50.000 Rupees. The treaty stipulated peace and friendship between the signatories, and most important for Britain, open and duty-free trade between the two sides.

The two decades following this Treaty saw progressive weakening of the central authorities and the increase of internecine conflicts in Bhutan between the regional princely rulers, the Penlops. The Shabdrung, in theory the supreme power, proved to be an institutionally weak office: as the successors were chosen by reincarnation, usually as boys of 2 to 4 years, one of the Penlops was ruling as regent in his place until the new Shabdrung came of age.

Misuse of the power and reluctance to give it up, regularly shown by the regents, resulted in growing instability. The struggle for power centred on the two rival factions headed by the Penlops of Paro and Trongsa who, by the beginning of the 20th century, emerged as the strongest political figures.

This instability in Bhutan was alarming the Anglo-Indian Government. Because with the expansion of the British Empire on the subcontinent, one of the most important questions in this area was: would Bhutan seek an accommodation with the new powerful southern neighbour or maintain the traditional ties with Tibet which was by now largely influenced by China. For some time Bhutan was able to balance these two alternatives, but in 1903 the matter came to a head. In Viceroy Lord Curzon's perception of the "Great Game" and in the context of his efforts to counteract the Russian expansion between the Black Sea and the Caucasus, into Turkmenistan and possibly into Tibet, the latter had to be brought under a certain degree of British control. So Curzon dispatched a large scale military expedition to Lhasa under Colonel Francis Younghusband.

While the Penlop of Paro was favouring the traditional ties with Tibet against British India, the Penlop of Tongsa, Ugyen Wangchuck, decided to offer his services as mediator and interpreter between Younghusband and the Dalai Lama. He accompanied the expedition to Lhasa.

Despite two bloody encounters of the victorious British corps with the Tibetan army, the subtle mediation of Ugyen Wangchuck with the Regent and the Tsongdu, the assembly of the monks, (the Dalai Lama had fled) was successful: a new British-Tibetan treaty, confirming and enlarging the previous one, in particular favouring trade between Anglo-India and Tibet, was signed in 1904. Through this apparent success, and the subsequent support from the British side, the position of the Penlop of Tongsa within Bhutan was strengthened. John Claude White of the Political Service of the Viceroy, an extraordinarily gifted diplomat, who had also been on the Lhasa-Expedition, was sent to Bhutan. He was instrumental to bring about the consensus of the Penlops and Abbots to agree to convert Bhutan into a hereditary Kingdom. On December 17th, 1907, Ugyen Wangchuck, the Penlop of Tongsa, was elected the first Druk Gyalpo, the Dragon King of Bhutan. Under his strong leadership, the country enjoyed, eventually, a stability unknown until then, and the beginning of a fruitful relationship with Anglo-India.

As the Chinese efforts to gain influence in Bhutan and their claims to rights over this Kingdom grew, the Viceroy decided to develop a "blocking policy" against such threat to the British interests. For that purpose it was decided to conclude a treaty with Bhutan which secured the external relations of the Kingdom.

Political Officer C.A. Bell was sent from his office in Sikkim to Punakha (the King had not agreed to station him in Bhutan), was authorized to negotiate a new treaty with the Druk Gyalpo. This treaty was signed on the 8th of January 1910: it stipulated de facto the full control of Bhutan's external relations by the government of India, however without interfering in the domestic affaires; and it doubled the annual compensation to be paid to Bhutan to 100.000 Rupees.

Bell was satisfied and wrote: "we have removed the Chinese threat for 220 miles off a very vulnerable frontier." Nevertheless in 1911, Peking reasserted officially that Bhutan (as Nepal) was a vassal state of China! It based this claim on former contacts between Bhutan and the Amban (the Chinese Agent) in Lhasa: gifts sent with Bhutanese visitors to Lhasa were interpreted as tribute payments of a vassal state, the acceptance of the Chinese imperial seal sent to Punakha as acceptance of Chinese dominance. Peking now even sent an official letter to Ugyen Wangckuk, addressing him only as Penlop of Tongsa, but ignoring his new office as Druk Gyalpo, and informed him of their intention to station Chinese troops in the Kingdom. This was the first opportunity for the King to refer any such matter to Bell as Political Officer who advised the King not to respond at all. The Chinese threat became, for the time being, immaterial as in 1912 the Chinese were expelled from Tibet after a successful uprising. On the other hand, in a secret memorandum of the Government of India, it was bluntly stated to the Secretary of State in London "that Bhutan is a native state of India under the suzerainty of H.M.G.!"

The relations between the British Crown and Bhutan remained, without interruption, friendly and fruitful also under the 2. King, Jigme Wangchuck (since 1926) until the independence of India 1947. As fruit of the Bhutanese diplomatic skill, the young government of India recognized Bhutan as an independent state, and the Indo-Bhutanese Treaty, adopting almost unchanged the text of the Treaty of 1910 with the Anglo-Indian Government, was signed in 1949: India undertook not to interfere in the internal affaires of the Kingdom, Bhutan agreed to be guided by New Delhi in its external affaires. It is obvious that this move greatly contributed to the preservation of Bhutan's independence, as limited as it may be, up to today.

A revolt against the Chinese in Eastern Tibet in 1958 set off political shock waves across the Himalayas. The rebels established themselves near the Bhutanese border. Nehru, fearing that this might lead to a Chinese invasion of Bhutan, demonstrated the "special relationship" between India and Bhutan, and visited the Kingdom. With this visit commenced, for strategic reasons, extensive Indian economic assistance to Bhutan including the construction of militarily important roads. During the nation-wide rebellion in Tibet in the following years, and the border clashes between India and China, Chinese military contingents penetrated several times into Bhutan, while in Peking, Chinese claims to suzerainty over Bhutan resurged. This led to a strong Bhutanese alignment with India, starting with the training of the Royal Bhutanese Army by a permanent training mission of the Indian army, and the deployment of Indian troupes and military advisors in Bhutan until today.

Economy

Bhutan is, judged by a BSP-per-capita of just over 700 $, one of the poorest countries in the world. The"Human Development Index 2000" places Bhutan to rang 124 out of 180 countries. But poverty in Bhutan is relative and nil compared, for example, to parts of neighbouring India. As all the original Bhutanese still belong to producing farmer families, nobody is starving. And the statistics do not give the correct picture as many goods and services, produced and exchanged in the rural areas, are not reflected in the monetary system. But is true that agriculture and animal husbandry, the economic backbone for the vast majority of rural Bhutan, are mainly still done on a subsistence basis and not yet developed to the aspired level which would allow to produce a constant surplus for cash income.

In a country which is covered for more than 60% by forests, forestry is a major factor. It is strictly controlled by the government in the framework of their exemplary environment policy. Export of raw wood has been stopped since 1999 in order to counteract the unlimited demand of Indian consumers and to promote Bhutanese wood industry.

Bhutan's hydropower potential is the most important single factor for the economy of the country. It is estimated to be over 30,000 MW, but at the end of 2001 only approximately 1.4 percent of that potential have been utilized. It is the largest source of revenue earnings for the Government, covering 45 percent of the total national revenue. More than 90 % of the power produced is exported to India. Annual domestic consumption of power in Bhutan has been growing at an average rate of about 10% percent over the past 5 years.

Domestic demand for electricity is now over 90 MW per annum; and more than 30 percent of Bhutanese households now have access to electricity. By 2005, when the Tala and Basochu Projects are fully commissioned, Bhutan will have 1.500 MW of hydropower capacity which still means that only 5 percent of its total hydropower potential will have been developed. This industry will then contribute about 60 percent of the total annual revenue generation for the state.

To show the realistic dimension of Bhutan's economy, here only 1 figure: the expenditure of the government in the fiscal year 2002/2003 were 11.200 Mio Ngultrum or about 250 Mio US $ (1 $ = 45 Ngultrum).

For the year 2002, the first year of the 9th Five-Year Plan, the real Gross Domestic Product GDP is estimated to have grown by 7.7% as to 6.6% in 2001. Bhutan continues to experience a strong macroeconomic performance, with a fall in inflation to 1,8 %, the lowest level in the last 20 years.

The contribution to GDP of the agricultural sector, comprising agriculture proper, livestock production, forestry and logging, is estimated to have fallen back to about 34 percent in 2002, after almost 36 percent in 2000. This sector provides occupation to about 75 percent of the total labour force. The manufacturing, mining, and electricity sector contributed to GDP 19,3 % in

2002, the electricity sector alone about 9,7 %, a drop from 12% in 2001. The construction sector is estimated to account for 17 % of GDP in 2002 from 15 % in 2001. The performance of this sector reflects to a large extent the activities related to the large power projects of Tala, Kurichhu and Basochu.

Tourism is the most important sector for the revenue in hard currency. It earned a net 8,4 Mio US $ (from 8 Mio $ 2001) as it saw an increase in the number of tourist arrivals to 6.100 in 2002 (from 5500 in 2001) but did not recover the all time high of 7600 tourists in 2000.

Annual inflation, as measured by the consumer price index (CPI), continued to fall, reaching 1,8 %, after 2.7 in June 2002 and 3.2 percent in December 2001.

For the 9. Five-Year Plan period, which began in July 2002, the economy is projected to grow at an annual rate of 8.2 percent, exceeding the growth of the last plan period. This optimistic projection is based on the potential direct and indirect contribution of the power projects (Kurichhu, Basochu, and Tala) during the plan period by spurring on other sectors, namely manufacturing, construction, transport, and trade.

In its foreign trade relations, Bhutan depends predominantly on India. 88 % of the imports come from India, 5% of the Bhutanese imports derive from Japan, only 1% each from GB, USA and Germany.

97% of Bhutans's exports go to India of which a good 60% are covered by electricity. Of growing importance for Bhutanese mostly agricultural exports are Bangladesh and Thailand. The Bhutanese currency, Ngultrum, is linked 1:1 to the Indian Rupee. Therefore, Bhutan has very little scope for an independent foreign currency politics. The government pursues a very prudent fiscal policy by limiting successfully the annual deficit to a maximum of 3,5%. Despite increasing expenditures for education, health and a growing bureaucratic apparatus, the government's portion of the BSP could be maintained constant.

Education and Health

Education has been one of the highest priorities of the Bhutanese Kings and governments since the 1960s. Until then, education was limited to the monasteries. At great speed public schools were established, now covering widely the whole country. Two colleges and an institute to train teachers followed. The Royal Bhutan University, the first, was established in June 2003. The education system is a government affair and free for all. Monastic schools have extended their curricula to the public requirements. Upon initiative of the present King, all pupils are to be educated simultaneously in theory and one or the other handicrafts. The general teaching language is English, Dzongkha is obligatory for all pupils. Besides education in modern matters, great emphasis is laid upon the conservation of the Bhutanese culture and tradition mainly in literature, arts, architecture, language, customs etc..

Enormous progress was made in the last decade to extend in number and quality the public medical services which are free for all. Existing hospitals were enlarged, new hospitals built. The Basic Health Units, medical stations in the rural areas mostly not accessible by motor traffic, were improved and enlarged. The number of medical doctors, paramedics and health-workers was considerably increased. The result is an impressive improvement of the health situation and life expectancy in the population.

BHUTAN AND CHINA, AND INDIA

India's strategic concerns about China arise from its emergence as the most influential player in Asia with the ability to shape the future balance of power that could be detrimental to Indian interests. Despite a dominant Indian desire at cooperation rather than competition with China, the vexed and unresolved boundary issue together with China's continued military modernization and incremental upgrade of its military posture in Tibet that enable rapid force deployment, backed by logistical capability and communication infrastructure complicates the relationship.

China's attempts at strategic balancing in South Asia by forging military and economic ties with all of India's neighbours, some of whom have fractious ties with New Delhi, and by expanding its naval power in the IOR further exacerbate bilateral tensions.

Bhutan, China, India and Nepal

Latest manifestation of this is the Chinese attempts to build in roads into Bhutan. The Chinese Premier Wen Zia Bao and Bhutanese Prime Minister Jigme Thinley's meeting on the side lines of Rio + 20 Summit was a result of Bhutan's ambition for a non permanent seat in the UNSC in 2013, which china appears to have exploited.

Implications of Chinese Moves

Chinese success in Bhutan together with moves in Nepal, where it is enhancing its economic, military and infrastructural footprints will have grave serious strategic implications for India. The landlocked Himalayan Kingdom of Bhutan has borders of some 470 km with Tibet and 650 km with

India. India has a special relationship with the Bhutanese Kingdom having signed a Treaty of Friendship way back in 1949, which was updated in 2007, that provides among others unilateral guarantee for the defence of Bhutan.

Whereas China officially does not recognise Bhutan and has no diplomatic relations, however it does conduct periodic talks to reduce border tensions. China claims some 300 sq miles of Bhutanese territory mainly in the Chumbi valley, the Torsa Nala, and some areas opposite Haa (Western Bhutan). The Chinese also claim some grazing areas in the north.

Strategic scenario on India's Northern borders will get greatly compounded if Bhutan and neighbouring Nepal were to fall into the Chinese sphere of influence. Bhutan sit's at the centre of Sino Indian Eastern sector, as long as it remains neutral any Chinese military adventurism in the Chumbi valley and Tawang would largely be through attritional mountain offensives invoking Indian reaction in self defence.

However, if Bhutan and Nepal were to come within the Chinese sphere of influence, the precarious land route along the the Siliguri corridor a virtual Chicken Neck of seven north eastern states would become vulnerable prone to being cut off by any determined Chinese push – isolating the entire eastern sector. It is for this reason Bhutan's neutrality is extremely important and absolutely imperative as it forms a barrier and buffer to Chinese desires of expansion to the South towards the Siliguri plains. Chinese designs in Bhutan plainly pose a threat in being to Indian security.

Two other issues are of importance. China is rapidly developing road infrastructure opposite the Chumbi Valley including plans to extend railway network from Lhasa to Zangmu, as well as Shigatse and possibly to Yadong at the opening of the Chumbi Valley. These developments point to Chinese attempts at upgradation of operational posture. What should be of concern to India is the fact that in the event of hostilities it is unlikely that China will respect Bhutanese neutrality. The defence of Bhutan therefore is irrevocably linked to the defence of India.

Strategic Perspective

It can thus be surmised that the Chumbi valley forms an essential ingredient of the China's forward policy. Chumbi Valley, a vital tri-junction between Bhutan, India and China, is significant as it is located mere five kilometres from the Siliguri corridor—the chicken neck which connects India to North East India and Nepal to Bhutan. At the same time, Chumbi Valley is of geostrategic importance to China because of its shared borders with Tibet and Sikkim.

It is this geo strategic context that has made New Delhi sit-up and take notice of recent Chinese overtures to Bhutan. China and Bhutan have held a range of boundary talks and both sides are moving towards a joint field survey, in order to harmonize the reference points and names of the disputed areas. The focus of the joint-field survey was supposed to be on the disputed areas in the western sector which constitute the pastoral lands of Doklam, Charithang, Sinchulumpa and Dramana.

This exclusive focus on the North-Western sector is important due to its close proximity to the Chumbi Valley. China realizes that to get requisite leverage against India, which it considers moving rapidly towards strengthening its military posture through structured modernization and communication infrastructure build up. For China, Bhutan and Nepal are critical cards against perceived Indian military maneuvering. It needs however to be underscored that the China- Bhutan reconciliation can only come with the settlement of the boundary issue where China seeks the Dhoklan plateau overlooking Chumbi Valley while making tradeoffs in the grazing grounds in North Bhutan. This complicates the China threat theory.

The moves in Bhutan together with rapid Chinese inroads into Nepal would greatly contribute towards China's desire to establish a continental bridge through Tibet. Bhutan on the other hand would provide PLA with the requisite launch pad to cut off the Siliguri Corridor either as pre emptive action or in concert with larger territorial designs. Trading off some territory in the North to Bhutan in lieu of the pastoral land of the Doklam plateau therefore appears to be a pragmatic step towards achieving larger strategic objective.

Nepal, Bangladesh, Myanmar and Sri Lanka are countries where India has ceded strategic space to China through acts of omission and commission land locking it from North and East. Restoration of diplomatic relations between China and Bhutan therefore would inevitably constitute a strategic shock for India.

India's Strategic Calculations

Strategically, Bhutan sits between Sikkim in the West and Arunachal Pradesh in the East. It's neutrality is an important construct in providing depth to the Chumbi Valley leading to Siliguri Corridor and Tawang – the centre of Tibetan spiritual abode in India. Should Bhutan diplomatically ally with China – these two vulnerabilities would be greatly exposed with all the attendant military ramifications. Access to Chumbi Valley through Bhutan, in addition to the traditional routes would severe and isolate North East in the event of a war with China. Simultaneously, Bhutan would open the Western flank of Tawang – Tenga sector exposing the threat to plains of Assam.

Indian economic investments in Bhutan are exemplified by Bhutan becoming a hydropower exporter to India. By 2020, India expects Bhutan to export 10,000 MW of power to India. In addition, there are a large number of other economic programmes afoot. As per Medha Bisht of IDSA, India is considered a trusted friend and an ally in Bhutan. At present, there is no anti-India lobby in the country and, given the geographical imperatives of Bhutan, India is likely to remain the most important partner in its foreign policy calculus in the coming years. Bhutan also leverages India's role as its strategic partner.

While geopolitics shapes the bilateral relationship in a major way, one need to take note of the fact that Bhutanese society is changing fast. With the youth constituting almost 50 per cent of the total population, a new generation is emerging in Bhutan. As evident in the India – Bhutan power cooperation, Bhutan is getting increasingly assertive in negotiating various issues with India. India needs to address these growing nuances, which could soon emerge as visible sores in India – Bhutan bilateral relations.

In initiating diplomatic ties with China thus, Bhutan will have to make some stark strategic choices. Replacing India with China would mean economic and ecological tradeoffs in a balancing strategy aimed at maintain harmonious relations with its two big neighbours. Bigger issue is how far Bhutan is ready in becoming a pawn in Chinese designs in Tibet and against India. The ultimate formula to settle the boundary dispute would dictate the extent of this engagement between the two.

Bhutan's strategic choices are thus of great geostrategic and military concerns to India. How it makes them would depend on the range and depth of Indo-Bhutan relations. Above discourse need not only be seen from the perspective of geo politics alone.

Is China pushing reconciliation with Bhutan to convert it into a continental bridge linking with the Bay of Bengal of course through connectivity with India to create another "Silk Route", in this regard recent resolution of boundary dispute between China and Tajikistan to create an access to Afghanistan in pursuit of its economic investments provides a possible window into Chinese designs. In case China is able to develop close political and economic ties with Bhutan and incrementally bring it into its circle of influence it will become a win – win situation for China and matter of grave concern for India.

The issue for India is that as sovereign independent nation state it has the rights to pursue an independent foreign policy commensurate with its larger interests. While being closely aligned with India it has sought to pursue a policy of neutrality. Will the Chinese overtures change this? How should India respond what are the policy choices, is the dilemma that India will need to deal with.

CHINA'S OBJECTIVES IN THE DOKLAM DISPUTE

At 14,000 feet above sea level and with a perpetually harsh climate, the Doklam Plateau is an enormously difficult place to defend. Meanwhile, those launching an attack face exponentially greater challenges—and that's before the Himalayan winter sets in.

This helps explain why China and India last week ended a military standoff there that had been festering since June. Beyond the sheer misery of preparing to fight on such a forbidding battlefield, however, both nations had every reason to deescalate one of the most serious showdowns since their sole war in 1962. The *status quo ante* has been essentially restored, but the dispute raised important questions about the balance of power in Asia, China's grand strategy, and what Washington can learn from the episode.

China and India share a border over 2,500 miles long, with almost all of it based on colonial-era agreements and surveys, and much of it still disputed. China claims pieces of territory held by India, mostly in the states of Arunachal Pradesh and Jammu and Kashmir, with smaller pieces claimed in Uttarakhand and Himachal Pradesh. India claims land held by China, most notably a piece of land called Aksai Chin through which Beijing built a road in the 1950s connecting Xinjiang to Tibet. Reflecting its unsettled nature, the portions of the border separating disputed territories are referred to as the Line of Actual Control. There are periodic skirmishes along the LAC, but both nations have carefully choreographed them to avoid escalation; as a result, there have been no casualties stemming from land disputes in half a century.

On June 8, a platoon-sized unit of Chinese border guards moved into territory claimed by both China and Bhutan, a client-state of India. They destroyed stone bunkers used sporadically by the Royal Bhutan Army, and shortly afterward a Chinese road construction crew arrived with excavators, bulldozers, and a larger military escort. On June 16, Indian troops arrived and blocked the road-building effort. The next two months saw periodic scuffles at Doklam, as well as a mass rock-fight (captured on video and posted to YouTube) by the disputed banks of the Pangong Lake 800 miles away. On August 28, both nations agreed to what India termed an "expeditious disengagement" of forces, and both declared this non-resolution a victory.

INDIA V. CHINA: IT'S A MEXICAN STANDOFF

India is now the belle of the ball, as most of the world and Asian regional powers make pilgrimages to New Delhi to flatter and flirt with India's dynamic Prime Minister, Narendra Modi. Modi and India come with a certain amount of unpleasant baggage, which its suitors do their best to ignore. Modi himself is an unrepentant Hindutva cultural chauvinist whose attitudes toward Muslims (and convincing circumstantial evidence of his involvement in an anti-Muslim pogrom in Gujarat—so convincing, in fact, he was previously banned from the United States) trend toward the fascistic.

In regional affairs, India has not been a particularly responsible or constructive actor, having mixed it up with Pakistan (abetted the split-off of East Pakistan a.ka. Bangladesh), Nepal (opened the door to the Nepalese Communists with its inept deposition of the King), and Sikkim (Sikkim, in case you noticed, doesn't exist anymore; it was annexed by India in 1975) and presided over a bloody insurgency and brutal counterinsurgency in Kashmir that has claimed the lives of at least 60,000 people. India birthed the horrific Tamil Tiger insurgency in Sri Lanka and its intelligence services played what may have been a decisive role in organizing and executing the successful electoral challenge on January 8, 2015, to the rule of the pro-Chinese (now-ex) president of Sri Lanka, Mahinda Rajapaksa.

And there's the People's Republic of China, and the contested issue of the borderlands of Arunachal Pradesh in the northeast and Aksai Chin in the northwest. Japan's Foreign Minister, Fumio Kishida, got himself tangled up in the Arunachal Pradesh issue during his recent visit to India.

China today lodged a protest with Tokyo after Japan's foreign minister was quoted as saying that Arunachal Pradesh was "India's territory." Japan's Sankei Shimbun, a conservative daily, quoted Fumio Kishida as having made the remarks in New Delhi on Saturday. Japan played down the issue today, saying it could not confirm Kishida's reported remarks. It added that it hoped India and China could resolve their border dispute peacefully. Kishida's reported remarks drew an angry response from China, which called on Tokyo to "understand the sensitivity of the Sino-India boundary issue."

A Japanese foreign ministry spokesperson said "the statement was made considering the reality that Arunachal Pradesh state is basically in reality controlled by India and that China and India are continuing negotiations over the border dispute." China disputes the entire territory of Arunachal, calling it south Tibet, especially Tawang, a key site for Tibetan Buddhism. The historic town briefly fell into Chinese hands during their 1962 war before Beijing retreated.

The Japanese Foreign Ministry backtracked expeditiously, indicating that Kishida's remarks were perhaps a slip of the tongue and not meant to inject Japan into the Arunachal Pradesh issue. Ever since Prime Minister Abe returned to office with an India-centric Asian policy, yearnings have been expressed that Japan might openly side with India on the Arunachal Pradesh issue. The PRC, was extremely leery of previous PM Manmohan Singh and his overt diplomatic and emotional tilt toward Japan and, with good reason, has expected the current officeholder, Nadendra Modi, to play off China, Russia, and the United States in a more pragmatic manner.

This, indeed, was the takeaway from President Obama's recently concluded trip to India. President Obama's decision to accept Prime Minister Modhi's invitation to attend the Republic Day extravaganza further buttressed Modi's prestige and popularity within India and elicited a wave of "Mobama" triumphalism in the press, much to China's discomfiture. However, in the end, Modi played true to form by publicly and bluntly rejecting President Obama's call to limit India's greenhouse gas emissions.

For the PRC, an important area of anxiety is Arunachal Pradesh and the threat that India might "internationalize" the bilateral border dispute by canvassing its actual and would-be allies for support on the issue, perhaps even to the extent of going tit-for-tat with Japan i.e. India backing Japan on the issue of Senkaku sovereignty in return for Japanese aid and comfort on AP. However, it looks like Japan—like the Asian Development Bank, which ran into a PRC buzzsaw when it tried to put an Arunachal Pradesh hydropower project on its agenda in 2009—is not quite ready to mix it up on AP.

Let's unpack the Arunachal Pradesh issue. I've written a lot about Arunachal Pradesh. It's a complicated situation and I scattered my narrative over a handful of posts: "China 'pivot' trips over McMahon Line," "Charm Offensive: China's Flank of Discontent," and "India Places Its Asian Bet on Japan: Roiling the Waters of the Asia-Pacific."

To summarize. Arunachal Pradesh is a region controlled by India in its northeast quadrant, between Bhutan and Burma, home to a variety of ethnic groups. One of those groups is Tibetan, centred on the town and district of Tawang in the western end of AP at the border with Bhutan.

The Arunachal Pradesh dispute is bookended with Aksai Chin, a blasted desert between India and the PRC in the northwest, and is controlled by the PRC. The Indian claim to Aksai Chin is not terribly robust, since it is based on an internal British Indian survey—the Johnson Line—which was never discussed or agreed with China. The PRC built a strategic road across Aksai Chin in the 1950s, and it took several years for the Indian government to even find out it was there.

There is a third slice of disputed territory, the "Trans-Karakorum Tract" bordering Kashmir, geographically distinct from Aksai Chin, which India claims Pakistan illegally ceded to the PRC in a land swap. For some reason, the PRC and India aren't arguing about this piece. Both Arunachal Pradesh (AP) and Aksai Chin territories have been openly disputed since before the 1962 Sino-Indian war. The PRC has at times offered a grand bargain in which the two sides acknowledge each other's regions of effective control, by which India got AP and the PRC gets AC. The official Indian response has been nothing doing and all territory it lost in the 1962 war must be recovered i.e. Aksai Chin is not negotiable. It has decoupled the two issues, and has focused its diplomacy on the insistence that its sovereignty over AP be confirmed. India's claim to AP is complicated in an interesting way.

In 1914, Great Britain was interested in creating an autonomous Tibetan buffer—"Outer Tibet"—between British India and Russia/China. To this end, Sir Henry McMahon, the Foreign Minister of British India, invited Tibetan and Republic of China delegates to the Indian town of Simla. Tibet, eager to be acknowledged as an autonomous power with its own rights to negotiate directly with foreign powers (and not just through China), generously conceded a delineation of Lhasa's sphere of control—the McMahon Line–that alienated Tawang, a market town that interested the Raj, to British India.

However, the Simla Agreement was negotiated between the Tibetan and British representatives in a provisional sort of way after the Chinese representatives had packed up and left. Since Britain's Foreign Office was protective of its China diplomacy and not interested in encouraging Tibetan pretensions to negotiate as an independent sovereign power, the absence of the Chinese representatives—and a Chinese endorsement of the border arrangement accepted by the Tibetan authorities–was a deal breaker.

The Simla Agreement was apparently treated as an aspirational document and was recorded in the most authoritative compendium of British Indian treaties, Sir Charles Umpherston Aitchison's Collection of Treaties, Engagements, and Sanads, with the notation that neither Great Britain nor

China had ratified the treaty. Since Tibet wasn't recognized as a sovereign power, whatever it hoped to achieve with the Simla Accord—and what it had tried to give away, namely Tawang– was, in the eyes of the British, moot.

Things puttered along until 1935, when the detention of a British spy in Tawang by Tibetan authorities awakened the cupidity of a diplomat in the Foreign Office of British India, Olaf Caroe. Caroe checked the files, found that Great Britain had no ratified claims on Tawang, and decided to amend and improve the record. He arranged for the relevant original volume of the 1929 Aitchison compendium to be withdrawn from the various libraries in which it was filed, discarded, and replaced with a new version—but one that still claimed to be compiled in 1929, thereby removing the need for awkward explanations or documentation concerning why the switch had happened. The spurious version claimed that Tibet and Britain had accepted the treaty.

The deception was only discovered in 1964, when a researcher was able to compare one of the last three surviving copies of the original compendium, at Harvard University, with the spurious replacement. Unfortunately, that was too late for Nehru, who staked his security strategy and his diplomatic exchanges with China to a significant extent on the fallacy that he had inherited from British India a clear and unequivocal claim to its borders.

In 1962 Nehru decided to move up military units to assert India's claim to territory in Ladakh/Aksai Chin and up to the McMahon Line in Arunachal Pradesh under a gambit optimistically named The Forward Policy. The PRC begged to differ—and Chairman Mao was itching to stick it to India's patron, Nikita Khrushchev–and attacked. India's entire strategy had been predicated on the assumption that the PRC would not respond (shades, I think, of Western confidence that Vladimir Putin would stay his hand in eastern Ukraine out of fear of sanctions and the wrath of his impoverished and disgruntled oligarchs) and the Indian Army, outnumbered, undersupplied, and disorganized, was completely unprepared to fight for the high ground in the north. India suffered a humiliating defeat at the hands of the PLA. After its victory, the PRC decided to take the high ground, diplomatically as well as geographically. It withdrew its forces to behind the McMahon Line and offered a swap of AP for AC. No dice, as we have seen. India clearly does not see any need to credit AP—territory that the PRC abandoned—as any kind of bargaining chip concerning Aksai Chin. This is, perhaps, a cautionary tale to the PRC as to the geostrategic minuses as well as pluses of trying to behave like Mr. Nice Guy.

This history is officially persona non grata in India. The report the Indian government commissioned on the 1962 war—the Henderson Brooks Report–

was so devastating to India's position and its legal, military, and diplomatic pretensions it was promptly banned and publication is forbidden to this day. In an ironic recapitulation of the case of the Atchison compendium, it was assumed that there were only two typewritten copies and they were securely buttoned up in safes in New Delhi. However, the Times of London correspondent, Neville Maxwell, got his hands on a copy and used it to write an expose on the tragedy of errors in 1962, India's China War, thereby earning himself the fierce hatred of generations of Indian nationalists.

Maxwell tried several times to put the report into the public domain. As quoted in Outlook India, Maxwell provided an interesting account of how the freedom of expression sausage gets made when the information involved is not necessarily a matter of national security (the report is classified Top Secret, but its content—the minutiae of military decisions and movements sixty years ago have no current strategic or tactical significance) but is a matter of supreme political embarrassment (to Nehru, the Congress Party, the Gandhi political dynasty, and to the army).

My first attempt to put the Report itself on the public record was indirect and low-key: after I retired from the University I donated my copy to Oxford's Bodleian Library, where, I thought, it could be studied in a setting of scholarly calm. The Library initially welcomed it as a valuable contribution in that "grey area" between actions and printed books, in which I had given them material previously. But after some months the librarian to whom I had entrusted it warned me that, under a new regulation, before the Report was put on to the shelves and opened to the public it would have to be cleared by the British government with the government which might be adversely interested! Shocked by that admission of a secret process of censorship to which the Bodleian had supinely acceded I protested to the head Librarian, then an American, but received no response. Fortunately I was able to retrieve my donation before the Indian High Commission in London was alerted in the Bodleian's procedures and was perhaps given the Report.

In 2002, noting that all attempts in India to make the government release the Report had failed, I decided on a more direct approach and made the text available to the editors of three of India's leading publications, asking that they observe the usual journalistic practice of keeping their source to themselves...To my surprise the editors concerned decided, unanimously, not to publish...Later I gave the text to a fourth editor and offered it to a fifth, with the same nil result.

Narendra Modi, a determined foe of the Congress Party and the Gandhis (I had to chuckle when I read these fawning articles about President Obama bonding with Prime Minister Modi over their shared Gandhi love, despite the awkward fact that Modi's BJP nationalist party had been and apparently still is the spiritual home of Gandhi's assassin), came to power promising to release the report,but didn't. And when Maxwell posted part of the report on his website, the site was symbolically blocked.

The Indian army, in particular, is wedded to a creation myth of PRC perfidy that is infinitely more utile than acknowledging that the PLA attack, rather than unprovoked, was a response to a strategically and diplomatically bankrupt Indian border gambit compounded by non-stop miscues by India's civilian leadership and a disastrous defeat for its military forces.

In 2005, the PRC and India started negotiations over the borders issue. Here's a nice explainer from the Daily Mail! in 2013 which signals that Aksai Chin might be on the table, but Tawang is off the table, and unfortunately omits the significant complication of the Caroe forgery.

India's move into Arunachal Pradesh in the 1950s is less than a slam dunk according to international law, complicated in particular by the issue of Tawang. Not only is there the problem of Olaf Caroe's bibliographic hijinks, there is the awkward fact that India forcefully displaced Tibetan theocratic rule in Tawang—nominally rule from Lhasa, actually local rule by the immensely powerful monastery.

Lhasa had apparently experienced cartographic remorse over Simla and implored India to recognize Tawang as Tibetan territory in 1947. Instead, India seized the district in 1951 in a quasi-official/quasi-military "liberating the Tibetan serfs" operation rather similar to what the PRC conducted in its part of Tibet.

In recent years, the Dalai Lama has been forced into the unpleasant position of affirming Indian sovereignty over Tawang, whose great monastery (the second largest in Tibetan Buddhism) first gave him shelter when he fled PRC control in 1959, and which had hosted the reincarnation of the 6th Dalai Lama way back when.

The Dalai Lama apparently verbally acknowledged, if not in writing, that AP and Tawang belonged to India on several occasions while he still served at the apex of power in the Tibetan government in exile (a position he relinquished in 2011). However, I assume twisting the Dalai Lama's arm to concede Indian sovereignty over Tawang falls a little bit short, since the Tibetan government-in-exile lacks international recognition (and with it the right to cede territory to India).

The PRC is happy to harp on Tawang's role in the AP situation, since it serves as a continual reminder that India is occupying territory in AP that, however you slice it, is a core component of the Tibetan homeland, thereby keeping alive a non-Indian or, if you want, a PRC-cum-Tibet claim to at least part of the region and attempting to balk India's attempt to claim full sovereignty over Arunachal Pradesh under international law.

To understand how this relates to the Senkakus requires reflection on another piece of suppressed history—that the United States returned the Senkakus to Japanese administrative control not sovereignty in 1973 as part of the Okinawa package with the stated expectation that the sovereignty of the rocks would be negotiated between China and Japan.

My personal opinion is that the PRC is in no hurry to unfreeze the conflict over Arunachal Pradesh, and its insistence on sovereignty over Tawang—a district, I suspect, that has extremely limited interest in reunification with the Chinese motherland—is something of a pretext. With the Simla Agreement tainted and no subsequent cession of Tawang by Tibet or China, the Indian position in Tawang is embarrassingly similar to that of the PRC in the matter of the Spratlys i.e. having expelled the previous rulers by conquest and achieved control of the territory without attaining international recognition of its sovereignty.

And it's somewhat similar to the Senkakus, where the United States effectively surrendered its sovereignty over the islands when it returned Okinawa and the Ryukyus to Japan, but didn't cede its claim to anybody else.

Maybe Arunachal Pradesh is another one of those Mexican-standoff situations like Kashmir vs. Tibet (a.k.a. the Indian temptation to make mischief in the ethnic-Tibetan areas of the PRC is inhibited by concern that the PRC, via Pakistan, might light the fuse in Kashmir).

The PRC keeps the Tawang/AP issue alive to forestall thoughts by India of giving aid and comfort to Japan on the Senkakus or, for that matter, Vietnam on the Spratlys.

Both the PRC and India are bulking up their infrastructure and military on their respective sides of the de facto McMahon-Line-based border, making it a virtual certainty that India will never alienate any part of AP, including Tawang. That's good news for reduced actual tensions (as opposed to defence ministry posturing) at the shared border, but India's heightened sense of security concerning Arunachal Pradesh may encourage it to be less tentative vis a vis the PRC in its Japanese and Vietnamese diplomacy.

So, paradoxically, greater security along the PRC-Indian border may lead to greater insecurity elsewhere.

DEVELOPMENT ON THE DOKLAM PLATEAU

Since the tense June 2017 standoff between China and India on the Doklam or Donglang plateau, China has taken significant steps to improve its defensive posture and military infrastructure in the region. These developments emerged at a significant pace.

The Doklam plateau is a disputed area between China and Bhutan, India supports the Bhutanese claim, but China currently controls the area. The area is strategically important to India and China as it leads to the Indian Siliguri corridor, often referred to the chicken's neck, which connects India's northeastern states to the rest of the country.

In June, Chinese road construction in the area prompted an Indian response on the behalf of Bhutan, attempting to halt the construction. The altercation resulted in a standoff and scuffles between Indian and Chinese troops. After online sources spent most January and February pointing out Chinese buildup in and around Doklam, the Indian Ministry of Defense gave a statement on March 7 that China and India "redeployed" after the summer 2017 disengagement.

Chinese developments on the plateau include a dense network of trenches densely covering areas surrounding the strategic road leading to India. Additionally, China has built helipads, storage sites for vehicles, and new roads, as well as widened existing roads to allow for greater logistical capabilities in the event of open conflict.

In the satellite image above, light turquoise lines mark new trench lines, while red lines mark new roads and old roads now widened or otherwise improved. White diamonds mark newly constructed vehicle depots and military installations. White circles mark newly constructed helipads. The entire area measures about 3.5 miles (5.6 km) across, and 2.5 miles (4 km) in depth.

The below provides imagery from just prior to the standoff, compared to imagery of recent Chinese development in the region. The slider also depicts some of the improved Indian infrastructure in the area directly adjacent to the Indian border. This includes, but is not limited to, a new paved road leading directly up to the Chinese Donglang border road.

Chinese developments use established roads under their control as a base for branching out with smaller roads and trench systems. This expansion occurred primarily in the western direction towards India, but also southward on strategically important hilltops, deeper into Bhutan. The mountainsides on the de jure Sino-Bhutanese border are covered in the most expansive and systematic trench systems in the area, whereas trench systems closer to the de facto Sino-Indian border are more organic.

The above satellite imagery originated from December 9, 2017, at which point most construction had reached its conclusion. Here, three helicopter landing pads have been added in a newly-constructed area for storing military materiel. A protective berm covered the backside of camouflage nets on the storage site in which the northernmost helipad resided.

The second graphic presented a much larger storage area, slightly further down the road, closer to the de facto Sino-Indian border. The site was still under construction in the imagery and trails left behind form temporary camps suggested that troops stationed in the area have moved to more permanent basing.

The third graphic, which was the closest of the samples to the Indian border, depicted an entrenched area for storage as well as a surrounding trench system. The presence of trench systems had nothing to do with their proximity to India, as more expansive trench systems exist further back.

Finally, the newly widened main road leading from China into Doklam is now radically different, and can accommodate better for more, heavier traffic. The road has also been lined with trench systems and various other infrastructure.

Naturally, the strengthening of forward positions did not occur in strategic isolation, but in the context of a bolstered military infrastructure in depth. According to open source research, China has been improving its capacity to accommodate a greater numbers of troops, materiel, and air power to rapidly deploy to the region.

2

Doklam Standoff Between India and China's Far From Over

This summer, Indian and Chinese troops were mired in a long-standing face off at Doklam – a once obscure patch of disputed territory between China and Bhutan.

In late August, both New Delhi and Beijing, with days to go before Indian Prime Minister Narendra Modi would meet Chinese President Xi Jinping at the BRICS summit in Xiamen, announced a mutual "disengagement" at Doklam.

In the days after, observers of the stand-off celebrated what was seen as the conclusion to the Doklam affair. However, nothing could have been further from the truth.

Today, the People's Liberation Army (PLA) remains on disputed territory in Doklam, as does the Indian army. August's "disengagement" was a reduction in tensions. In practice, troops on both sides retreated their positions from the stand-off point by 150 meters each.

Reporting clarifying this state of affairs at Doklam emerged some weeks after the "disengagement" was announced. In effect, this should somewhat dampen Indian celebrations about a tactical victory at Doklam.

Yes, New Delhi successfully attained an outcome where the PLA was unable to extend a road that terminated just 60 meters from the Indian border post at Doka La, but an extended and increasingly robust PLA presence at Doklam is foreboding.

For India, the prospect should be cause for concern. Even as the stand-off continues, heading into the harsh winter months, there is little prospect currently of a comprehensive diplomatic resolution. The damage done over the course of the crisis at Doklam – particularly to bilateral agreements and understandings since 1993 – will have important spillover effects in the coming years. While Xi and Modi were able to maintain face during their meeting in Xiamen, the mistrust generated in India over the duration of the Doklam crisis will linger, with implications for the development of bilateral ties. It also remains to be seen if the conclusion of the ongoing 19th Party Congress in Beijing leads to an inflection point at Doklam in early November. While the PLA remains in place and with his power consolidated, Xi may emerge from the Congress with an elevated appetite for risk-taking.

For China, there are good reasons to keep up the heat at Doklam. First, the stand-off made plain to Beijing its quantitative and even qualitative disadvantages against the Indian armed forces in the Himalayas.

Beijing's slow but steady build-up on the disputed plateau can serve as an opportunity to rectify this imbalance along this sector of the border, where Indian strategic planners remain particularly concerned given the proximity to the vulnerable Siliguri Corridor – a geographic choke point between northeast India and the rest of the country measuring just 23 km at its narrowest point.

The so-called "turning point" that served as the summertime epicenter of the stand-off is no more following the disengagement. Now, the PLA may look to buttress its position farther north, near China's undisputed border with Bhutan in the southern reaches of the Chumbi Valley.

Even if matters at Doklam remain static for an indefinite duration, there is the renewed possibility of new PLA incursions in eastern Ladakh or Uttarakhand. Beijing may choose to test India's patience in other sectors of the two countries' disputed border.

The silver lining is that despite China's insistence that India withdraw before diplomacy could take effect, the "disengagement" itself was the result of hard-fought negotiation. The mutually agreed sequential withdrawal was no doubt a positive reduction in the temperature at Doklam, but it remains unclear what concessions either side may be willing to offer to reach a more comprehensive agreement to put an end to the stand-off once and for all.

What should be clear is that the Doklam stand-off is far from over. What began presumably as a dispute over the extension of a road is now something far greater. It is a test of how India and China will come to manage their relationship and whether each can manage its ambitions in Asia without irreversibly thrusting the bilateral relationship into decline.

BEIJING'S REGIONAL GOALS

China's initial move, even if it appeared to be the opening gambit in a geopolitical chess-game, was likely not intended as such. Beijing has been on a nationwide infrastructure building-spree since the 1990s, and sensitive border areas have not been left out of this program. To Indian eyes, the creation of a paved highway on highly strategic terrain looked like the laying of a foundation for a potential invasion; but to China, it may have been nothing more than the same sort of gravel-to-asphalt upgrade underway throughout the country.

In fact, Chinese and Indian troops frequently push one another's border positions a few hundred yards (or more) one way or another, depending on how much ground they can seize before higher authorities intervene. In April of 2013, for example, a Chinese platoon advanced 12 miles into Indian-held territory near Daulat Beg Oldi in Kashmir, but it withdrew about three weeks later, after intensive diplomatic wrangling. Another factor suggesting mishap rather than high-level premeditation is the tactical set-up: India commands the high ground, which means if the People's Liberation Army tried to push beyond Doklam toward the Siliguri Corridor it would be forced to attack largely uphill for about 90 miles.

Regardless of its origin, this unprecedented face-off—the first of this magnitude in 30 years—dragged from days to weeks to months. After the first week or so, it went from being a field-level initiative to a policy choice undertaken at the highest echelon of the Chinese government. Indeed, Beijing stoked nationalist sentiments among the Chinese public by running inflammatory (and in some cases baldly racist) stories in the state-controlled press and social media. The Chinese government arguably had four key objectives in the dispute, two directed squarely at India and two of with more direct implications for the U.S. and other nations around the world.

India's leaders increasingly describe Pakistan as their nation's rival of the past, and China as the rival of the future. Beijing's first strictly regional goal may have been to keep India from thinking it was at parity with China. The 1962 war—in which China invaded India without great difficulty, and unilaterally withdrew a month later while retaining the only pieces of territory it wanted to keep—shattered any illusion that the two giant nations of Asia were either friends or peers. In subsequent decades, Indian leaders were generally wary of offending Beijing. Through the Mao Zedong years and after, the military and economic gap (especially from the 1990s onward) between the two nations seemed to grow ever wider. In the new century, however, India's confidence has steadily grown: leaders of both major political parties increasingly describe Pakistan as their nation's rival of the past, and China as the rival of the future. Under Prime Minister Narendra Modi, this attitude has been matched by action. Modi has stepped up India's construction of military and dual-use infrastructure along the LAC, and increased security cooperation with its Pacific partners, including Australia, Japan, and Vietnam.

This increased desire for security cooperation extends straight across the ocean. During the four summit meetings over the past three years, Indian and U.S. leaders have pushed to advance security cooperation as speedily as possible. During Modi's visit to Washington in June 2017, for example, India announced that it would purchase 22 Guardian MQ-9B unmanned aerial vehicles from the United States for maritime surveillance. On July 10, the United States and India began the twenty-first edition of their annual Malabar naval exercise, which for the first time featured aircraft carriers from these two nations as well as Japan. In the past, India had generally shied away from multilateral exercises involving Washington, or from any actions which could be read by Beijing as a step toward a de facto U.S. alliance. China, understandably, would like to keep it that way.

Perhaps the most important Chinese concern in the Himalayas, however, deals with the future of the 82-year-old Dalai Lama. Indian leaders have given the Dalai Lama sanctuary in the town of Dharamsala for nearly six decades, but Modi has been more willing than any of his recent predecessors to press China's Tibetan sore spot. In 2014 he broke protocol by inviting Lobsang Sangay, prime minister of the Tibetan government-in-exile, to his inauguration. In April 2017, six months after encouraging a similar tour by the U.S. ambassador, Modi permitted the Dalai Lama to visit Tibetan communities in the state of Arunchal Pradesh—territories claimed by China.

Beijing has objected vociferously to each of these steps, with the Foreign Ministry noting in April, "China will firmly take necessary measures to defend its territorial sovereignty and legitimate rights and interests." China intends to select the Dalai Lama's successor—as it did in 1995 for Tibetan Buddhism's second-ranking cleric, the Panchen Lama. China's claim to the areas held by India (and Bhutan) flows from its claim to Tibet. If Tibet is an integral part of China, then all territories ever controlled (or claimed) by Tibet are also integral parts of China. A high-profile scare on the Doklam Plateau—inhabited only by seasonal Tibetan and Bhutanese yak-herders—may have been intended to send India an implicit message: namely, not to repeat its decision to shelter the Dalai Lama in 1959, a key cause of China's 1962 invasion.

Takeaways for U.S. Policy

The Doklam episode holds lessons for the United States and any other nation interested in Beijing's global strategic calculus. Although China claims more than 35,000 square miles of Indian-held land along the eastern portion of the LAC alone, it did not choose any part of this area as the site for an international incident. By focusing on Bhutan instead, China may have been trying to drive a wedge between India and its most vulnerable ally. New Delhi would defend its own sovereign territory, but Beijing may have wanted to see whether India would go to war against a much stronger adversary to defend someone else's real estate. Perhaps India would back down and compromise in some way: for example, permitting Bhutan to trade its claim on Doklam for China's dropping its quest for two other disputed areas held by the tiny kingdom. Several nations in South Asia (the Maldives, Nepal, and Sri Lanka) look to India for some degree of security protection, and several in Southeast Asia (including Indonesia, Malaysia, and Vietnam) have expressed interest in greater security engagement; a failure to fully protect its most direct client would have grave implications for India's credibility as a partner.

In addition, China's speedy movement of road-construction equipment into the disputed area suggests that Beijing could be replicating its approach in the South China Sea where it is building infrastructure to establish de facto ownership. China's strategy in the South China Sea has been unfolding in public view for years. Since December 2013, Beijing has reclaimed more than 2,900 acres, essentially building islands on top of barren reefs in the Paracel and Spratly chains. So far, this strategy has been successful. None of its rivals has accepted Beijing's claims—but none has taken a meaningful step to remove China's new array of landing strips, naval facilities, and surveillance stations.

But Doklam may not be the last such move outside of the maritime arena. China not only has unresolved land disputes with India, but it could also conceivably use a build-it-and-own-it approach to reopen long-dormant border disputes with Vietnam or Myanmar. It could even leverage its investment in infrastructure projects throughout Asia, Africa, and Latin America to extract political concessions—a tactic that European imperialist powers employed for hundreds of years.

The crisis at Doklam is over for now, but the episode's true impact will only unfold in the weeks and months to come. The crisis at Doklam is over for now, but the episode's true impact will only unfold in the weeks and months to come. From a U.S. perspective, the most important signs to look for are any concessions by the involved parties to China. This could involve Bhutan quietly acceding to Beijing's claims on the disputed Jakarlung and Pasamlung territories, which are less strategically threatening to India. New Delhi might subtly dial back its support for the Tibetan exile community. Or perhaps Vietnam will find India less responsive to future requests for economic or security engagement. Any such development might indicate that Beijing had not been stopped cold in the Himalayas, but had leveraged this conflict to its advantage.

If China regards Doklam as a success, it may be tempted to reuse the same template elsewhere, whether at an atoll in the Pacific or at a copper mine in the Democratic Republic of Congo. That is why Washington mustn't relax now. It should pay close attention to the aftermath of the dispute, which is the most serious Sino–Indian confrontation in a generation. Although troops are backing off their mountain-top positions, only time will tell whether their rumblings have actually subsided or rather, created the conditions for an avalanche.

THE CHINA-INDIA BORDER STANDOFF: WHAT DOES BEIJING WANT?

The trouble began on June 16, when Chinese construction workers were spotted in disputed territory on the remote Doklam Plateau. The workers were building a road that would extend China's strategic position further into territory claimed by Bhutan. India responded immediately, sending troops into Bhutan to halt the road-building. Soon thereafter, troops from both sides were seen pushing and shoving each other, a form of low-intensity conflict known as "jostling."

Over the weeks that followed, each side held its ground. For its part, Beijing demanded that India withdraw its troops before any negotiations could begin. Chinese officials also fired various verbal darts at New Delhi. On August 4, Wu Qian, a Chinese Ministry of Defense spokesman, issued a thinly veiled threat to India to stand down. "Here is a wish to remind India, do not push your luck and cling to any fantasies," Wu said. Statements by semi-official Chinese media outlets were even more blunt and aggressive in tone, assuring India that it would lose any conflict with the much stronger and richer China.

On August 21, the Chinese Foreign Ministry pronounced China "extremely dissatisfied" with Indian actions. Foreign Ministry spokeswoman Hua Chunying faulted India for altering the status quo, stating that Chinese forces had been "obstructed" in their "normal patrols." The dispute ended — for now, at least — with one final parting shot from Beijing: rather than acknowledging that both sides had agreed to pull back their troops, the Chinese Foreign Ministry instead highlighted the withdrawal of "trespassing personnel and equipment to the Indian side." (A Foreign Ministry spokesperson did, however, acknowledge that the People's Liberation Army would "make adjustments" in light of changing conditions.) Key Chinese media outlets echoed the Foreign Ministry's somewhat one-sided account.

For many observers, the uptick in tensions and even India's decision to increase its troop presence on and near the Doklam Plateau were nothing out of the ordinary. After all, there have been scores of such mini-confrontations between China and India over the years, most of which have led to nothing more serious than a series of sharp-edged statements by both sides. Once temperatures cool, Beijing and Delhi usually pledge to renew their efforts to find a diplomatic solution, and move on. One could argue that this is what has happened here.

One wonders, however, whether this particular standoff highlights rising China's disinterest in actually resolving its border disputes with India and Bhutan. After all, it was Chinese border activity that provoked the standoff. Once the scuffle began, Beijing maintained an aggressive and aggrieved tone. Its public rhetoric was all stick and no carrot. Beijing also insisted, both publicly and privately, that an Indian withdrawal of troops should precede any negotiated solution, a demand that was hard to square with the fact that, in this case, it had moved first to change the status quo. None of these moves indicate that China is anxious to conclude a final deal anytime soon.

Its dispute with India and Bhutan aside, China actually has a reasonably strong record on resolving border disputes with its neighbors. Its dispute with India and Bhutan aside, China actually has a reasonably strong record on resolving border disputes with its neighbors.

According to one authoritative study, China has resolved a full 17 of 23 border disputes with other states, and in many of those cases was willing to make significant concessions in order to reach a settlement. The disputed territory on the Doklam Plateau is a key exception, as are various pieces of disputed terrain along the so-called Line of Actual Control on the China-India border.

As the political and economic relationship between China and India has grown in recent decades, many hoped that some sort of deal could be reached, thus permanently removing a potentially significant stumbling block. And yet, despite years of bilateral talks, no solution has been found. It may well be the case that, for China, the territorial dispute serves an important function: it allows Beijing to grab New Delhi's attention whenever it ever needs to.

At any time, China can create a security crisis for India, merely by placing more troops in the disputed territory. John Garver, a top scholar of India-China relations, believes that China keeps the border disputes alive to remind India that it should respect Chinese sovereignty over Tibet. This theory seems plausible: India gave up on its longstanding pre-1949 influence in Tibet only with reluctance, and would likely seek to resurrect it if possible.

No doubt the Tibet factor remains central to Beijing's thinking. Given this context, the provocative comments by Arunachal Pradesh Chief Minister Pema Khandu in April 2017, openly suggesting that Tibet is not a part of China, were not helpful. New Delhi should warn all of its government officials to avoid such comments in future.

Khandu's comments notwithstanding, officials in the region and in Washington need to ask whether China's strategic evaluation of the border disputes is evolving in such a way as to require a new kind of response. Put simply, China's rise over the past two decades has altered the balance of power between China and India: China is much stronger than it once was across Asia, economically, politically, and militarily. While Southeast Asia has borne the brunt of China's expanding power and influence, South Asia has been affected as well: states like Bhutan, Nepal, and Sri Lanka — all closely tied to India — have seen their relations with Beijing grow, in ways that inevitably cut into India's sway. India remains the clear leading power in the region, but the trends must be troubling for New Delhi.

In this rapidly changing context, China will likely reconsider its strategic interests and goals in the sub-continent. In this rapidly changing context, China will likely reconsider its strategic interests and goals in the sub-continent. When it comes to the border disputes with India and Bhutan, for example, might not China start asking for more of the disputed territory, all the better to improve its strategic position in the Himalayan highlands? Or might it use the signal-sending function that the border disputes provide to send a message to India on a broader range of issues, including India's opposition to China's One Belt, One Road economic initiative, or its growing security relationship with the United States?

Another puzzling element of the border scuffle has been Washington's conspicuous silence. For over a decade, both the Bush and Obama administrations sought to strengthen U.S.-India political and security ties.

In its first months in office, the Trump administration has sought to build on this warming trend. In fact, word of the border spat with China broke just before Indian Prime Minister Narendra Modi paid his first visit to the United States since Trump took office. During Modi's visit, the two sides further cemented their security relationship, with the Trump administration agreeing to sell India advanced drone surveillance equipment that could be used to track Chinese naval movements in the Indian Ocean.

And yet, neither the White House nor the State Department have given a firm and clear statement on this most recent spat. The Trump administration's reticence may stem at least in part from the well-documented disarray within the ranks of the U.S. foreign-policy apparatus: as with many other seemingly less pressing foreign policy concerns, the Trump White House may not yet know exactly how to balance competing interests and objectives, including the need to maintain good relations with China and to allay Pakistani concerns that Washington is getting too close to its arch rival.

Any effort to formulate and execute a policy response is made all the more difficult by the fact that key South Asia posts remain unfilled. Any effort to formulate and execute a policy response is made all the more difficult by the fact that key South Asia posts remain unfilled. Seven months into the Trump presidency, his administration has yet to nominate either an assistant secretary for South Asia or an ambassador to India, and the State Department has offered to no sign as to when these posts will finally be filled.

On Sunday, August 27, roughly 70 days after the spat began, an unnamed Trump administration official gave what appear to be the first public comments from the U.S. government on the matter. The official told an Indian newspaper that the United States is closely monitoring the situation. "We are concerned," the official said. "We support a return to the status quo."

A blind quote to an Indian media outlet, provided more than two months into the border standoff, can hardly be considered a robust response. The Trump administration's reticence is unfortunate: without some sort of signal from Washington, Beijing might conclude that it can escalate its activities in the disputed area without worrying about any interference from the United States. If India responds in kind, the potential for military conflict between the two nuclear-armed regional powers will grow.

It is still too early to tell whether the latest border scuffle represents a shift in Beijing's strategic thinking. That said, what would a more aggressive Chinese approach to the border dispute look like? First, it would include an increased militarization of the disputed border regions by China. The second prong would be a higher prioritization of political and economic ties with Bhutan, Nepal, Bangladesh, and Sri Lanka, in an effort to make those governments more open — over time — to Chinese strategic priorities in the region. Finally, it would include a decreased emphasis on the geopolitical costs of a more assertive strategy. Beijing could conclude that, as much as New Delhi is distressed over any assertive Chinese moves, India simply won't be able to respond for fear of damaging economic ties.

A key signal to watch for: Now that this latest squabble has been resolved, will Beijing avoid any additional provocations along the border? Or will it once again seek to provoke New Delhi just a few months down the line? Absent a firmer response from Washington, it may only be a matter of time before Beijing looks to probe India's resolve once again. At the earliest opportunity, the Trump administration should signal to all concerned that it would not look favorably on a military buildup by any party in the Himalayas, and that the United States expects all parties to peacefully negotiate a final resolution to their border woes.

CHINA-INDIA BORDER STANDOFF

The 2017 China India border standoff or Doklam standoff refers to the military border standoff between the Indian armed forces and the People's Liberation Army of China over Chinese construction of a road in Doklam near a trijunction border area, known as Donglang, or Donglang Caochang (meaning Donglang pasture or grazing field), in Chinese. On 16 June 2017 Chinese troops with construction vehicles and road-building equipment began extending an existing road southward in Doklam, a territory which is claimed by both China as well as India's ally Bhutan. On 18 June 2017, around 270 Indian troops, with weapons and two bulldozers, entered Doklam to stop the Chinese troops from constructing the road. On 28 August, both India and China announced that they had withdrawn all their troops from the face-off site in Doklam.

BHUTANESE REACTIONS

After issuing a press statement on 29 June, the Bhutanese government and media maintained a studious silence. *The Bhutanese* clarified that the territory on which China was building a road was "Bhutanese territory" that was being claimed by China, and it is part of the ongoing border negotiations. It also defended the policy of silence followed by the Bhutanese government, saying "Bhutan does not want India and China to go to war, and it is avoiding doing anything that can heat up an already heated situation." However,

ENODO Global, having done a study of social media interactions in Bhutan, recommended that the government should "proactively engage" with citizens and avoid a disconnect between leaders and populations. ENODO found considerable anxiety among the populace regarding the risk of war between India and China, and the possibility of annexation by China similar to that of Tibet in 1951. It found a strengthening of Bhutanese resolve, identity and nationalism, not wanting to be "pushovers".

The New York Times said that it encountered more people concerned about India's actions than China's. It found expressions of sovereignty and concern that an escalation of the border conflict would hurt trade and diplomatic relations with China. ENODO did not corroborate these observations. Rather it said that hundreds of Twitter hashtags were created to rally support for India over China and that there was a significant blowback over the *Xinhua* video "7 sins". Scholar Rudra Chaudhuri, having toured the country, noted that Doklam is not as important an issue for the Bhutanese as it might have been ten years ago. Rather the Bhutanese view a border settlement with China as the top priority for the country. While he noticed terms such as "pro-Chinese" and "anti-Indian" often used, he says that what they mean is not well-understood.

Disengagement

On 28 August 2017, India and China announced that they had agreed to pull their troops back from the face-off in Doklam. By the end of the day, it was reported that the withdrawal was completed.

The Indian troops withdrew back to their original positions at their outpost at Doka La, located in a militarily advantageous position on the Bhutanese border, less than 500 meters away down the ridge slope. *The Times of India*, citing a source, reported: "Our soldiers sit on the top, hold the ridge and can swiftly intervene, as they pro-actively did in mid-June, if the People's Liberation Army once again tries to unilaterally change the status quo by constructing a road near the Sikkim-Bhutan-Tibet tri-junction."

Ministry of External Affairs (MEA) of India released a press statement stating that India and China had mutually agreed to disengage. It said that India and China had maintained diplomatic communication in recent weeks and that India was able to convey its "concerns and interests".

In Beijing, the foreign ministry spokeswoman said that the Chinese forces on site have verified that the Indian troops pulled out, and implied that Chinese troop numbers would be reduced. She said that the Chinese troops would continue to patrol the area, to garrison it and to exercise "sovereign rights". However, she made no mention of road-building activities. The statement from the Chinese Foreign Ministry spokesman, as *The Diplomat* reported, "offered Beijing a face-saving way out of the impasse." Indian MEA issued a second statement later in the day that both the sides have withdrawn "under verification". The Indian news channel NDTV reported that, by the end of the day, Chinese road-building equipment was removed from the face-off site. Some experts warned that one shouldn't be overly optimistic as another standoff is entirely possible.

The Washington Post commented that it was not clear if China had offered any concessions in return for the Indian withdrawal, such as agreeing to halt road construction. It said that the deal allowed both sides to save face. However China was continuing to be "cagey" in its official remarks. *Al Jazeera* said that China was not giving up its historical claims and it expected India to respect its "historical borders". Scholar Taylor Fravel pointed out that there are plenty of options available to China to garrison the area other than extending the road.

On 29 August, Bhutan welcomed the disengagement and hoped that it would lead to the maintenance of peace and tranquility as well as status quo along the borders.

On 5 September, Prime Minister Narendra Modi and President Xi Jinping held hour-long discussions on the sidelines of the BRICS summit. They agreed on a "forward-looking" approach and vowed to make efforts to ensure that situations like the Doklam standoff do not recur. They reaffirmed that maintaining peace and traniquillity in the border areas was essential for the relations between the two countries.

On 7 September, some media reports claimed that both nation's troops still were patrolling the area at the face-off site, simply having moved 150 meters back from their previous position.

CHINA AND INDIA'S BORDER DISPUTE AND NEW STANDOFF

China and India, never great friends, suddenly ended a military standoff this week on a plateau in the Himalayan mountain kingdom of Bhutan. For 70 days Chinese troops defending a highway project on the Doklam Plateau faced Indian counterparts called by Bhutan for help. China claims the plateau, which lies on its own border, hence its rush to defend the roadwork. The standoff between Asia's two biggest and among the two most militarily powerful countries had scared a lot of people to fear a hot war like one the same two sides fought in 1962.

The two would-be combatants are likely to bring their forces back someday for failure to resolve underlying issues such as whether China has rights to build. "The standoff has ended without resolving the dispute over the Doklam plateau," says Brahma Chellaney, strategic studies professor at the Center for Policy Research in New Delhi. China is seeking the glow as a good neighbor now as it prepares to host Indian Prime Minister Narendra Modi next week at the BRICS Summit, an 11-year-old event aimed at building cooperation across emerging markets. Before year's end, Chinese President Xi Jinping faces a performance review of sorts at his country's 19th National Congress of the Communist Party. He wouldn't want to be burdened then with a knotty foreign affairs problem as the Congress considers him for another five-year term as party head.

In those contexts, the agreement Monday for an "expeditious disengagement" of troops on the plateau rings perfectly logical. "The Chinese apparently backed off temporarily to ensure the success of the BRICS Summit and the Party Congress," says Mohan Malik, professor at the Asia-Pacific Center for Security Studies in Honolulu.

But the disengagement doesn't mean either side trusts the other more now than before, meaning watch out again once the scheduled events end in China. The two sides could easily retrench at the plateau, experts say.

"The fact that Indian and Chinese statements have described the mutual withdrawal deal in completely different language means that there remain strong disagreements," Malik says. "So neither side is going to lower its guard by pulling back troops."

Indian forces pulled back 500 meters to a ridge-top post, Chellaney said, and "can quickly intervene" if China restarts the roadwork on Doklam plateau. China has withdrawn troops and construction equipment but lashed out verbally this week at India. One Chinese state-run media reportaccuses India of "trespassing" at the plateau and possibly "pretending to go to war in the hope of forcing China into making concessions," for example. Beijing officials say they reserve the right to send their troops back.

The two sides separately dispute two other border tracts, China controlling one and India the other. India further resents China's military support for Pakistan, which has its own territorial disputes with New Delhi. Over the past decade Beijing has tried to solidify claims to disputed lands along its borders as well in the East and South China seas. It shows little signs of stopping despite push-back from other countries. "A fresh crisis could flare if the PLA tries again to build the controversial road to the Indian border," Chellaney says.

FUTURE SCENARIOS FOR CHINA AND INDIA AND THEIR IMPLICATIONS

In the country studies for China and India, analysis was undertaken using the Global Trade Analysis Project (GTAP) model and projections of future growth were made to the year 2020. Through this exercise the implications of rapid growth for production and consumption of agricultural products and trading opportunities for other countries in the region and the world have been assessed, based on certain assumptions.

Prospects for Growth and Domestic Implications

The analysis conducted in the China case study projects average annual growth in GDP of 8 percent in 2006 to 2010 gradually slowing to 6-7 percent in the following decade. Several factors favour this strong growth performance, including macroeconomic stability, high domestic savings, increased spending on research and development, continued high levels of FDI, improved market environment and trade liberalization, and the commitment to greater equity – granting higher purchasing power to lower income groups. Also noted are obstacles that will tend to reduce growth particularly in the long run – a decline in the domestic savings rate, an ageing population and pressures on the natural resource base for sustained agricultural production.

While China's growth rate is projected to decline somewhat in the near future, the India study suggests that GDP growth could be rising from the current levels of 6-7 percent to 7-8 percent. It should be noted that these growth projections apply to two economies of considerably different size. Nevertheless, how does one explain the divergence? Part of the explanation is related to the incremental capital output ratio (ICOR).

In India it is currently about 4 and expected to decline. In China while the ICOR was 4 in the early 1980s it has steadily risen since then and in 2002 was 5.4. In short, despite reforms in state-owned industries in China, India uses capital more efficiently. Also favouring India is the demographic dividend, with the percentage of the population in the 15 to 59 age group increasing from 59 percent in 2001 to over 63 percent in 2011 which could add 1 percent to GDP growth. In China, by contrast, the ageing population and sharp decline in population growth due to the one child policy will eventually slow overall economic growth.

The picture for agriculture is somewhat mixed. The land area used in crop production is gradually shrinking due to urbanization and in some instances environmental degradation. Thus for staple crops, production growth depends on an increase in yields. China has already achieved high yields in staple crops, and further gains will depend on technological breakthroughs.

Indian crop yields are low by comparison with China and other countries. This is attributed in part to the neglect of investments in research and extension beyond the early Green Revolution years. In both China and India the yields for the principal Green Revolution crops, rice and wheat, have plateaued, due in part to falling groundwater tables and environmental degradation. However, if priority can be given to investment in research and development and infrastructure, there appears to be ample scope, particularly in India, for increasing yields and agricultural productivity.

As a result of continued rapid economic growth and increase in income per capita, demand for high income elasticity products, like milk, livestock and horticultural products will continue to grow. China and India are committed to maintaining cereal grain self-sufficiency. The projections for both economies indicate that food security can be maintained at a national level without resorting to significant imports. The baseline scenario presented in the China study, for example, indicates that in 2020 China will maintain or surpass self-sufficiency in rice, horticulture, pork and poultry, fish and processed foods, and come close to self-sufficiency in wheat, fibre and beef and mutton. In the case of India, despite low current growth rates of output for many crops, the expectation is that self-sufficiency can be maintained in rice, wheat, coarse grains, sugar, cattle and meat, fish and other foods.

The country should also come close to self-sufficiency in other crops (although the model predicts significant decline in both production and consumption of these crops) and milk. However, both countries will need to adopt policies that ensure food security at a regional and household level where hunger and poverty still persist.

China's agricultural production structure is expected to shift more towards labour-intensive products such as vegetables, fruit, fish and processed foods, while self-sufficiency in land-intensive products such as oilseed, fibres and coarse grains is predicted to fall further from current levels. The largest increases in Indian agricultural production are predicted for oilseed, sugar, fibres, milk, fish, other agricultural products and other foods, while negative or low growth rates are expected in cattle and meat, rice, wheat, coarse grains and other crops. Nevertheless, for some of the high growth products India will continue to require significant imports, especially of oilseed, fibres and other agricultural products.

The dollar-a-day-poverty index had fallen to 16 percent in China in 2002 while it was 34 percent in India. Poverty is projected to continue to decline in India. With a GDP growth rate of 8 percent or more the poverty rate should fall from 26 percent in 1999-2000 to 14 percent in 2010 and then to 8 percent in 2015. There appears to be an implicit assumption in these figures that the reduction in poverty will come largely from growth in employment in the non-farm sector. The analysis of the Chinese experience suggests that the impact of rapid economic growth on poverty reduction tends to slacken eventually if the rural sector does not grow hand in hand. As incomes have grown, the impact and effectiveness of general economic growth on poverty reduction have weakened.

Implications for Asia and the Greater Pacific Region

Trade liberalization, globalization, and pressures to meet WTO and FTA agreements are generating a substantial growth in trade. China will have the largest impact on Asia and the Pacific region because China's economy is two-and-a-half times larger than that of India, it is growing faster and it is more integrated with the rest of the world.

For example, China received some US$60 billion of FDI last year while India received only US$5 billion. FDI and multinational investments are a means of importing technology and entrepreneurial and management skills. By 2020 China is projected to be the world's second largest importer and exporter.

At the level of the overall economy, both China and India will be major importers of energy and minerals principally from Australia, the Russian Federation and the Middle East. China is projected to drop from 92 percent self-sufficiency in energy in 2001 to 67 percent in 2020. Recognizing this as a potential constraint to growth, China is taking steps to improve efficiency in the use of energy. The high total factor productivity (TFP) growth projection in the China country report indicates that reliance on energy imports can be reduced by as much as 60 percent and minerals by 50 percent. Aided by FDI and information technologies, China and India along with other developing countries are finding it increasingly easy to transfer technology from developed countries to exercise their comparative advantage in manufacturing. However, both countries have historically made low use of external resources, relative to their economic size, and national initiatives will continue to play an important role in determining their growth paths.

As noted previously, both China and India are projected to be self-sufficient in cereal grains and do not provide a serious threat to global food security. India is projected to continue its current role as a major net exporter of rice. Both China and India will be major importers of oilseed, plant-based fibre and forestry products. Soybean meal, for example, will come from destinations as distant as Brazil. In China there is already a trend in trade away from land-intensive crops such as food and feedgrains and sugar, and towards export of labour-intensive, high value commodities — horticultural crops, livestock, and aquaculture products. The predictions of the two country reports with regard to net exports and imports in 2020. The use of different scenarios in the China report indicates that China presents considerable opportunities for other agricultural exporters under the baseline and high GDP growth scenarios, but these opportunities are significantly reduced under the high TFP growth scenario. The Indian data, on the other hand, under-represent opportunities for catching up in productivity via technological change.

The China report examines changes in the patterns of agriculture and food trade that are likely to emerge by 2020. Interestingly, Chinese exports to India are predicted to increase by 1 179 percent over their 2001 level, while Indian exports to China are predicted to grow by only 79 percent. The Indian study did not undertake a comparable analysis, but the figures presented in the China report tend to reflect the relatively narrow range of India's net agricultural exports at present — mainly rice, followed by wheat and sugar.

The major diversification in China's exports is predicted to take place in Southeast Asia and "other" Asia, while exports to Japan, Republic of Korea, Hong Kong Special Administrative Region, China, and Taiwan Province of China are predicted to remain fairly stable. Less important growth areas for China include the Russian Federation, Australia and New Zealand, and Central and South America.

On the import side, however, major growth in agricultural trade should come from the more developed Asian countries as well as most other parts of the world excepting Southeast and other Asian countries. For the developing countries in Asia, China is emerging as a significant competitor in agricultural products. In particular the current trade surplus in agricultural products that the Southeast Asian region enjoys with China is predicted to turn negative. Meanwhile many Asian countries will find it difficult to compete with non-agricultural exports from India and China such as textiles, given the comparatively low wages in these two economies.

3

Moving Beyond Doklam in India-china Relations

The narrative of what went down in the Himalayan frontier region in the summer of 2017 has come under scrutiny once again ahead of a series of high-level meetings between Indian and Chinese officials. Indian External Affairs Minister Sushma Swaraj and Defense Minister Nirmala Sitharaman are expected to visit China next week to attend ministerial meetings for the Shanghai Cooperation Organization (SCO) summit, while Prime Minister Modi has planned a visit in June for the SCO summit. During her visit next week, Swaraj is also set to meet the newly-promoted Foreign Minister and State Councilor Wang Yi, who oversees negotiations with India over territorial disputes, on the sidelines of the SCO summit.

Looking ahead to these high-level meetings, the question is whether last summer's 73-day military standoff over the Doklam plateau located in the India-China-Bhutan tripartite region will remain at the forefront of discussion between the two sides. Recently, in an interview, New Delhi's ambassador to Beijing, Gautam Bambawale, blamed China for the standoff, saying it "changed the status quo in the region." Reacting to the ambassador's remarks, Chinese Foreign Ministry spokesperson Hua Chunying said, "Donglong (Doklam) belongs to China because we have historical conventions...China's activities there are within our sovereign rights. There is no such thing as changing status quo."

The events at Doklam brought to light the negative consequences that both sides accrue when the national interests of China and India collide.

These strong statements reinforce the significance of the protracted territorial dispute in clouding bilateral relations for more than half a century. Issues that came to the fore in 2017—India's hosting of the Dalai Lama, the securitization of shared river water, and China's ambitious Belt and Road Initiative (BRI)—have only added layers to the already-complex border issue. However, the events at Doklam brought to light the negative consequences that both sides accrue when the national interests of China and India collide. Heading into the SCO meetings, there are incentives for both New Delhi and Beijing to move beyond the Doklam dispute, balancing relations for mutually beneficial outcomes on both the political and economic fronts.

A TRYING YEAR IN SINO-INDIAN RELATIONS

The Doklam crisis must be taken into the full context of 2017, a year that witnessed several downturns in Sino-Indian relations. Tensions soared around the Dalai Lama's visit to the disputed state of Arunachal Pradesh, the growing security dilemma in the Indian Ocean region, Beijing moving to block India's bid to join the Nuclear Suppliers Group (NSG), as well as its veto of an Indian effort to sanction the head of a Pakistan-based terrorist group through the United Nations. Moreover, India decided to boycott Xi's flagship Belt and Road Initiative (BRI) summit on the grounds that the project violated Indian sovereignty as it involves infrastructure running through Pakistan-administered Kashmir.

Compounding these issues, in the immediate aftermath of Doklam crisis, Beijing breached a bilateral agreement by withholding hydrological data—crucial for flood forecasting and warning—from lower riparian India while sharing data on the same river with lowest downstream country Bangladesh. According to the agreement, upstream China is to share hydrological data with India during the monsoon season between May and October. However, Indian officials confirmed in August last year of not receiving any data. Chinese authorities cited technical reasons for not having data to share, but Bangladesh confirmed receiving said data from China. A third of India's total freshwater supply comes from rivers originating in Tibet. I Iad China provided the necessary data, it could have prevented some of the deaths in the flooding that hit India's northeast.

Worsening matters, the Doklam standoff also impeded crucial military confidence-building measures between the Indian Army and China's People's Liberation. The two armies did not hold their traditional border personnel meeting (BPM) along the Line of Actual Control (LAC) nor did the annual "Hand-in-Hand" exercise take place.

POST-DOKLAM STATUS QUO

In an unprecedented move that is markedly different from New Delhi's earlier supportive stance towards Tibetan activities in India, a directive from the government urged officials not to partake in the celebrations commemorating the Dalai Lama's 60 years of exile in India in March this year. It bluntly stated that the timing of the events coincided with a "sensitive time" for New Delhi's relations with Beijing.

However, the directive can be seen as India's decision to tone down its aggressive language towards China in a move to reset relations than a forced political concession due to Chinese aggression on the LAC. After all, the Indian Foreign Ministry issued a statement clarifying there is no change in India's position towards Tibet, and that "His Holiness is accorded all freedom to carry out his religious activities in India." Moreover, India has balanced its competing needs to counter and court China by being involved in strategic partnerships like the newly revived Quad with powers like Japan, the United States, and Australia, while at the same time engaging China in multilateral forums like BRICS and SCO.

It appears there is enough political will on both sides to move past the downturns in relations that occurred in 2017—including the Doklam crisis—at the soonest. New Delhi has already indicated this by implicitly acknowledging that Tibet has been a sore subject for Beijing. In turn, around the same time, China agreed to resume sharing hydrological data with India. Amid a trade war with the United States, China has indicated its keenness to sign a free trade agreement with India and address the huge trade deficit that India has with China. Moreover, China agreed to place Pakistan on the FATF (Financial Action Task Force) terror financing grey list earlier this year in a move supported by India.

China does not want an adversary in India, while New Delhi, in hopes of maintaining the status quo in Doklam while keeping a check on China's activities in the Indian Ocean, does not wish to antagonize Beijing.

Behind these moves on both sides are political and economic considerations. A tense military standoff or worse—war—will not be favorable to either Modi or Xi domestically. With upcoming general elections in 2019, Modi will not want to be embroiled in any scuffle with China lest he is seen as having lost Doklam to the Chinese. Meanwhile, President Xi just won a second term and is driven to build his image as a world leader in his own right as a champion of global free trade. The flagship $174 billion BRI project is poised to position China as the focal point in the next chapter of globalization, necessitating cooperation and allies across the region. China does not want an adversary in India, while New Delhi, in hopes of maintaining the status quo in Doklam while keeping a check on China's activities in the Indian Ocean, does not wish to antagonize Beijing.

MOVING PAST DOKLAM

What began as a dispute over road construction has invariably become a bigger issue in the Asian geopolitical climate. The upcoming SCO meetings in the post-Doklam status quo will be a litmus test of how well India and China will be able to manage their relationship without plunging bilateral relations off the deep end. If the latest round of boundary talks held last month is anything to go by, New Delhi and Beijing have not been able to move beyond complaining about transgressions supposedly committed by the other side. Yet, both countries have much to lose if they let the territorial dispute over Doklam continue to define bilateral relations. If India and China are to move beyond the current stalemate for shared political and economic gain, as both sides seeming willing to do, then the Doklam dispute will likely take a backseat in the days ahead.

SINO-INDIAN RELATIONS: A CHRONOLOGY

On the eve of the 11th meeting of the Sino-Indian Joint Working Group (JWG) to discuss bilateral relations, with special reference to the pending border dispute, it would be useful to analyse the set-back to the bilateral relations since May, 1998, and the Chinese perception of its relations with India in the bilateral and global context after the Pokhran II nuclear tests. An attempt has been made to cover all important Chinese statements since May 1998 in this chronology. From the chronology, one could notice three phases in the Chinese reactions. In the first phase (May to July, 1998), there was a strong barrage of criticism of the statements of George Fernandes, the Indian Defence Minister, and Prime Minister Atal Behari Vajpayee's letter to President Clinton portraying the threat from China as a motivating factor for the Pokhran II nuclear tests.

The characterisation of the Chinese threat was condemned by China as hurting the Chinese people and projected as a mere pretext to cover India's hegemonistic ambitions. The tests were viewed as also indicative of India's desire to acquire a new political status through the possession of nuclear weapons. During this phase, the Chinese criticism of India related to the bilateral (damage to Sino-Indian relations) as well as global (damage to the global non-proliferation regime) aspects. There was rigidity in the Chinese attitude to both these aspects. In the second phase (July-middle to December, 1998), there were signs of a mellowing down of the Chinese rigidity on the bilateral aspect. There was once again stress on the importance of Sino-Indian relations and repeated calls to India to make amends in a suitable manner so that the bilateral relations could be put back on track. After the initial hard-line comments on Kashmir suggesting a multilateral conference on the issue, Beijing reverted back to its 1996 and pre-1996 stance of neutrality as between India and Pakistan on this issue.

In the third phase (since January, 1999), while welcoming the Indian initiatives for mending the damage to bilateral relations, Beijing continued to be rigid in its insistence that the international community should not accept India's concept of a minimum nuclear deterrence and that India and Pakistan should sign the NPT and the CTBT unconditionally and immediately. There was also a note of concern in Chinese pronouncements that other permanent members of the UN Security Council might ultimately accept India's need for a minimum nuclear deterrence.

During all these phases, Chinese inconsistencies in possessing a nuclear and missile capability for itself and opposing a similar capability for India were sought to be explained as follows:

- The Chinese capability was acquired in self-defence in the context of the cold war. China did not view the capability as conferring a political status on it. Moreover, China was already a permanent member of the Security Council.
- On the other hand, the Indian capability was acquired after the cold war was over when the contemporary trend was towards peace, harmony and non-proliferation. The Indian nuclear aspirations marked a revival of its hegemonistic designs and had the ulterior motive of seeking a new political status in the international community.

It is evident from the chronology that China's two-pronged policy is to continue to oppose India's nuclear aspirations and deny it any new political status at par with that of China through its emergence as a de facto nuclear weapon power, while at the same time not allowing this to affect the bilateral relations.

The Chronology

The setback process started with a statement by George Fernandes, the Indian Defence Minister, in the beginning of May 1998, in which he reportedly described China as a major military threat to India. However, he subsequently claimed that his observation made to a private TV channel was distorted.

On May 5,1998, Zhu Bangzao, a spokesman of the Chinese Foreign Office, described Mr.Fernandes' remarks as "absolutely ridiculous and unworthy of refutation" and added that China had noted with the "utmost regret and resentment" his statements on China since coming to office.

He said:" The remarks by the Indian Defence Minister George Fernandes have seriously sabotaged the friendly atmosphere for improving bilateral relations between China and India...China does not pose any threat to neighbouring countries. His accusation concerning China's relations with relevant countries is utterly fictitious and has no basis in facts...His statement that China has built a sophisticated electronic surveillance base in Myanmar's Coco Islands and has installed missiles in Tibet targeting India is absolutely fictitious and entirely baseless.... It is extremely irresponsible."

On May 8,1998, an unidentified spokesman of the Chinese Foreign Office told pressmen that China had twice protested to India through the Indian Embassy in Beijing over the "ridiculous and fragile" statements of Fernandes.

On May 12,1998, Lin Shanglin, the Chinese CDA in New Delhi, issued a written statement at New Delhi stating as follows:" The so-called issue that China has been building a naval base in Myanmar is utterly fictitious, whose aim is to find grounds to the so-called China threat...Allegations of Chinese involvement in the development of Pakistan's Ghauri missile are a fabrication. It is irresponsible to assume that China is engaged in nuclear proliferation. The co-operation between China and Pakistan in the peaceful utilisation of nuclear energy is under the safeguards and supervision of the International Atomic Energy Agency (IAEA) and conforms to the international general practices."

After the suspected leakage to the "New York Times" by the US State Department of the letter written by Indian Prime Minister Atal Behari Vajpayee to President Clinton citing India's perception of a possible threat from China as one of the reasons for Pokhran II, Chinese Government spokesmen, govt-controlled media and strategic analysts started a barrage of vigorous criticism of India.

The Xinhua news agency said on May 18,1998: "Political analysts are of the view that with the nuclear explosion, India seeks to develop nuclear weapons, barge into the world's club of nuclear powers and then seek regional hegemony."

Ye Zhengjia, a former Chinese diplomat posted at New Delhi and subsequently posted to the Chinese Foreign Ministry's Institute of International

Studies, told Japan's Kyodo news service on May 18,1998: " By presenting a China threat scenario, India is trying to extract mileage out of ideological differences between China and the West while New Delhi is actually masking its own contradictions with the West to lessen the blow of sanctions." He denied that China's nuclear tests were carried out to raise the country's political status in the new world order. He added: " In any case, a country's international standing does not depend upon its capability to do a nuclear test. That time has passed."

The official "China Daily" wrote on May 20,1998: " India's improper move of attributing its nuclear tests at Pokhran to potential threat from China has made the international community realise that the new Indian Government is not only irresponsible, but also immoral. This is the first time in history that a nuclear country has denied its own responsibility for its nuclear tests and shifted the blame to others..To justify its series of nuclear tests, India uses the political tactic of making India-China ties tense....China had been taking a reserved attitude towards provocative statements from India in order to push forward Sino-Indian ties. However, India took China's forbearance as weakness."

Xinhua reported on June 2,1998, that at a meeting between the Chinese Vice-Premier Qian Qichen and the US National Security Adviser Sandy Berger both sides "believed that the international community must take effective and feasible measures to halt the nuclear arms race in the South Asian region and prevent nuclear proliferation in order to restore and safeguard peace and stability in the region." Sandy Berger had gone to Beijing to prepare the ground for Clinton's visit.

In an interview to the AFP news agency on June 3,1998, President Jiang Zemin denied that China had helped Pakistan make nuclear bombs and said: "The nuclear co-operation between the two countries is strictly peaceful in the area of technology of nuclear reactors and all the installations concerned are under the control of the IAEA."

He recalled his historic visit to India in 1996 "after a number of signals of friendship from New Delhi" and said he had received a warm welcome, " but the Prime Minister then was not the same person as the one today."

Jiang further said that Pokhran II which clearly showed that "India is targeting China and Pakistan" surprised him He added: "China hopes that Pakistan will not respond and will make a wise decision. But the Pakistani Government is faced with strong public pressure on the subject."

In an article on June 5,1998, the "Liberation Army Daily", the journal of the PLA, accused George Fernandes of recklessly using China's name as an excuse for India's nuclear ambitions and warned: " If this arrogant boast and military expansionism are not effectively checked, the consequences will be serious."

A signed editorial in the "China Daily" of June 6,1998, urged India to show wisdom by renouncing its nuclear weapons programme and said that a 14 per cent rise in India's defence budget was an unwise decision which would further escalate the arms race in South Asia.

It added: "Such a rise in defence spending reveals the South Asian country's ambition to be a military power and is adding fuel to the already heated arms race...It is unwise for the Indian Government to develop nuclear weapons and raise defence spending with no regard for its relations with the international community." It described Fernandes' statement in the Indian Parliament about the occupation of Indian territory by China as a "concocted excuse."

In an interview to the "Newsweek" on June 21,1998, Jiang Zemin said: "In November 1996, I paid a successful visit to India. I was accorded a very friendly reception by the Government and people of India. That visit has left me with very good memories. I was very surprised that they conducted the nuclear tests. I was even more surprised that they cited China as a reason for their nuclear testing. I really don't know what kind of threat China poses."

Jiang also said that if Clinton raised the question of alleged Chinese supply of missiles to Pakistan, "the answer very simply is that we don't plan to sell missiles."

A joint statement issued by Jiang Zemin and President Clinton on June 27,1998, after the latter's visit to Beijing in the last week of June, 1998, said: "Recent nuclear tests by India and Pakistan and the resulting increase in tension between them are a source of deep and lasting concern to both of us.

"Our shared interests in a peaceful and stable South Asia in a strong global non-proliferation regime have been put at risk by these tests, which we have joined in condemning.

"We have agreed to continue to work closely together, within the P-5, the Security Council and with others, to prevent an accelerating nuclear and missile arms race in South Asia, strengthen international non-proliferation efforts and promote reconciliation and the peaceful resolution of differences between India and Pakistan. "The P-5 joint communiqué of June 4, which was endorsed by UN Security Council Resolution 1172, set out clear and comprehensive objectives and a plan for action to address the threat of a South Asian nuclear and missile arms race.

"We pledge our full support for the steps outlined in the joint communiqué and again call on India and Pakistan to stop all further nuclear tests and adhere immediately and unconditionally to the CTBT, to refrain from weaponisation or deployment of nuclear weapons and from testing or deployment of missiles capable of delivering nuclear weapons and to enter into firm commitment not to weaponise or deploy nuclear weapons or missiles capable of delivering them.

"The United States and China remain firmly committed to strong and effective international co-operation on nuclear non-proliferation, with the NPT as its cornerstone.

"We will continue to bolster nuclear non-proliferation efforts and reiterate that our goal is adherence of all countries, including India and Pakistan, to the NPT as it stands, without any modification.

"States that do not adhere to the treaty cannot expect to be accorded the same benefits and international standing as are accorded to NPT parties. Notwithstanding their recent nuclear tests, India and Pakistan do not have the status of nuclear weapon states in accordance with the NPT."

Speaking at the Beijing University on June 29,1998, Clinton said: "We (the US and China) are now pursuing a common strategy to move India and Pakistan away from further testing and engage in a dialogue to resolve all outstanding issues."

Commenting the same day on the reference in the Clinton-Jiang statement to the nuclear issue in South Asia, the "China Daily" said that the US-China understanding on this subject "signified a healthy, stable China-US relationship." It added: " Such a relationship is not only in the interest of China and the US, but of the world peace and stability at large. "

Tang Guoqiang, a spokesman of the Chinese Foreign Office, rejected on June 30,1998, India's criticism of the Clinton-Jiang statement. He said that as major powers, the US and China had to act in the common interest of the international community to prevent a nuclear arms race in the region and promote reconciliation between New Delhi and Islamabad.

Accusing India of starting a nuclear arms race in South Asia, he said: "The joint statement expresses the strong determination of China and the US in further preventing nuclear proliferation and also promoting reconciliation and peaceful settlement of the differences between India and Pakistan.

"There is nothing reproachful about the joint statement on South Asia. While India opposed the joint statement, Pakistan has welcomed it. However, we have taken note of India's comments."

Writing in "The Hindu" of July 2,1998, F.J.Khergamvala, its Tokyo correspondent, quoted Robert Manning and James Przystup, former senior US State Department officials, who had visited China, as having stated in an article in the "Wall Street Journal" (date not mentioned) that during their visit a prominent Chinese analyst told them that "transferring material or technology to Iran is negotiable, but Pakistan is our Israel", implying thereby that Pakistan's security was as important to China as Israel's was to the US.

However, in an interview to the State-run China Central Television before leaving China, Clinton said that the US and China had agreed to work together to prevent the spread of nuclear and missile technologies to countries like Pakistan that might misuse it.

He added: "China has agreed to work with the US to stop the transfer of technologies to countries that might misuse it, to not assist unsafeguarded nuclear facilities like Pakistan's and to consider joining the worldwide system that prevents the exportation of dangerous technologies."

At a meeting of the leaders of China, Russia, Kazakhstan, Kyrgyzstan and Tajikistan held at Almaty in Kazakhstan on July 3, 1998, Jiang Zemin failed to have a critical reference to the nuclear and missile arms race in South Asia included in the final communiqué. However, during a joint press conference by the leaders after the summit he condemned India for starting a nuclear race in South Asia.

While briefing pressmen on July 9,1998, Tang Guoqiang, the Chinese Foreign Ministry spokesman, avoided commenting on India's offer of a pledge of no-first-use of nuclear weapons. He merely said: "The most urgent task for India is to immediately abandon its nuclear programme and sign the NPT and the CTBT unconditionally as soon as possible."

However, in an interview to K.K.Katyal and C.Raja Mohan, the New Delhi correspondents of "The Hindu" the same day, Zhou Gang, the Chinese Ambassador to India, gave the first indication of the beginning of a mellowing down of the Chinese criticism of India. He made the following points:

- "It is up to the doer to undo the knot". Beijing would like India to provide responsible explanations for totally "unreasonable and groundless" accusations against China and, thus, create a favourable atmosphere for a new beginning in bilateral relations. The initiative for this must be taken not by China, but by India. It was China's set policy to develop a "constructive and co-operative partnership" with India towards the new millennium.

- It was impossible to call for a dialogue and establish best relations while keeping up attacks on China, which had been the victim of baseless accusations. China would like these charges to stop and "actual actions" initiated. China would not like the present situation to go on. "As two big powers, the high-level political contacts between India and China should be normal."
- He hoped that India and Pakistan would peacefully resolve their differences "including the Kashmir issue" through talks. "The position of the Chinese side is consistent". After the nuclear tests by India and Pakistan, the growing tension on Kashmir and the issue of peace and security in South Asia had caused widespread concern in the international community. "We will do whatever is beneficial for the improvement of India-Pakistan relations and peace and stability in South Asia, but never do otherwise."
- China's ties with Pakistan were State-to-State relations between two sovereign countries. China had not transferred to any country equipment or technology that could be used for making nuclear weapons. Some of India's concerns over Sino-Pakistan military co-operation were caused by misunderstandings and others arose out of unnecessary misgivings. China would like to exchange views on this subject with India through diplomatic channels, as used to be done in the past. He disapproved of the resort to media and exaggerations based on "rumours from the West."
- There was peace and tranquillity on the India-China border. "We hope the two sides would make joint efforts to maintain this situation." China had taken "a series of flexible measures" on Sikkim and he hoped that the Indian side " would also adopt a positive and flexible attitude so as to create a proper atmosphere and conditions for the disposal of this issue."

In a lead article on July 14,1998, the "China Daily" called for " a multilateral meeting attended by India, Pakistan, the US, China and Russia to help resolve the Kashmir dispute, over which India and Pakistan have fought two wars since 1947."

The article, quoting Ma Jiali of the China Institute of Contemporary International Relations, said: "Indian Government officials should stop spreading the China menace theory which will create suspicion and hostility between the two peoples. The Indian Government's unreasonable attacks on

China deeply hurt the feelings of the Chinese people and undermined the mutual trust the two countries have been trying to build over generations." Quoting Ouyang Liping, another expert of the same Institute, the article said that China had consistently adhered to the policy of non-proliferation of nuclear weapons and denied that China was aiding Pakistan's clandestine nuclear programme.

Commenting on the annual report of the Defence Ministry of the Government of India for 1997-98, the article said: "In the report, the Indian Government did not examine its mistake in provoking a dangerous nuclear arms race. It vilified China as the main reason for the deterioration of South Asia's security environment instead."

The article described the BJP-led Government as head strong and alleged that the real purpose of Pokhran II was to gain regional hegemony.

It further quoted Ouyang Liping as saying: "India's recent nuclear explosions reflect a dangerous ultra-nationalism and its ambition to build a regional hegemony and become a major political power."

The article added: "Continuously denying its faults and spreading lies will not win sympathy or trust from others, but will make the international community more vigilant against its ambitions. India should first abandon its nuclear development plan unconditionally so as to convince Pakistan to follow in its foot steps."

The article again quoted Ouyang Liping as saying that the international community must press India and Pakistan to completely abandon their nuclear programmes and convert South Asia into a non-nuclear area. In this connection, he cited the examples of South Africa and Ukraine and said: "They (South Africa and Ukraine) abandoned their nuclear capability in the 1990s under international pressure and for the good of their own peoples."

Despite this article, there was another indication of a possible mellowing down of the Chinese official criticism in an address by Zhou Gang, the Chinese Ambassador, in the India International Centre at New Delhi on July 25,1998. He made the following points:

- India's nuclear tests had led to "temporary difficulties" in Sino-Indian ties, but had not diluted Beijing's commitment to building a long-term friendly relationship with New Delhi." It is a firm policy of the Chinese Government to develop with India a long-term neighbourly and constructive partnership of co-operation for the 21st century.
- India and China could play an influential role in promoting Asian stability. "As the two most populous developing countries in the

world, China and India can exert important influence in the affairs of South Asia and Asia as a whole."

- China did not seek hegemony in the region though it was naturally interested in the developments between India and Pakistan. China had normal relations with Pakistan, which were based on the five principles of peaceful co-existence. Pakistani nuclear weapons programme could not be linked to China's. Pakistan had, however, received conventional weapons from China, but the quantum of these exchanges was much smaller to the defence trade between India and a "powerful country" (an apparent reference to Russia).
- "Friendly relations between China and any country are not directed at any third country." China did not pose any security threat to India. "Fictitious charges against China have gravely hurt the feelings of the Chinese people and harmed Sino-Indian relations."
- China wished India "stability, progress and development" and sought "neighbourliness, friendship and progress" from New Delhi. The Chinese pronouncements were a refutation of some wanton attack and accusations by certain personages in India. They were meant to "safeguard the friendly relations between our two countries and bring them back on track."

Co-operation between India and China must diversify and should not be held hostage to the pending resolution of the border dispute. The boundary question could be resolved on the principle of mutual understanding and mutual accommodation. The Peace and Tranquillity accord of 1993 and the subsequent agreement of 1996 on confidence-building measures continued to be the cornerstone of the Sino-Indian security relationship.

In an interview to the "Al Ahram" of Cairo on July 26,1998, Prime Minister Zhu Rongji said: "I assure there is no Chinese threat to India. I confirm our keenness on good neighbourly relations and peaceful co-existence. Beijing had no time to threaten or scare other countries, as it is busy with its own economic development. Any view on China's fearful size came only from India. No other State took this view. India has utilised this theory as a pretext to conduct its nuclear tests. However, the real target behind the nuclear tests is practice of hegemony as well as settling the internal crisis facing the ruling party. Due to limited economic capabilities, China sets aside a limited percentage of its resources for defence purposes. It is less than that allocated by India and Japan. In fact, China needs some defence capabilities."

Jaswant Singh, who attended the ASEAN meeting at Manila as the Indian Prime Minister's special representative, met Tang Jiaxuan, the Chinese

Foreign Minister, on July 27,1998. A Chinese spokesman later said that "both sides conducted frank discussions on the Indian nuclear explosions and Sino-Indian relations." He added that during the discussions, the Chinese Foreign Minister stressed that India, running counter to the world trend, conducted nuclear tests and that India, "in an attempt to find an excuse for the tests, groundlessly alleged that China poses a threat to India."

A joint statement issued by Tang Jiaxuan and his Filipino counterpart, Domingo Siazon after bilateral talks on August 2,1998, expressed the support of the two countries for the Security Council Resolution 1172 of June 6,1998. The two countries expressed "their grave concern over and strongly deplored the recent nuclear tests in South Asia. These had exacerbated tensions in the region and raised the spectre of a nuclear arms race." In a statement in the Lok Sabha, the lower House of the Indian Parliament, on August 4,1998, Prime Minister Vajpayee said India was keen on improving its relations with China and asserted that his Government had never dubbed China as an enemy or a threat. He also said that India wanted to accelerate the efforts for a solution to the border problem.

Commenting on this statement on August 7,1998, Tang Guoqiang, spokesman of the Chinese Foreign Office, said: "We have taken note of the Prime Minister's statement in Parliament. We hope that the Indian side will take concrete actions so that the bilateral relations will return to normal." Replying to a question on the Kashmir issue on August 11,1998, the same spokesman distanced himself from the views mentioned in the "China Daily" article and re-stated the traditional Chinese position. He said: " Kashmir is an outstanding issue between India and Pakistan. The Chinese position on that is consistent. The Chinese side hopes that India and Pakistan will solve their dispute through peaceful negotiations and maintain calm and restraint before the solution of the problem."

Addressing a meeting of industrialists organised at New Delhi on August 12,1998, by the Federation of Indian Chambers of Commerce and Industry, Zhou Gang, the Chinese Ambassador, made yet another reassuring statement. He said that despite the setback to the Sino-Indian bilateral relations, there was scope for increased bilateral trade and economic relations "because the reforms and the opening up of the economy in both the countries have provided great opportunities for expanding trade and economic relations." He expressed his optimism that "on the eve of the next century trade and economic relations and cooperation between China and India would be pushed on to a new high." However, while talking to journalists after the meeting, he added that India's nuclear tests had severely damaged bilateral relations and "this will spill over to the economic relations also." In reply to questions during the daily press briefing on August 13,1998, Tang Guoqiang, the Chinese Foreign Office spokesman, again evaded comments on China's reaction to India's no-first-use of nuclear weapons offer and repeated the Chinese demand that India should first give up its nuclear programme and sign unconditionally the NPT and the CTBT.

Addressing a meeting at the Bharat Chamber of Commerce at Calcutta on September 14,1998, Zhou Gang, the Chinese Ambassador, said differences between the two countries should not be seen as an obstacle to fostering trade. He added: "Expansion of economic relations, trade and technological co-operation between our two countries is beneficial for the overall development of bilateral relations and in conformity with the fundamental interests of the people of our two countries." He also claimed that China's nuclear tests were undertaken in the interest of self-defence.

China reacted sharply to a courtesy call by the Dalai Lama on Prime Minister Vajpayee in the third week of October 1998. On October 22,1998, a Chinese Foreign Office spokesman described it as a violation of India's commitment to keep itself away from the Dalai Lama's anti-Chinese activities. Rejecting the Chinese criticism, a spokesman of the Indian Foreign Office pointed out the next day that the Dalai Lama had been received in his capacity as a religious leader by successive Indian Prime Ministers and that leaders of other countries had similarly received him too. The 11th meeting of the JWG, which should have been held in the second half of 1998, could not be held due to the misunderstanding in the bilateral relations. While talking to a group of visiting American journalists at New Delhi in the middle of November, 1998, a diplomat of the Chinese Embassy said that China had adopted an "active approach" to the subject and that the matter was under discussion through diplomatic channels.

In his briefing for the US journalists, the unnamed Chinese diplomat reportedly made the following points:

- China acquired a nuclear weapon capability in the context of the cold war. After the end of the cold war the trend was towards non-proliferation.
- The Indian tests were against the contemporary historical trend and seriously affected peace and stability in South Asia. The Indian tests had also dealt a heavy blow to international nuclear disarmament and the global non-proliferation regime.
- China did not agree that there was a nuclear apartheid. "The nuclear status of the five permanent members of the UN Security Council is

a product of history. In our opinion, favouring the NPT doesn't mean that the nuclear weapon states will enjoy the permanent privilege of possessing nuclear weapons. China had all along urged countries with the largest nuclear arsenals to speed up the process of nuclear weapon reduction. As a nuclear state, China will never shirk its own responsibility for the complete prohibition and thorough destruction of nuclear weapons in the end."

- "China has always been committed, on the basis of the Five Principles of Peaceful Co-Existence, to the development of good neighbourly and friendly relations with its neighbouring countries, including India. China has made unremitting efforts to improve and develop Sino-Indian relations. This stand of China has not changed. Before and after India's nuclear tests, the Indian Defence Minister and other senior officials preached the China threat theory and made wanton accusations against China. All this cannot but affect the normal development of the bilateral relations. The responsibility for upsetting Sino-Indian relations at present is totally on the Indian side. As the ball is now in the Indian court, we hope that apart from expressing its willingness to improve the relations in words, what is more important for the Indian side is to take concrete actions to improve the relations."

A joint declaration signed by Russian President Boris Yeltsin and Jiang Zemin, at the end of the latter's visit to Russia on November 25,1998, cited South Asia along with Kosovo, Afghanistan and Korea as regions of "the most acute conflict situations, which, if they escalate, may pose real threats to the international community." It added: "On South Asia, Russia and China confirm their position expressed in the UN and at other international fora and stress the paramount importance of the NPT and the CTBT for the global efforts to promote the non-spread of nuclear arms and nuclear disarmament. Russia and China call upon all countries which have not yet joined these treaties so far to do so without delay and without conditions."

Russian Foreign Office officials tried to play down the significance of the reference by saying that they had succeeded in toning down a harsh statement which Jiang wanted and in ruling out any reference to India by name. According to them, since Jiang insisted on some reference to it in the joint declaration they had to agree to a mild formulation which need not cause embarrassment to India.

In a letter to Jaswant Singh on December 15,1998, congratulating him on his taking over as the Minister for External Affairs, Tang Jiaxuan, the

Chinese Foreign Minister, hoped that Sino-Indian relations could be consolidated and further developed during Singh's tenure. In his reply to the message, Jaswant Singh said:" India remains committed to the process of dialogue to address and resolve outstanding issues." He referred to his meeting with Tang at Manila and said that he looked forward to "continuing our interaction to further mutual understanding, co-operation and friendship, so essential for our two countries and peoples."

In his first press conference after taking office, Jaswant Singh stated that India was committed to improving its ties with China so that all outstanding issues were resolved in accordance with the five principles of peaceful co-existence.

In his daily press briefing on December 28,1998, Zhu Bangzao, the spokesman of the Chinese Foreign Office, said: " We welcome Minister for External affairs Jaswant Singh's remarks. China has always attached importance to the growth of its good neighbourly, friendly and co-operative ties with India on the basis of the five principles of peaceful co-existence. Normalisation of Sino-Indian relations complies with the fundamental interests of the people of both the countries."

The "Jane's Defence Weekly" reported in the last week of December, 1998, that the Chinese authorities had assessed that India would take at least 10 years to establish an operational nuclear strike capability and, hence, India did not pose an immediate threat to China's security.

China strongly expressed its annoyance over the remarks of Ram Jethmalani, the Indian Urban Affairs Minister, that there was a strong case for India to recognise Taiwan as an independent country. He made these remarks in an interview to "The Week" of Kerala in the last week of December 1998.

The "People's Daily" wrote on December 31,1998: "We strongly urge certain Indian politicians to stop interfering in China's internal affairs and work towards improving rather than damaging the bilateral ties. Jethmalani's remarks have further hurt the feelings of the Chinese people. "

In a despatch on January 1,1999, Xinhua described Jethmalani's remarks as "evil-minded and dangerous." In an article on January 6,1999, the "China Daily" asked Indian leaders "not to test China's patience with irresponsible comments" and to adopt a coherent policy towards China. It added: "China's goodwill and repeated patience should not be returned with vile language." The criticism came down after the Government of India, through the Indian Embassy in Beijing as well as through its press spokesman in New Delhi, assured China that there was no change in India's policy on Taiwan.

There were clear indications in January 1999, that while showing readiness to restore the pre-Pokhran II normalcy to the bilateral relations, China remained determined in its opposition to India's acquiring any nuclear deterrence capability. Addressing a meeting of non-proliferation experts in Washington in the middle of January 1999, Sha Zukang, head of the Department of Arms Control and Disarmament in China's Foreign Office, reportedly stated as follows:

- "It is a direct violation of UN Security Council Resolution 1172 to negotiate, or to even discuss, with India on India's so-called minimum nuclear deterrence capability."
- "It is also unhelpful to publicly support India's permanent membership in the UN Security Council soon after its nuclear tests."
- The South Asian tests had become a litmus test for the effectiveness of the global non-proliferation regime. The international community should do its best to stop and reverse the nuclear weapons programmes of India and Pakistan.
- There were two essential requirements for the success of the international nuclear diplomacy in the sub-continent. First, " the international community should have sufficient patience and perseverance and should not lose hope because of the lack of progress in the short run." Second, "the major powers must have a consensus view and take concerted actions in this matter."
- "If any country seeks to exploit the South Asian situation to obtain unilateral, short-term political, economic or strategic benefits at the expense of the other countries and the international solidarity, it can only further undermine the already badly-damaged international non-proliferation regime, and, in the end, the long-term interests of that country will also be jeopardised."
- "We have noted with concern that after the Indian nuclear tests, some Nuclear Suppliers' Group members have taken a more pro-active stand on issues of nuclear co-operation with India. We hope that these countries could be more cautious in this area."

In an interview to the "Handelsblatt" of Germany on February 2,1999, Tang Jiaxuan, the Chinese Foreign Minister, rejected indirectly the idea of a Russia-India-China strategic triangle to which Prime Minister Yevgeny Primakov had referred during his visit to India in December, 1998. Tang spoke of China's "very good strategic partnership with Russia, which is full of vitality and regularly produces new elements" but clarified that Beijing's partnership with Moscow "includes neither alliances nor confrontation with third countries such as the US."

He described relations with India as far from ideal and blamed India for the deterioration in the relations. He urged India "to take practical steps towards the restoration of normal and healthy relations."

In an interview to the Press Trust of India on February 4,1999, Zhou Gang, the Chinese Ambassador to India, said: "India, instead of maintaining the so-called minimum nuclear deterrent, must accede to the CTBT and the NPT without delay and conditions."

Referring to speculation about the possible easing of sanctions against India by the US in the wake of the latest round of Jaswant Singh-Strobe Talbott discussions, he said:"Basically, China does not advocate sanctions."

On Primakov's strategic triangle idea, the Ambassador said:" China handles international affairs by proceeding from the fundamental interests of the people of China and the whole world and does not enter into alliances with any big power or group of countries. China's developing relations with any other country are not directed against another country." In his daily press briefing on February 23, 1999, a spokesman of the Chinese Foreign Ministry welcomed the Vajpayee-Nawaz Sharif summit and the resulting Lahore Declaration. He added: "We hope the two sides will keep the momentum of dialogue and solve their differences through peaceful negotiations and consultations."

In his inaugural address to the budget session of the Indian Parliament on February 22,1999, President K.R.Narayanan said that India "seeks to strengthen and deepen its historic and friendly relations with China" and "is looking forward to continuing the dialogue with that country."

Addressing a seminar on Sino-Indian relations at New Delhi on February 25,1999, Zhou Gang, the Chinese Ambassador, said as follows:

- "We have consistently believed that the problems that cropped up in the Sino-Indian relations are temporary and can be surmounted. There exist extensive common interests between China and India and our commonalties far outweigh our differences."
- 'The outstanding issue between China and India is no more than the boundary dispute left behind by history." These differences could be resolved on the basis of the five principles of peaceful co-existence and in accordance with the principle of mutual understanding and mutual accommodation.
- "We have noted that the Indian side has recently expressed its

willingness to attach importance to its relations with China, not to view China as an enemy,and resume the dialogue, so as to find solutions to mutual concerns."

- China was not involved in the Pakistani nuclear and missile programmes."All co-operation between China and Pakistan in the field of peaceful uses of nuclear energy is under the safeguards of the IAEA. Non-existent is the issue of nuclear and missile proliferation to Pakistan. In fact, the Chinese side has already taken note of some concerns of the Indian side and, proceeding from the overall interests of friendly relations between China and India, it has taken a positive, flexible and pragmatic approach and made proper re-adjustment of certain policies concerned."
- The entire historical baggage of Sino-Indian differences could not be shed overnight, but only on the basis of reciprocity in a step by step manner. "All this needs a favourable atmosphere in our bilateral relations. Therefore, we hope that the Indian side will also adopt a flexible and pragmatic approach and solve the Chinese side's concerns earnestly."
- The attribution of a Chinese threat to justify India's nuclear tests by some personalities was mainly responsible for the recent deterioration in the Sino-Indian relations. "All this has deeply hurt the feelings of the Chinese people and seriously harmed the Sino-Indian relations. This is the main cause upsetting Sino-Indian relations."

The Ambassador's presentation coincided with the visit of a team of officials of India's Ministry of External Affairs to Beijing for three days from February 25,1999, to prepare the ground for holding the delayed JWG meeting.

In the daily press briefing on March 1,1999, Ms. Zhang Qiyue, a spokesperson of the Chinese Foreign Office, commented as follows on the talks with the Indian team: "Both sides discussed India's tests and their impact on Sino-Indian ties and expounded their respective positions on the issue. The two sides also focused on bilateral issues and re-affirmed their faith in the five principles of peaceful co-existence. The two sides agreed to work for the restoration and improvement of bilateral relations."

A spokesman of the Indian Embassy in Beijing said that India stoutly defended its position on the Pokhran tests and added: "We pointed out to them India's rejection of the UN Security Council resolution and our stand on the NPT and the CTBT." Addressing a press conference during the session of the National People's Congress, Tang Jiaxuan, the Chinese Foreign Minister, said on March 7.1999: "I expect, may be soon, the JWG on the boundary question between China and India will resume its activity." He again appealed to India and Pakistan to roll back their nuclear programme.

Addressing a seminar on "India, China and Russia in the 21st century" organised by the Indian Council of World Affairs at New Delhi on March 9,1998, Zhou Gang, the Chinese Ambassador, said:

- The recent consultations in Beijing between officials of the two Foreign Offices marked a "new starting point" to improve bilateral relations.
- "We have noted that the Indian side has recently expressed its willingness to attach importance to and improve relations with China and not view China as its enemy. All this is welcome."
- China was pursuing an independent foreign policy vis-à-vis Russia, the US and India. "As powers of major influence and permanent members of the UN Security Council, China and the US share common interests on major issues related to peace and development in the Asia-Pacific region and the world as a whole. The two sides have decided to work together for the establishment of a constructive strategic partnership."
- The concept of a Sino-Russian strategic partnership did not have any military connotations. "Building a Sino-Russian strategic partnership is not aimed at forming an alliance and is not directed at any third party, but is aimed at abandoning confrontations between the two countries so as to create conditions for the broadest equal exchanges and co-operation."
- "It is the firm policy of the Chinese Government to develop with India, a long-term neighbourly, constructive and co-operative partnership into the 21st century. The two countries had the foundation and potential for evolving mutually beneficial co-operation. India and China shared similar or common views on such issues as peace and development, human rights, environmental protection and population control."
- "Strict adherence to the five principles of peaceful, co-existence, mutual trust and shedding a threat image of each other were the key for laying a credible foundation for a healthy Sino-Indian relationship."
- China hoped that "South Asian countries will treat one another on an equal footing, live in harmony, develop friendly co-operation and settle their differences and disputes through peaceful means."

- When the bilateral relations were developing without a hitch, some personalities in India accused China of posing a threat to India's security so as to justify the nuclear tests. This was the main cause for upsetting the bilateral relations. Beijing's policy was defensive in nature and any fear of a China threat was entirely "unfounded and fabricated with ulterior motives."

In an interview to the PTI on March 21,1999, Sha Zukang, Director-General of the Department of Arms Control and Disarmament in the Chinese Foreign Office, said:

- "We have never posed a threat to India and history clearly shows that...We didn't have New Delhi in mind when we decided to go nuclear."
- Since China became a nuclear power, it had never threatened any country. "On the contrary, because of our own bitter experience of being blackmailed, we have declared to the world that we would never be the first to use nuclear weapons. To say China's nuclear weapons are threatening the security of India is hurting."
- China was willing to resume dialogue with India in the post-Pokhran phase, provided New Delhi took concrete actions to normalise strained bilateral relations. "We are prepared to enhance dialogue with India so as to clear misgivings, further mutual understanding and promote the goal of establishing a constructive and co-operative partnership between China and India. We hope that the Indian side will also take concrete actions in the same direction."
- "We continue to maintain that India and Pakistan should fully implement the UN Security Council Resolution 1172. To maintain peace and stability in South Asia and establish a nuclear-weapon-free world, both South Asian neighbours should abandon their nuclear weapons programmes and unconditionally accede to the NPT and the CTBT."

In an address to the United Services Institution (USI) of New Delhi on March 24,1999, Zhou Gang, the Chinese Ambassador, said as follows:

- "There exists profound traditional friendship between the people of the two countries. China and India sympathised and supported each other during their struggles of national independence and liberation against foreign aggression. The two countries share similar or identical views on many major issues such as economic development, human rights, environmental protection, combating drug trafficking and crime and population control."

- "There is nothing abnormal about some differences between the two countries. As long as both sides proceed from the overall interests of bilateral friendly relations and handle these concerns on the basis of mutual trust, with a positive, flexible and pragmatic approach and in a truth-seeking and forward-looking spirit, the differences will be narrowed gradually and problems resolved instead of coming in the way of the normal development of the bilateral relations."
- "Good neighbourly relations between India and China will not only conform to the fundamental interests of the two countries, but will encourage peace, stability and development in Asia and the world at large."
- "The outstanding issue between China and India is no more than the boundary dispute left behind by history. The Chinese Government has maintained that while positively seeking a solution to the boundary issue, the two sides should work hard to develop bilateral relations in various fields so as to create a favourable atmosphere for the final solution of the boundary issue. China stood for a peaceful, fair and equitable solution to the boundary issue on the basis of the five principles of peaceful co-existence, in accordance with the principle of mutual understanding and mutual accommodation through friendly talks, while taking into account the historical background and the present reality and the national feelings of the people of the two countries."
- "China welcomed the resumption of talks between the two Foreign Office officials in February. This useful meeting provides a new starting point for the improvement of Sino-Indian ties." He hoped that the two sides trust each other and treat each other with sincerity and strictly adhere to the five principles of peaceful co-existence.

Talking to pressmen on April 2,1999, Brajesh Mishra, Principal Secretary to the Indian Prime Minister, said that an official dialogue with Beijing had already commenced and that the forthcoming JWC meeting might result in a visit to China by the Indian Minister for External Affairs.

During a meeting with a visiting delegation of the Congress (I) led by K.Natwar Singh, at Beijing on April 8,1999,Hu Jintao, the Chinese Vice-President, asked India to pursue a long-term policy on Sino-Indian relations in view of the "complex and dynamic international situations unfolding at the turn of the century." He said that under the changing international situation today, India and China should "look closely at and handle the relations between the two countries from the historical perspective and a long-term viewpoint." He noted that the bilateral relations had progressed on the normal track over the past decade "thanks to the joint efforts of the leaders of the two countries ", and regretted the chill in the bilateral relations after Pokhran II. The process of progress had consequently suffered "undesirable disturbances", he said.

Reports of Chinese reaction to the Agni II missile test available so far indicate that the spokesman of the Chinese Foreign Office expressed regret and concern at the test which, he pointed out, was a violation of the Security Resolution 1172 and added:" We have taken note of the remark by the Indian Prime Minister that this test is not directed against any country."

The annual report of the Indian Defence Ministry for 1998-99 released on April 16,1999, said as follows on Sino-Indian relations:

- Sino-Indian relations have improved in recent years and New Delhi regards China as "a great neighbour."
- India does not regard China "as an adversary and would like to develop mutually friendly relations with it."
- India has expressed its interest time and again in resolving its boundary dispute with China peacefully and through bilateral negotiations as quickly as possible.
- The September 1993 agreement on peace and tranquillity and the subsequent accord on confidence-building measures provided a reliable framework for the maintenance of peace and tranquillity in the border areas.
- Contacts between the two sides such as the meeting between Jaswant Singh and Tang Jiaxuan at Manila and the earlier visit to India by the Chinese Chief of General Staff serve the objective of furthering mutual understanding between the two countries and reassuring each other about their peaceful intentions.

THE MODI-XI SUMMIT AND CHINA-INDIA RELATIONS

Chinese President Xi Jinping will travel to India for a three-day visit to meet with Indian Prime Minister Narendra Modi and others there in government and business. The bilateral environment for this trip is better than last year when Chinese Prime Minister Li Keqiang went to India a few weeks after a border standoff and former Prime Minister Manmohan Singh traveled to Beijing in his last few months in office. Mr. Xi's visit is part of what have been three-plus months of intense Indian activity in the foreign policy realm since Mr. Modi took office in May. It comes a couple of weeks after the Indian prime minister's visit to Japan and the Australian prime minister's trip to India, just after the Indian president visited Vietnam, and less than two weeks before Mr. Modi meets with U.S. President Barack Obama in Washington.

The Chinese president's visit, in particular, involves a country that poses both an opportunity and a challenge for the Modi government. As a result of this, and the fact that the state of China-India relations can potentially affect the situation in Asia and beyond, this visit is being watched closely.

This piece looks at where the China-India relationship stands, the backdrop of the Xi visit, what the two sides will be looking for and trying to signal, the trip agenda, as well as what all this means for the United States.

Recently, the Indian foreign minister frankly noted that India's relations with China were currently "good," but involved both "competition and cooperation."

Arguably, there is also a potential for conflict. The cooperative elements of the relationship include a burgeoning economic relationship, greater dialogue on issues like Afghanistan and counterterrorism, as well as cooperation in multilateral forums, including BRICS (Brazil, Russia, India, China and South Africa) and on multilateral issues such as climate change.

The competitive and conflictual elements that will hang over Mr. Xi's visit include the long-standing boundary dispute between the two countries, China's concerns about the presence of the Dalai Lama and other Tibetan leaders in India, as well as India's concerns about Chinese dam construction on its side of the Brahmaputra river and cyber-espionage and cyber-security threats. Each country also has broader concerns about the other's relationships with third countries. In China's case, India's developing relationships with countries in the Asia-Pacific, especially Japan and the U.S., and perhaps Australia and Vietnam. In India's case, particularly China's relationship with Pakistan, but also its overtures to India's smaller neighbours and Beijing's increasing interest in playing a role in the Indian Ocean region.

In addition, the very issue that was supposed to bind the two countries—economic ties—has been a source of trouble. Bilateral trade has actually fallen over the last few years from $74 billion in 2011 to about $65 billion in 2013. From India's perspective, what's also been problematic is its growing trade deficit with China ($31 billion in 2013). Furthermore, bilateral investment has remained limited, with both sides complaining about market access in the other country.

The Backdrop: A New Government in Delhi; A Beijing Looking for Partners

None of these problems is new, but what is new is the government in Delhi. The majority government in India—the first of its kind in two and a half decades—is led by someone who is no stranger to China. Mr. Modi traveled there when he was chief minister of the state of Gujarat in order to seek investments and markets for his state and its companies.

In the past, he has expressed concern about China on the security front. However, he has also stated his admiration for its economic achievements and a desire to do business with that country, especially in order to deliver on his campaign promises of growth and development. Mr. Xi's visit thus offers an opportunity to attract Chinese investment, as well as elevate India's role on the world stage. Furthermore, there will be an underlying hope that the visit (and other recent ones) will encourage competitive courting by the U.S.

Chinese officials, in turn, welcomed Mr. Modi's election, emphasizing that they were ready to work with someone they see as a business-minded leader.

The first senior official to visit India from the P-5 was indeed the Chinese foreign minister, sent as Mr. Xi's special envoy. For Mr. Xi, his own visit offers an opportunity to establish a relationship with the new Indian government and especially Mr. Modi. A stable relationship with India could ease pressure on one of China's borders.

Furthermore, a good relationship could limit how far Delhi takes things with Tokyo and Washington. Mr. Xi's task, at least on this visit, has been made easier by the fact that he postponed his visit to Pakistan. But he will be cognizant of the fact that he is not the only one wooing India right now, and not the only country that India, on its part, is wooing. Moreover, in the outgoing Indian visits to Japan and Vietnam, China was a publicly unspoken theme and it'll likely be so when Mr. Modi visits the U.S. later this month.

Mr. Xi's Visit

These and other issues provide the backdrop to Mr. Xi's visit and in some cases will be agenda items. Economic issues will be a key focus of the visit. The Chinese government is aware that an imbalanced economic relationship poses a problem for broader ties and is not sustainable, not least because Mr. Modi stressed this point when he met Mr. Xi on the sidelines of the BRICS summit in Brazil. It is also an issue the Indian commerce minister discussed with her Chinese counterparts recently in Beijing. Chinese officials have noted that in order to help address this imbalance, Mr. Xi will take with him investment commitments of over $100 billion over five years. They have suggested that these will especially be targeted towards the infrastructure and manufacturing sectors, which are focus areas for Mr. Modi, and will likely involve the establishment of industrial parks, including one in Mr. Modi's home state. Offers of more Chinese financing for Indian companies are also likely to be on the table. Mr. Xi is also likely to seek Indian participation in Chinese initiatives for regional connectivity, an offer that India will likely consider but not to the exclusion of other such initiatives.

The economic component of the relationship is likely to be one of the main points of focus during Mr. Xi's first stop in Ahmedabad in Gujarat. This leg of the visit will also give Chinese officials a chance to highlight that the bilateral relationship does not just involve the central governments in both countries, but also states and businesses. Overall, the economic dimension is also providing Mr. Xi's government a way to try to one-up Japan, with the Chinese consul general explicitly comparing China's potential economic offers to the recent Japanese commitment of $35 billion over seven years.

Some believe that this moment also offers an opportunity for the two countries to move ahead on border talks, especially transitioning from managing the dispute to trying to solve it. Indeed, a former Indian foreign secretary has urged the Indian government to press this issue at what he sees is an advantageous time when China is courting India. During Mr. Xi's visit, we might see the announcement of the next step on this front.

In addition, there will likely be discussion of a number of global and regional issues, not least the situation in Afghanistan, as well as the Middle East.

This visit, however, is not just about substance, but also about style. Just as Mr. Li did last year, Mr. Xi has been trying to use this visit to (a) signal that China considers India to be important and (b) add a personal dimension to the relationship. An underlying irritant for many in India has been the sense that Beijing has, at best, treated India as irrelevant or peripheral and, at worst, been trying to contain India or prevent India's rise—not least through China's support of Pakistan, as well as its reluctance to endorse a permanent seat for India on the U.N. Security Council and past objections to Indian membership in the Nuclear Suppliers Group (NSG). In the lead up to the visit, Chinese policymakers have tried to mitigate some of these concerns, indicating support for India's membership in the Shanghai Cooperation Organization and inviting Mr. Modi to the Asia-Pacific Economic

Cooperation meeting in Beijing. One thing to watch during Mr. Xi's visit is whether China will take further steps on this front—even if just rhetorical.

On his part, Mr. Modi is going out of his way for Mr. Xi in some respects, sending his national security advisor as his special envoy to Beijing to, among other things, stress the importance the government is placing on the visit. More significantly, he is making a "special gesture," possibly against the advice of a number of his diplomats, since it is a departure from Indian protocol, to greet Mr. Xi in Ahmedabad.

While the Chinese president perhaps can't compete with the personal relationship that Japanese Prime Minister Shinzo Abe has established with Mr. Modi over the last many years, Mr. Xi has tried to inject a personal dimension, saying that when he first met Mr. Modi he "felt like meeting an old friend." He is also travelling first to the prime minister's home state, and will visit the Sabarmati Ashram that is linked to Mahatma Gandhi and India's struggle for independence.

The Chinese president has tried to emphasize the commonalities not just between the two countries, but particularly between the tasks that lie ahead for Mr. Modi and him. There are indeed commonalities between Mr. Modi and Mr. Xi, two Asian leaders that have tried to emphasize that they will take "strong economy, strong security" approaches. Yet the contrast in terms of how the two leaders came to be in power couldn't be more different: one was elected democratically; the other was selected by a chosen few. As Dhruva Jaishankar of the German Marshall Fund has noted, the disparity in their backgrounds is also striking: one, a former tea seller; the other, a prince-ling.

Challenges and Questions

For this visit and beyond, challenges and questions lie ahead for the China-India relationship.

There are open questions with regard to China, including: How much can and will Mr. Xi do to assuage Indian concerns, particularly on the border and Pakistan? How will China react if the Modi government follows through with its plans for military modernization, border infrastructure upgradation and the development of India's northeast? What will Beijing do with regard to Tibet, particularly in the event of a transition in Tibetan leadership?

There are also a number of questions with regard to the Indian government:

Can Mr. Modi deliver domestically? A common challenge to all India's key relationships is that they are both motivated by and dependent on domestic transformation in India, especially on the economic side. Chinese capital, companies and attention will come to India if Mr. Modi's government is seen as delivering on his promises of growth, governance and getting things done. If there is a sense that he can't deliver, they might lose interest.

What happens if and when there's a crisis or if China crosses an Indian red line? We haven't seen major Sino-Indian tension or setbacks since Mr. Modi took over, but we have seen in his government's approach to Pakistan that its reaching out is contingent on a sense that the other country is acting in good faith. But the relationships with China and Pakistan aren't equivalent, and many will watch to see how Mr. Modi will respond if and when there's a sense that China hasn't acted in good faith.

Mr. Modi's predecessors have found that even minor crises can derail the bilateral relationship or at least result in a two-steps-forward-one-step-back dynamic. This is partly because the Indian media and public are not inclined to give Beijing the benefit of the doubt. There is still a lack of trust in the relationship, especially in India where narratives related to the 1962 Sino-Indian war continue to resonate. There remain questions in India about Chinese intentions, evidenced from the fact that in the press conference to preview Mr. Xi's visit, the Indian foreign ministry spokesperson found himself fielding skeptical questions about allegations of Chinese border transgressions. This lack of trust is compounded by a lack of (or limited) knowledge of the other on both sides.

Can Mr. Modi's government walk the China-India tightrope effectively, with the fine balance necessary to reconcile competing interests? The Indian diplomatic corps is no stranger to this challenge and we've already seen the new Indian government try to grapple with it. For example, the foreign minister stating that China "should understand and appreciate our sensitivities regarding Arunachal" while the foreign ministry has avoided answering the question of whether Indian minister of state for home affairs Kiren Rijiju (who is from the state of Arunachal Pradesh, which China claims) will attend the dinner for Mr. Xi. Or, the government making clear that the Dalai Lama and Tibetans will continue to be welcome in India while they will likely try to limit Tibetan protests—or at least their visibility—during the Chinese president's visit.

Mr. Modi has a base, a media and, arguably, a population that tends to be skeptical, if not suspicious, of China. It won't be lost on Mr. Modi that he's taking a risk; that some will question the nature of his welcome for the Chinese president, that some will draw comparisons with former Indian Prime Minister Nehru's embrace of the Chinese leadership before Sino-

Indian relations turned sour. But Mr. Modi is likely calculating that the opportunity is worth it and that his "strong" credentials will dampen criticism.

The tag line that the Indian government is propagating is that its foreign policy will have a strong face, a sensitive face and a proactive face. And while the "sensitive" face will perhaps be more visible during Mr. Xi's visit, the Modi government has also been finding ways to convey that they will neither be push-overs nor hesitate to express Indian concerns, and will speak from a position of strength. Hence, early on, the invitation to Tibetan leader Lobsang Sangay to attend the government's swearing in. Last week, the Indian foreign minster asserted that her Chinese counterpart has been told, "If we believe in one China policy, you should also believe in one India policy." In Japan, we've seen Mr. Modi criticizethose who encroach on others' lands and seas, and state his preference for countries that emphasize a development-focused rather than an expansionist mindset. While the Indian foreign minister refused to confirm or deny that these were references to China, they only reiterated a sentiment Mr. Modi had explicitly expressed about China in Arunachal Pradesh during the election campaign. The just-concluded Indian presidential visit to Vietnam has, in turn, resulted in a joint communique that expresses support for "freedom of navigation in the East Sea/South China Sea," with India welcoming the chance to host the Vietnamese prime minister in October and the offer of additional oil and gas blocks for exploration by an Indian state-owned company.

The "strong face" is also being signaled through statements and suggestions that India is politically stronger and will be economically so as well. Furthermore, there is an attempt to convey this by taking on any suggestion that China is India's superior in civilizational terms—witness Mr. Modi's statements and tweets on how Buddhism traveled from India to China, a connection that China used to try to downplay. Finally, the government will try to signal this strength through the continued pursuit of a diversification strategy, highlighting that India has options by engaging with a number of countries, including Australia, Japan, Russia, Vietnam and the U.S.

Where Does the U.S. Fit In?

The India-U.S. relationship is partly driven and shaped by the two countries' perceptions of and relationships with China. Delhi and Washington, therefore, watch closely how the other is interacting with Beijing.

It's a complex, dynamic triangle. On the one hand, the U.S. would like to see a stable China-India relationship, especially given other tensions in Asia and the world. Furthermore, it won't necessarily mind if Chinese investment in India leads to a better Indian economy and, particularly, infrastructure that can redound to the benefit of American business as well. On the other hand, the U.S. would not like to see China and India grow too close, China dominate the Indian economy or for the two countries to form a tag team—with Russia possibly in tow as well—in multilateral fora.

Similarly, on the one hand, Indian concerns about a potential G-2 persist—the idea that China and the U.S., which are economically interdependent, will act together in a fashion that will be to India's detriment.

A different manifestation of this concern is the assessment that the U.S. is not a reliable partner vis-à-vis China because it will choose China when push comes to shove. On the other hand, Indian officials don't want to see Sino-U.S. tensions that might destabilize the entire region, jeopardizing Indian domestic goals.

In addition, the Indian leadership recognizes that American concerns about Chinese intentions and the nature of the Chinese government are partly what make India important to key constituencies in the U.S.—something Delhi finds useful—but it also doesn't want to be asked to choose between China and the United States. Defense Secretary Hagel indeed recently acknowledged this Indian concern in Delhi.

Another dimension for India is that its officials realize that what is partly driving China's diplomatic and economic interest in India is its relationship with countries like Japan and the U.S. Thus, India will continue to reach out to these countries bilaterally and even in a trilateral context.

Furthermore, even if not explicitly, the U.S. is also considered to be part of India's strategic insurance policy. The U.S. can help manage China's rise and assure the kind of Asia that India would like to see. The Indian government does not share what some have outlined as Mr. Xi's vision of Asia, with China the dominant country and with the U.S. playing a minimal role.

The fact that India would like to see a different kind of Asia is reflected in the Tokyo declaration that notes that the responsibility that India and Japan share to shape "the character of this region." It is also evident in the repeated statements from Indian officials that they would like to see a continued, effective U.S. role in the Asia-Pacific.

While they have various concerns about each other, however, it's also worth keeping in mind that China, India and the U.S. also share some common concerns—including those related to Afghanistan (and even Pakistan), the Middle East and climate change—and this offers the prospect of cooperation, or at least, consultation in the future.

PROSPECTS FOR SINO-INDIAN RELATIONS

As the need to enhance cooperation and dialogue is the consensus of decision makers in both countries, Sino-Indian Strategic partnership is entering a new phase of development. This general orientation would not be affected by changing domestic political circumstances in both countries. Looking ahead, one needs to take note of the following developments in Sino-Indian relations:

Near-term Uncertainties and Variables

As the General Election is approaching in the coming year, rivalry among all political forces in India will be in full swing. Current top leaders and policy makers, such as Prime Minister Singh, National Security Advisor Menon, and Minister of External Affairs Salman Khurshid, might leave their posts in addition to other personnel changes. This might affect China-Indian relations.

There are not many "China hands" among Young Turks in the National Congress Party and their position and views on India's China policy are not quite clear. If "Right-deviant" party as represented by Bharatiya Janata Party (BJP) comes into power, Sino-Indian relations may proceed in a "learning curve". Of course, whichever political force assumes power in the coming election in India, India's fundamental policy toward China would not change dramatically, but one would definitely see some "fine-tuning" of the strategic tendency and certain specific issues in India's China policy.

Sino-Indian relations

Though years of concerted efforts, China and India have learned hot to treat each other in good terms and properly handling their differences while working for peaceful development. The two countries will gradually rid themselves of the negative impact of old scores and historical disputes and construct a normal relationship as between two close neighbors, a cooperative relationship as between two major powers and a new-type relationship as between two emerging powers sharing weal and woe. Sino-Indian relations will have a more salient and stronger impact on regional and international patterns of relationship. As it rises, India will be more and more confident and poised in its relations with China. The growth of India's own strategic deterrent and increasingly close ties with the United States and other western powers have somewhat alleviated its feeling of insecurity and mentality of being encircled. As India is more confident and is deporting itself in a calmer manner in handling its relations with China, it will more firmly believe that the two countries will mutually benefit from cooperation and friendly exchanges. India has realized that as rapidly rising power, China has a pivotal impact on India's development and security. The mainstream view in India is that maintaining a stable, cooperative and mutually beneficial relationship with China is in India's national interests. Even those strategic analysts and politicians in India who still stubbornly cling to their view that China is "a long-term threat to and a rival of India" tend to think that India can keep such threat and rivalry under control by way of economic engagement, military preparation, diplomatic skill and a balancing strategy of maneuvering among big powers, thus making the bilateral relationship less vulnerable to contingencies.

China and India should not Fight Again

In the foreseeable future, the outbreak of a planned, long-scale military conflict in the border areas between China and India is virtually impossible. A major constraint is the fundamental national interests of both countries for which the top priority is to grasp strategic opportunities in the coming years and shape a secure and stable domestic and international environment for national rejuvenation. This is also the primary concern in formulating their military and security policies. Moreover, the military strength of both countries has grown markedly in the past several decades. Both countries possess large quantities of conventional arms and a significant nuclear deterrent force, each side having a greater capability to deter and defend against the other. With all these factors at play, war would mean an unbearable disaster fraught with danger ever afterwards for both sides.

Focus of Sino-Indian Relations Shifting

In future, bilateral trade, economic ties and mutual investment will be an increasingly important factor that will affect the evolution of Sino-Indian relations. In other words, more "low politics" issues will affect bilateral relations. Some issues and matters which seemed to be less important or less sensitive in the past may now have major impact on bilateral relations.

While economic cooperation, trade and investment are favorable assets for strengthening and promoting Sino-India relations trade and economic frictions will likewise affect the vital interests of the peoples of the two countries, thereby upsetting the overall bilateral cooperation. National sentiments in the two countries, individual cases of economic disputes and different lobby groups and interest groups would exert more influence on bilateral relations. "High politics" issues such as the border dispute, the Tibetan question and military issues would undoubtedly continue to affect bilateral relations, but they would be less and less important and sensitive. This objectively will be conducive to the solution of such issues.

CLOSER RELATION OF INDIA, CHINA AND BHUTAN

Till the 1960s, the official, economic and military capacities of the Bhutanese leadership to enhance the kingdom's international relations were severely limited by the country's geographical isolation, lack of modern communications and general economic backwardness. As it is, Bhutan being a landlocked country, with enormous mountainous barriers, was far away from mainstream international commercial and political activities. Its leadership and officials may also have been unaware or unconcerned with the world beyond the immediate border regions. They seem to have had no need to venture beyond relations with bordering countries, and that too, only when its own interests mattered. There was almost a complete absence of all forms of communications starting with motor roads, telephones and news media. Even for communications within the country this was possible to some extent only from 1956-57 onwards when wireless sets powered by generators run on imported petroleum carried on human or animal backs to various centers, began to replace mail runners.

Motor roads were constructed into the interior areas of Bhutan from the Indian border from 1961 onwards. Nationwide and viable telephone services were possible only when the Japanese assisted Bhutan with satellite and digital communications as late as the 1980s. The earlier system set up in a tardy fashion was only to meet basic official needs after development plans were begun and could hardly be termed functional or modern, and even then not available for private use. Up to 1985, the Bhutan embassy in Delhi had to communicate with Thimphu by wireless, and this communication was extended to the Permanent Mission of Bhutan to the United Nations in New York through "telex" by the Delhi embassy. As the Bhutanese Ambassador in New Delhi in 1985, the author recalls informing Thimphu about Mrs. Indira Gandhi's tragic assassination through the embassy's wireless facility as phone calls were not possible.

Radio broadcasting began in the country in 1973 as a "youth broadcasting" service through the personal initiative of Karma Tenzing, a graduate from the United States and an officer of the Ministry of Trade, Industries and Forests who seemed to do it out of sheer nationalistic and patriotic feelings. A few years later the government converted this service to a national one and named it Bhutan Broadcasting Service (BBS). Bhutan also did away with its own restrictions on satellite television and the Internet as late as 1999.

During and prior to the rule of the third King there were certain historical legacies and threats, though considered distant and even absurd today, could not be easily ruled out and had to figure in the strategies followed by Bhutan's leaders.

The first was the fear of China and the possibility of this giant neighbor compromising Bhutanese sovereignty. In 1910, when China intervened in Tibet it declared that the Himalayan region including Bhutan, Sikkim, Nepal and Ladakh were parts of China. This fear of China could be said to have manifested in the Treaty of Sinchula with the British, which essentially made Bhutan a "protectorate" of Britain. Henceforth, Bhutan's relations with the outside world would be conducted on the "advice" of Britain, and after the 1949 treaty, by independent India. The concerns over Chinese intentions were again enhanced after the Chinese army intervention of Tibet in 1951 and the violent suppression of the Tibetan revolt in 1959 after which Bhutanese-Tibetan relations of the past effectively came to an end. Bhutan closed its borders and avoided doing anything to antagonize China.

After the 1962 Sino-Indian war over their boundaries, China may have become much more amenable and enthusiastic in giving recognition to Bhutanese sovereignty if only to compromise the 1949 Indo-Bhutan Treaty and India's foothold in the kingdom. At the same time, India may also have been more forthcoming in recognizing and giving more substance in its relations to Bhutanese sovereignty. There was therefore some advantage in Bhutan's geopolitical situation in strengthening its sovereignty.

A more substantive relationship with the Chinese at the time would have been inconceivable for Bhutan. Given the Chinese threats and its announced views of the Himalayan kingdoms, the absorption of Bhutan into Tibet, and therefore, China, loomed as a fearful possibility. The Cultural Revolution of Chairman Mao Zedong would have destroyed all of Bhutan's traditions and the young monarchy. Bhutan would have no longer existed as a distinct cultural and political entity. While considering this possible relation with China in the early 1960s it should be remembered that this was not mere conjecture. There were strong views among some prominent members of the then Bhutanese leadership that Bhutan should move closer to China rather than India, especially from ethnic and cultural points of view. These persons, who fortunately were in the small minority, failed to comprehend that when it comes to safeguarding a nation's sovereignty and independence, ethnicity or racial policies and approaches may not prove to be in one's true interests. One needs to simply look at the histories of Asia, Africa and Europe. The Indians and the Pakistanis, the Japanese and the

Koreans, the Chinese and the Japanese, the Chinese and the Tibetans, the Chinese and the Taiwanese, the Kuwaitis and the Iraqis, don't really get along politically despite racial and cultural similarities. In the 21st century, Africa has faced history's most serious problems in Rwanda, Sudan, Nigeria, Uganda and elsewhere. Again, if Bhutanese consider themselves closer to Tibetans, it should be remembered that the latter have demonstrated attitudes of condescension towards Bhutanese. So a one-sided approach will not succeed. Therefore in national politics, the urge to reach out to other peoples based on preconceived notions that ethnicity and race will better serve one's interests may not be the best of politics for a nation, and leaders and people with such notions should be simply ignored and not permitted to play any significant national role. A nation has to base its international politics on safeguarding its vital interests of sovereignty, independence and security–no matter with which entity or race or ethnicity its leadership may have to deal with. In Bhutan's case this has been glaring. India, rather than Tibet or China, has served Bhutan's interest the best.

Setting the Stage for Indo-Bhutan Relations

King Jigme Dorji Wangchuck ascended the throne in 1952 when Bhutan, Tibet and the region as a whole were going through trying times. In the north, the Chinese intervention in Tibet had acquired a violent and ominous character resulting in the fleeing of the Dalai Lama and thousands of Tibetans into India. The Chinese communists of the times seemed to be in no mood to make any compromises on their claims over Tibet. At the same time they were bent upon integrating the Tibetan region into the "motherland" by all means, including militarily. The Cultural Revolution in China attempted to achieve this through the destruction, and if this was not possible, the dilution of Tibetan religion, culture, language, geographical boundaries and demographics. Thousands of Tibetans fled their homeland and scattered all over the Indian subcontinent and beyond to Europe, the United States and Canada. The Cultural Revolution resulted in the tragic destruction of Tibet's ancient civilization that had for centuries influenced Bhutan and the Himalayan region including Mongolia and parts of China. The "it looks like me" revered statue of Guru Rimpoche in Samye, Tibet, was also destroyed during this period. The Tibetans expected support from an international community that knew or cared very little about them or their struggle. The United States, through its Central Intelligence Agency (CIA), made some half-hearted attempts to provide training and arms to the Tibetan resistance movement but as soon as they felt that their interests were not threatened and Tibet was of little importance to them politically and economically, they dropped even the token assistance being provided. In fact, the resistance put up by Tibetans with CIA assistance may have only helped to make the Chinese reactions harsher. When US aid was abruptly cut off, the Tibetans suffered more as a result.

Neither was Nehru's India in any mood to aid the Tibetans militarily or in the United Nations. In fact, India initially inherited the British view that Tibet was an autonomous region under Chinese "suzerainty" as opposed to "sovereignty"–a legal position that British diplomats had devised to avoid Chinese wrath but seemingly to show some sympathy for Tibet's cause. India, of course, now fully recognizes the sovereignty of China over Tibet, as does China regarding India's Sikkim. From the Indian perspective, Indian diplomats seemed to have had this concept that India's sphere of influence should be paramount south of the Himalayan range and that of China in the north. This was a colonial concept, but the hangover may persist in New Delhi.

Prime Minister Jawaharlal Nehru's government in India after 1947 was in a dilemma on how to react to the developments taking place on the yet-to-be demarcated borders of the Himalayas with China. Nehru seemed basically an idealist who believed that the Indians and Chinese, the two great civilizations and peoples of Asia, and who had both emerged from the yoke of colonialism, could not afford any rivalry. Now, as independent developing countries he expected that both would concentrate on socioeconomic development and deal with neighbours and other countries on the basis of respect for each other's sovereignty and national pride. He was so carried away by the idea of friendship and cooperation that the term "Hindi Chini Bhai Bhai" was coined. Nehru's expectations were shattered in 1962 when the Chinese invaded parts of northern India and disputed India's concept of the borders with China as inherited from the British.

India, Bhutan and Nepal have to be nevertheless given the credit for the help provided and the generosity shown to the waves of Tibetan refugees. India has given a lot of space for Tibetan refugees to sustain their religion and culture in Dharamshala and other parts of India. In the case of Bhutan, those Tibetans who wanted to integrate into Bhutanese society found it easy in view of the ethnic and cultural similarities. Officially Bhutan could not afford to antagonize the Chinese, and hence, had to curb all political activities of the Tibetans that were directed towards China. Internationally, Bhutan could say nothing about Tibet's status even if it wanted to, and politically it became expedient to accept Chinese claims over Tibet. After all, where did Bhutan stand when powers like the United States, the erstwhile Soviet Union, the United Kingdom, India and all major nations acquiesced to the fait accompli in the face of China's evolving global economic and political clout.

Despite the 1949 Treaty with Bhutan, the Government of India was unclear on how it should deal with Bhutan under the circumstances, especially with the Chinese takeover of Tibet and claims over the Himalayan region. Besides Bhutan and Nepal being a consideration, what was more important were the Chinese claims of what India considered its territories like the North East Frontier Agency (NEFA)–later renamed Arunachal Pradesh by Prime Minister Indira Gandhi of India, and Aksai Chin. The Indian army which had just emerged from the partition of their country and the grant of independence by the British, was still not well trained and equipped to meet a threat like that of Mao Zedong's revolutionary China.

In the case of India's relations with Bhutan, Pandit Jawaharlal Nehru provided an unambiguous interpretation in his public speech in Paro on September 23, 1958. He declared: "Some may think that since India is a great and powerful country and Bhutan a small one, the former might wish to exercise pressure on Bhutan. It is, therefore, essential that I make it clear to you that our only wish is that you should remain an independent country, choosing your own way of life and taking the path of progress according to your will. At the same time, we two should live as friendly neighbours helping each other. Freedom of both Bhutan and India should be safeguarded so that none from outside can do harm to it." This statement of Nehru's has proved to be enduring for Indo-Bhutan relations, and was quoted by Prime Minister Dr. Manmohan Singh during his visit to Bhutan in May 2008.

An outsider's assessment of the thinking within the Indian leadership at least till now shows that India decided to accept Chinese claims north of the Himalayas, that is, in Tibet. As for Bhutan, Nepal and Sikkim, India felt that these should be under its sphere of influence both in international relations and security considerations. The problem for India was and still seems to be, is that China has not conceded to this view of the region, and neither have these Himalayan entities all gone the way India wanted. Indira Gandhi's government managed to annex Sikkim by taking advantage of the political upheaval in that country begun by Kazi Lhendup Dorji Khangsarpa. Nevertheless, China put off recognizing this annexation for a long time but has now given in to the fait accompli in exchange of India's consistent stand recognizing China's sovereignty over Tibet. India avoided dealings with Taiwan and supported mainland China's seat at the United Nations just as trade and economic links between the two giants grew, and the enhanced position and role of China on the world stage. This was formally done during

Prime Minister Vajpayee's visit to China in 2003 and further confirmed when the Chinese presented India with revised maps showing Sikkim as a part of India. Nepal has always tried to resist or minimize India's influence while still expecting all the trade and transit advantages in India, emphasizing when it could that this was an international right of landlocked countries. At the same time, Nepal from time to time attempts to play off India and China to its advantage, and which sometimes has backfired. It also refused to accept any defense arrangements with India vis-à-vis China and instead made attempts to import Chinese weaponry including ground to air missiles, which India felt was not in keeping with the treaty relationship between the two countries. This attitude of Nepal has resulted in constant friction in Indo-Nepal relations, and at times has reached seritous proportions when at one time Prime Minister Rajiv Gandhi even decided to close down all transit routes and trade between the two countries–reportedly "to teach Nepal a lesson."

The most recent attempt by Nepal to play off India and China came when the newly elected Prime Minister, Pushpa Kamal Dahal, or more popularly known by his revolutionary name, Prachanda, snubbed New Delhi and made his maiden visit to Beijing in August 2008. When undertaking the boundary negotiations with China, these same principles seemed to find no place in negotiations with the Government of India. The Bhutanese cabinet in the 1970s frequently questioned the Survey Department as to how the boundaries with India had been finalized without explicit cabinet consent let alone through deliberations and approval in the National Assembly. This discussion in the cabinet never resulted in a satisfactory conclusion except to be informed that the basis would be the boundary line finalized with the British, which were most likely unilaterally drawn up by colonial surveyors as in the case of most boundaries in the subcontinent. On the other hand, the border discussions and the periodic outcomes between Bhutan and China have rightly been subjected to lengthy debates in the National Assembly with displays of large detailed maps and sand models at the Royal Bhutan Army headquarters in Lungtenphu, Thimphu. For the sake of mentioning it, the author had been made responsible by the fourth King to lead the border negotiations with China for the first time in Bhutan's history in the summer of 1984.

THE KING OF BHUTAN IS GUIDE BY INDIA

A young monarch and his red-robed Buddhist lamas are trying to assert Bhutan's independence without endangering India's stranglehold on this

Himalayan kingdom. Wedged between India and Chinese-occupied Tibet, the relatively unknown, lightly populated medieval kingdom is one of the poorest nation on earth, Bhutanese officials say. Gigantic 16th century Buddhist fortresses dot the pine forested mountains while villagers, often barefoot, trundle past turbulent rivers toward houses of rough stone. Bhutan has no choice but to maintain friendly relations with India to gain aid, trade and expertise needed for development. "We are in a strategic situation and it is in India's interest that Bhutan remains close neighbours to India, so she would not face any threat from Bhutan," Bhutan's King Jigme Singye Wangchuck told United Press International in a rare, 90-minute interview.

"And for Bhutan too, we need trade with India, aid from India," the 27-year-old king said while sitting on a leopard-skin sofa in his throne room. "We trust the government in power in India and know their thinking. We would not do anything which would endanger our relationship," King Wangchuck said.

Land-locked Bhutan has no heavy industry. It imports almost every daily and essential item from India including gasoline, oil, electricity, medicine and appliances. Though largely self-sufficient in food, Bhutan also depends on India's military to aid the kingdom in times of peace and tension. Bhutan depends on Indian teachers, engineers and advisers.

Goods and people are transported across the few mountain roads, mostly on Indian vehicles. Such total dependence on India by Bhutan has raised concern that New Delhi could one day take over the kingdom, which is populated by only 1.2 million people.

Bhutanese officials, however, publicly insist they trust India has good intentions for their nation. The most frequent phrase used by Bhutanese when describing their fledgling kingdom is "sovereign and independent." Maintaining good relations with New Delhi, however, means shunning China — which beat India during a brief border war in 1962.

Thimpu's refusal to engage in relations with Beijing has destroyed Bhutan's traditional ties with Tibet. For centuries, Bhutan's Drukpa sect of Buddhism, culture, ornate art and much of its heritage came down the snowy mountain passes from Tibet. Bhutan's known history began in the seventh century when Tibetan King Songtsen Gampo built two monasteries in Bhutan. "Bhutan's past was always with the north, with Tibet," one historian said in an interview. "Then, after the Chinese invaded Tibet in the 1950s and the 1962 India-China war, Bhutan turned almost 100 percent to the south, to India. This is a new phase of Bhutan's history." One Bhutanese government official said in an interview, "If we were not bordering China, India probably would not be so concerned about aiding us." The only Chinese-made goods in Bhutan — such as clothing, utensils, and cosmetics — are illegally smuggled in, though sold freely in many shops. The king asked Beijing in 1981 for a bilateral meeting to demarcate their glacier-covered border, 110 miles south of Lhasa, the capital of Tibet. Though Bhutan says China does not occupy any of its territory and the demarcation would be to establish sophisticated markers, Beijing never responded, King Wangchuck said.

Asked if relations with China would improve after the proposed demarcation, the king replied: "We don't have any strategy or idea to have changes in the status quo. We are friendly with the Chinese and the government of India." Bhutan has few troops and no air force. India has a few thousand soldiers stationed in Bhutan, mostly building and maintaining roads while training Bhutan's small army.

Within minutes, however, Indian warplanes could fly over the 8,000-foot high Bhutanese capital of Thimpu from air force bases at Hashimara and Bagdogra in India's West Bengal state, which borders southern Bhutan. Indian personnel stationed inside Bhutan also serve as New Delhi's eyes and ears on Bhutanese affairs. Of vital concern to India is the so-called "Chinese knife" — especially its Chumbi valley at the tip of a dagger-shaped region controlled by China and separating Bhutan from India's Sikkim state.

If Chinese forces charge southwest down the Himalayas across India, they could reach Bangladesh after crossing only 45 miles of Indian territory. The Chinese could then cut off India's road and rail links to seven northwest states, including Assam which produces 30 percent of New Delhi's petroleum. Bhutan's only major airport — built and operated by Indians at Paro town near Thimpu in western Bhutan — is 25 miles from China's Chumbi valley.

Bhutan, meanwhile, also has no lawyers, large universities or opposition political parties which could disrupt the monarchy, so the king enjoys a relatively stable position to develop his nation. In a still-valid 1949 Bhutan-India treaty, "Bhutan agrees to be guided by the advice" of India in foreign relations. The clause is seen by many outsiders as permission for New Delhi to manipulate the kingdom.

Cautiously, however, Bhutan is trying to develop a mind of its own. King Wangchuck, dressed in a yellow scarf and traditional autumn-colored robe and knee-socks, insisted, "The interpretation was, if the government of India wants to express its views. But if we want to take the advice, it is up to the royal government of Bhutan. "Even in foreign affairs, the government of India does not interfere with Bhutan," the king added.

Any interpretation may be academic if relations between India and Bhutan sour because New Delhi could merely cut off supplies to Bhutan and strangle Thimpu until the Bhutanese obey. Bhutan, meanwhile, is slowly opening to the outside world with India's help. The kingdom is a member of several international organizations including the United Nations, the World Bank and the Non-Aligned Nations movement.

Each new organization Bhutan joins increases its international image as an independent nation and enables it to gain support, Bhutanese officials say. The king's main objective in developing and decentralizing his mountainous country is to create exports. "The lifeline for us in the future is trade. We have no internal market for the goods we produce, so we have to export," the king said.

Products include industrial minerals, timber and agricultural items. Bhutan is preparing for the May meeting in Geneva of the ALDC – Asian Least Developed Countries – which also includes Afghanistan, Bangladesh, Western Samoa, Maldives, Nepal and Laos. Asked about direct aid from Washington, Moscow or Beijing, Deputy Development Minister Lam Penjor said in an interview: "We have left the three superpowers out. They are all too big for us. "We have just come of age, and we have to learn world politics. We have to learn to play the game," Penjor said.

The scenic "land of the dragon" will not, however, open to mass tourism to earn money. Only 2,125 tourists will be allowed in next year, Tourism Commercial Organization General Manager Jigme Tshultim said in an interview. "Maybe in five years we will allow 5,000 tourists in a year," Tshultim said. Each tourist must come in a government-controlled group and pay either 75 US dollars or 130 US dollars a day, depending on the style of the tour, Tshultim added.

The government limits the influx of tourists because it fears spoiling Bhutan's traditions and losing antiques, he said. Bhutan is also strengthening relations with nearby Bangladesh, mostly to export items south to Dhaka. Only India and Bangladesh have embassies in Bhutan, but the establishment of diplomatic ties with nearby Nepal was being discussed in the National Assembly, King Wangchuck said. Bhutan established honorary consuls in Hong Kong and Singapore in 1982, mainly for trade contacts in Southeast Asia, and hopes to eventually also export products to the Middle East.

The serious Wangchuck is the fourth king in a monarchy established with the help of the British Empire in 1907. If the king dies before marrying and giving birth to an heir, the throne would pass to his eldest sister, Finance

Minister Sonam Chhoden, born in 1953. Bhutan's 153-member National Assembly includes 10 Buddhist monks as representatives, plus 100 "peoples representatives" elected throughout the nation.

INDO-BHUTAN RELATIONS: PORTION JOINT INTERESTS

"...the Indo-Bhutan ties are a model in international relations today. India is a big power and Bhutan is a small land locked kingdom. Still, we get along very well. What can be more satisfying than this model relationship?" The then Foreign Minister Dawa Tsering of Bhutan in an interview to The Tribune, March 11, 1996.

In a region characterised till not so long ago by the familiar trend of mistrust and suspicion primarily directed towards India, there has been one exception—the Indo-Bhutan relations. Both countries have been able to strike the right note and sustain their friendship. The treaty of 1949 between India and Bhutan is said to be central to the two countries' relations. However, this cordiality has not come about by freezing relations as they were in 1949. If anything, Bhutan of today has changed in all respects, including its economy and international stature since 1949. The relationship has, thus, been one of dynamism and change.

What are the factors which link the two countries? Are Indo-Bhutan relations really free of tensions? Is the "perpetual peace and friendship" phrase used in the 1949 treaty to describe Indo-Bhutan relations really true for all time to come? Is it a relationship where India as the big power, puts pressure on Bhutan? Does the relationship serve only Indian interests or is it equally beneficial to Bhutan? What are the challenges that the relationship will face in the future in the context of the changing domestic, regional and international environment? Which factors, in spite of the challenges, will keep the two countries together in the face of the choices that they have? This essay attempts to answer these questions to understand the unique relationship that the two countries share.

The Treaty of 1949 and its Working

The Treaty of 1949 provides the basic framework for conducting relations between the two countries. This section examines the Treaty in terms of its provisions and working.

Provisions of the Treaty

The Treaty of 1949 has ten Articles. The very first Article tries to perpetuate Indo-Bhutanese friendship for all time to come by stating, "There shall be perpetual peace and friendship between the Government of India and the Government of Bhutan." However, the most important provision in the treaty is its Article 2, according to which, "The Government of India undertakes to exercise no interference in the internal administration of Bhutan. On its part, the Government of Bhutan agrees to be guided by the advice of the Government of India in regard to its external relations." The point that has provoked some amount of critcism or controversy pertains to the second part of this Article since it tries to qualify Bhutan's external relations.

Other Articles of the treaty deal with the annual payment of Rs. 5 lakh by the Government of India to the Government of Bhutan in continuance of the compensation which was paid by British India.

Independent India however, has increased the amount to Rs 5 lakh from Rs 1 lakh earmarked earlier. To mark the friendship between the two countries, India agreed to return to the Government of Bhutan about 32 square miles of territory in the area known as Devangiri and the same was spelt out in the treaty. The treaty also establishes a free trade regime between India and Bhutan.

Further, the citizens of both countries residing in each other's territory will be treated on par with own citizens. The treaty also has provisions for extradition of Indian citizens in Bhutan and of Bhutanese citizens in India when required, and the procedure for the same has been spelt out. The mechanism for settling disputes arising out of differences in interpretation or application of the treaty is also mentioned. It is also stated that the treaty shall continue in perpetuity unless terminated or modified by mutual consent. Another important article is Article 6 of the treaty which refers to Bhutan importing arms and ammunition, machinery, warlike material or stores for the strength and welfare of its country. The clause is qualified by stating that such imports shall be undertaken with the assistance and approval of the Government of India from or through India into Bhutan. The Government of Bhutan, according to the treaty, agrees that there shall be no export of such arms and ammunition, etc. across the frontier of Bhutan either by the Government of Bhutan or by private individuals.

SINO-INDIAN RELATIONS IN CHANGING CIRCUMSTANCES

Having gone through a decade of exploratory efforts by the two sides in the new century, Sino-India relations at present display the following outstanding features:

Top leaders of both countries define Sino-Indian relations as one of the most important sets of bilateral relationships in their foreign relations and an increasing higher priority in their diplomatic agenda. As the two largest countries in Asia and the developing world as well as countries with an ancient civilization and major emerging market economies, China and India have great potentials for bilateral cooperation and more and more common interests and carry growing strategic weight in the restructuring of regional forces in Asia. Clearly, Sino-Indian relations have an increased impact on the international trading system, the international financial order, the global development agenda and regional cooperation in Asia and the Pacific.

If one used to observe Sino-Indian relations by gradually shifting one's perspective from South Asia to the Asia and the Pacific at large five or six years ago. One should now shift one's focus from Asia and the Pacific to the world at large in analyzing Sino-Indian relations. Just as Indian Prime Minister Singh points out, "Today, both India and China are in the midst of rapid transformation. The development agenda has taken centre-stage in both our societies. Our systems are different, but people in both countries are united in their aspiration for a better future. When countries of the size of China and India, together accounting for 2.5 billion people begin to unshackle their creative energies, it impacts on the whole world."

Pragmatically and Rationally

Due to the lack of strategic mutual assurance in the past several decades, anything in the offing or any contingency might easily stir emotions on both sides. This has always been a major deficiency in the bilateral relations. In recent years, however, under the guidance of top leaders of both countries, Sino-Indian relations have again become more practical and rational. The manifestation of this are: 1) Leaders of the two countries have reiterated that the earth is a vast planet which allows for the rise of China and India as new emerging powers; 2) in 2012, the year that marks the fiftieth year after the border conflict, the mainstream view in the media and public opinion in both countries was that the two sides should reflect on and learn lessons from the past with a conclusion that the two countries should never fight again and work together for a better future; 3) Each side is more keen on discovering and learning from the strong points of the other, refraining from treating it emotionally or with preconceived ideas, and drawing on good experiences and valuable assets of the other side to the good of its own development. This is particularly the case in the areas of trade, economic cooperation and the mutual investment. Such changes have markedly highlighted the importance of cooperative Sino-Indian relations and facilitated the growth of friendship mass organizations and associations as a valuable asset in Sino-Indian relations.

Reserving or Solving Differences

In the past fifty years and more, an important principle governing Sino-Indian relations has always been to bear longer interests of bilateral relations in mind and seeking common ground while reserving differences. While "freezing", controlling and shelving major differences, the two sides taking store by the overall interests of bilateral relations, have been working hard for cooperation and common development in other areas so as to prepare conditions for resolving such differences and contradictions in the future. In recent years, both sides have realized that an important way of enhancing strategic mutual reassurance and future promoting bilateral relations as well as freezing Sino-Indian relations from interference of third parties is to iron out their disputes through better communication, dialogue and consultation. While continuing to find out and expand the convergence of interests, the two sides should proactively try to narrow down or resolve the differences. Despite the fact that the two sides are yet to prepare all necessary conditions for the resolution of the boundary dispute and that one has not seen a marked increase of favorable factors, they wish to talk and settle this issue and act accordingly with a deeper understanding of the importance of maintaining peace and stability in the border areas. With this in mind, China and India have made progress on some "theory issues" in their relationship. They have launched, or are ready to launch, talks on establishing new mechanisms for the border issue, strategic and economic dialogue, maritime security dialogue, dialogue on the Tibetan questions in addition to steady progress in the consultations on trans-border water resources, combating terrorism and mil-to-mil relations.

Bilateral Relationship

In the past ten years, China and India have gradually found out how to keep on good terms through properly handling their differences and disputes and making cooperative efforts for common development and better bilateral relations.

First, new ideas and suggestions for enhancing Sino-Indian relations have kept emerging, such as "new concept of China-India relationships", "2.0 edition of China-India relations", "Five Principles of Peaceful Coexistence", "How emerging powers should treat one another", etc. Of late, Mr. Sanjaya Baruÿformer Press Consultant of Prime Minister Singh has made a comparative analysis of President Xi Jinping's recent "Five –Point proposal" on Sino-Indian relations and Prime Minister Singh's five principles governing Indo-China relations. The fact that leaders of both countries are thinking of putting bilateral relations more on a theoretical basis indicates that Sino-Indian relations are becoming more and more important and that the bilateral relationship now stands at a critical juncture of reaching a new height.

Second, each side tends to take a more pragmatic and forbearing approach to the presence and activities of the other side in the region of its pivotal interests. The joint "China-Indo-Japan ship escorts" in the Gulf of Aiden and China-Indian consultation and collaboration at East Asia Summits point to the fact that the two countries have less "zero-sum mentality" and more cooperation and win-win in mind.

Third, the two sides are less on the alert and more accommodating towards each other in exchanges of views in multilateral fora. Cases in points are their collaboration in G20 events, BRIC meetings and UN conferences on climate change.

FRESH PROGRESS OF SINO-INDIAN RELATIONS IN RECENT YEARS

China is now on of India's largest trade partners whereas India is China's largest trade partner in South Asia. According to statistics released by China's Ministry of Commerce, bilateral trade between the two countries reached $ 66.47 billion in 2012, China's export to India was $ 46.47 billion and China's import from India was $ 18.8 billion, falling by 10.1%, 5.7% and 19.6% respectively from the year before. India had a deficit of $ 28.87 billion in its trade with China with an increase of $ 1.79 billion from 2011. Chinese companies had signed contract projects to an accumulated amount of $ 60.131 billion with a turnover of business of $ 33.518 billion by the end of 2012. In two way investments, the Chinese Ministry of Commerce had approved or put on record $ 725 billion of direct investment from China in non-financial projects in India while Indian companies had actually invested $ 486 million in 800 non-financial projects in China by that time. This indicates that despite the negative impact of the overall international economic environment and growing trade frictions between the two sides, Sino-Indian trade and economic cooperation have continued to grow steadily as smooth progress of the contract projects portends enormous potentialities for mutual investment.

Tortuous Path of Security Cooperation

The Indian side unilaterally suspended military exchanges with China in 2009 when the Chinese side began to issue stapled visas to inhabitants residing in the Indian-controlled zone in Kashmir.

Nevertheless, after the Fifth Round Defense and Security consultation between the Ministries of National Defense of the two countries in January 2013, the two sides argued to resume defense cooperation and launch the third joint military exercise scheduled this year.

As the two countries' international roles grow, the maritime interaction between the two sides has become a focus of concern as they begun to explore for dialogue on maritime security as of 2012. It should be noted that the two countries are prepared to start "dialogue on the Tibetan issue" in the post-Dalai Lama time with a view to reducing the frictions over this issue left over from history. In April 2010, the two sides signed the*Agreement between China and India on the Establishment of a Hotline between Prime Ministers of the Two Countries.*

This is one of the latest actions taken by the two sides for enhancing mutual assurance. This will be an effective way of dispelling misunderstandings on both sides at a time of crisis and preventing the escalation of the crisis. Therefore, it is of great significance for an exchange of view on strategic issues between leaders of the two countries. Just recently, the two sides held the Sixth Round Consultation on Anti-terrorism in Beijing, during which the participants had in-depth discussions of international and regional developments against terrorism and bilateral cooperation in this area. By and large, the two sides have made progress in the negotiations over sensitive and complex security and strategic issues and slowly but effectively reduced the "deficit" in strategic mutual reassurance.

Border Areas under Effective Control

Given that no major breakthrough is in sight in a short time, the two sides are prepared to tighten their control over the border areas and prevent contingencies. For this purpose, the Special Representatives' Meeting for boundary negotiations is charged with a wider scope of responsibilities and functions. Moreover, the two sides formally signed the*Agreement between the Government of the People's Republic of China and the Government of the Republic of India on the Establishment of a Working Mechanism for Consultation and Coordination on India-China Border Affairs*. This consultative body is comprised of diplomats and military officers from both sides, led by principals at the Director-General level of Ministries of Foreign Affairs.

It is mandated to handle all matters concerning peace and stability along the China-India borders and study how to carry out exchanges and cooperation between military personnel and agencies of the two countries in border areas so as to serve as a proper channel and platform for enhancing information exchange and better collaboration and ensure for handling border affairs through the diplomatic channel in a more timely and effective manner, thereby preparing good conditions for resolving the boundary question through negotiations and promoting better relations between the two countries.

In April 2013 when "troops face-off at tents" occurred in the western sector of the Sino-Indian border, the two sides successfully prevented the escalation of the event, which might lead to the deterioration of the bilateral relationship through such a consultative and collaborative mechanism for boundary affairs and through timely diplomatic contact and meetings between frontier officers of both sides at the border.

The successful "soft-landing" of the troops face-off indicates that the two sides still have different views on and perceptions of the line of Actual Control. It also proves that the cooperative regimes and institutions for the boundary issue are truly helpful in crisis management. Generally speaking, border control is a kind of preventive measure of "negative assurance", but it is indispensable in the course of resolving the boundary questions between China and India, and serves as an important institutional guarantee which has prevented major military conflicts over the past several decades along the Sino-Indian border that has not been formally delineated to date.

Bilateral Cooperation

In recent years, as India plays an increasing salient role in the reshaping of international order, it has become one of the strategic partners China counts on. The two countries support each other in regional cooperation and made joint efforts to promote peace, stability and development in Asia. China and India join hands in handling many global issues such as international trade and financial issues and sustainable development, energetically safe guarding the tights and interests of developing countries and new emerging powers and facilitating improvement and reshaping of the existing international economic order.

All these are outstanding highlights for bilateral cooperation which provides a convincing footnote for Sino-Indian strategic partnership. The United States and some other western countries feel hard pressed by the common positions of China and India on energy security, climate change and some other global issues. The BRIC countries, G20 Summit and the East Asia Summit (EAS) have now become important venues for close interaction between leaders of the two countries in sustainable development of bilateral relations.

A Plus in Bilateral Relations

To commemorate the both anniversary of the establishment of diplomatic relations, China and India co-launched "India Year" and "China Year", an exchange program of culture activities in 2010. In 2011, the two sides hosted more people-to-people exchange programs under the auspices of "Sino-Indian Year of Exchanges". And in 2012—defined as "Sino-Indian Year OF Friendly Cooperation", the exchange programs in the field of humanities helped to reduce the negative memory of the border conflicts that had broken out 50years before. Moreover, the exchange of visits of "hundred-member" youth delegations were well received in the host country. Indian audiences very much enjoyed the shows put up by Chinese artists' troupes on their commercial performance tours in India in recent years. India is now one of major tour destinations for Chinese cultural and theatrical troupes. This has injected new vitalities into cultural exchanges between the two countries and energetically promoted non-governmental exchanges and mutual understanding between the two peoples.

SINO-INDIAN CONVERGENCE: BILATERAL AND GLOBAL

Bilateral relations between India and the People's Republic of China (PRC) have indeed come a long way after they touched their nadir in the immediate aftermath of India 's nuclear tests in May 1998. China had been singled out as the "number one" security threat for India by India's Defence Minister just before the nuclear tests. After the tests, the Indian Prime Minister wrote to the US President justifying Indian nuclear tests as a response to the threat posed by China. Unsurprisingly, China reacted strongly and diplomatic relations between the two countries plummeted to an all time low.

However, some six years later, the relations between the two countries seem to be on an upswing. The visit of the Indian External Affairs Minister to China in 1999 marked the resumption of high-level dialogue and the two sides declared that they were not threats to each other. A bilateral security dialogue was also initiated that has helped the two countries in openly expressing and sharing their security concerns with each other. India and China also decided to expedite the process of demarcation of the Line of Actual Control (LAC) and the Joint Working Group (JWG) on the boundary question, set up in 1988, has been meeting regularly. As a first step in this direction, the two countries exchanged border maps on the least controversial middle sector of the LAC.

The Indian Prime Minster visited China in June 2003, the first such visit in a decade. The joint declaration signed during the visit stated that China was not a threat to India. The two states appointed special representatives in order to impart momentum to border negotiations that have lasted twenty two years, with the Prime Minister's principal secretary becoming India's political-level negotiator, replacing the India-China JWG. India and China also decided to hold their first joint naval exercise later in the year and discussions on joint air exercise continue. India also acknowledged China 's sovereignty over Tibet and pledged not to allow "anti-China" political activities in India. On its part, China has acknowledged India 's 1975 annexation of the former monarchy of Sikkim by agreeing to open a trading post along the border with the former kingdom and later rectified official maps to include Sikkim as part of India.

India and China have found substantial convergence of interests at the international level. Both share similar concerns about the growing international dominance of the US, the threat of terrorism disguised as religious and ethnic movements and the need to accord primacy to economic development. India and China have both expressed concern about the US ' use of military power around the world and publicly opposed the war in Iraq. This was merely a continuation of the desire of both states to oppose the US *hyperpuissance* ever since the end of the Cold War.

Like other major powers in the international system, India and China favour a multipolar world order where US unipolarity remains constrained by the other "poles" in the system. China and India zealously guard their national sovereignty and have been wary of US attempts to interfere in what they see as domestic affairs of other stares, be it Serbia, Kosovo or Iraq. Both took strong exception to the US air strikes on Iraq in 1998, the US-led air campaign against Yugoslavia in 1999, and more recently the US campaign against Saddam Hussein arguing that these violated the national sovereignty and undermined the authority of the United Nations system.

Both nations also favour more democratic international economic regimes. They have strongly resisted efforts by the US and other developed nations to link global trade to labour and environmental standards, realizing clearly that this would put them at a huge disadvantage vis-à-vis the developed world, thereby hampering their drive towards economic development, a top priority.

Both have committed themselves to crafting joint Sino-Indian positions in the World Trade Organization (WTO) and global trade negotiations in the hope that this might provide them greater negotiating leverage over the developed states. They would like to see further liberalization of agricultural trade in the developed countries, tightening of the rules on anti-dumping measures and ensuring that non-trade related issues such as labour and environment are not allowed to come to the WTO.

In recent years, India and China have attempted to build their bilateral relationship on the basis of their larger worldview of international politics. As they have found a distinct convergence of their interests on world stage, they have used it to strengthen their bilateral relations. They have established and maintained regular reciprocal high-level visits between political leaders. There has been a sincere attempt to improve trade relations and to compartmentalize intractable issues that make it difficult for their bilateral relationship to move forward.

India and China have strengthened their bilateral relationship in areas as distinct as cultural and educational exchanges, military exchanges, and science and technology cooperation. Bilateral trade has recorded rapid growth from a trade volume of US $265 million in 1991 to US $3596 million in 2001. In 2001, bilateral trade saw an increase of 23.4 percent over 2000. It is expected to rise to $10 billion this year. The two nations are even evaluating the possibility of signing a comprehensive economic cooperation agreement and a free trade agreement by the end of this year, thereby building on strong complementarities between the two.

Both states are also taking steps to upgrade their military-related cooperation, leading to greater understanding on the bilateral military front, something that would have been unthinkable just a few years ago.As a first step in this direction, the Chinese and Indian navies carried out joint search and rescue operations off the Shanghai coast in November 2003. Both states are also seeking to cooperate on the nuclear front with China planning to import heavy water from India to be utilized in the pressurized heavy water reactors near Shanghai.

Many observers have also pointed out a subtle shift in Beijing 's stance on Pakistan vis-à-vis India. China 's "neutral" position during the Kargil conflict and the intense Indo-Pak crisis following the terrorist attack on the India 's Parliament is seen by many as a reflection of China 's sincerity in its attempts to improve ties. In keeping with China's attempts to project itself as a responsible regional player, China is seen by some as supporting peace and anti-terrorist efforts in South Asia by cooperating with the US and India. China is also seen as playing a central role in encouraging Pakistan to negotiate with India by using its leverage over Pakistan.

After assuming office Prime Minister Manmohan Singh's government made it clear that it favoured closer ties with China and would continue to work towards improving bilateral relations with China. In his first address to the nation, the Prime Minister, Manmohan Singh, also emphasized the carrying forward of the process of further development and diversification of Sino-Indian relations. The late J.N. Dixit, National Security Advisor in the current government, wrote that "the Congress will continue the process of normalizing, strengthening and expanding India's relations with China, which is the most important factor affecting Asian security and stability". One of the first foreign visits of the new Indian foreign minister, Natwar Singh, was to China to attend the Asia Cooperation Dialogue in Qingdao, in East China's Shandong province and apparently had "substantive discussions" with his Chinese counterpart.

All this reflects on India continuing to build its relations with China on the convergence of interests that the two nations have achieved in recent years. Aside from the positive developments, one should not ignore the enormous obstacles that confront this bilateral relationship. There has been a dominant tendency in the Indian foreign policy establishment to focus on the strengths of its bilateral relations with China while pretending that problems confronting the relationship would somehow take care of themselves. The challenges in the Sino-Indian relationship are by no means insignificant nor will China take care of Indian interests. It is for India to recognize them for what they are and evolve a coherent strategy to tackle them.

Divergences and Challenges

The number one priority for China 's leadership today is economic growth and social stability. China soon underwent one of the most peaceful and orderly political transformations in its recent history, even though its exact ramifications remain far from clear. Hu Jintao became Communist Party chief in 2002 and President of China in 2003 replacing Jiang Zemin. He also finally ceded the effective control of the armed forces to Hu Jintao in September 2004. Hu Jintao is now formally in command of the vast party, government, and military bureaucracies that rule China. This shift, although important for the smooth working of the Chinese government, is unlikely to produce any radical change in China 's foreign policy. China 's focus is going to be on maintaining its high rate of economic growth in the coming years. It should be remembered that Hu Jintao is a product of the "evolutionary policies" of Deng Xiao Peng that emphasize economic growth and orderly governance. President Hu Jintao has made it amply clear that Western-style multiparty democracy is something that would not serve the Chinese people well, terming it a "blind alley" for China. Therefore, one can expect China to continue on its current economic trajectory and shaping its foreign policy accordingly.

China has enjoyed average annual rates of real income growth of around 10 percent in the last two decades of the twentieth century, something unprecedented historically. China accounts for about 5 percent of world trade and foreign direct investment (FDI) to China is predicted to reach an annual utilized rate of 100 billion in 2005. After its accession to the WTO, China 's already-high global economic profile is set to rise manifold. China will continue to focus on maintaining its high rates of economic growth in the coming years, even as some of the economic challenges China faces will become more acute. The burgeoning income disparities, restructuring of its states owned enterprises and the problem of non-performing loans in its banks are just a few of the economic problems China 's economy is likely to face in the coming years. So far China has managed remarkably even though the future remains uncertain.

Broadly speaking, Indians either view China 's economic growth as a façade or envy it. While India has achieved some remarkable growth rates in the last few years enjoying average annual rates of real income growth of six percent in the last two decades of the twentieth century, it still lags behind China. India accounts for less than one percent of world trade in goods and services. Currently, China outperforms India in terms of levels of growth, education, health, and living standards of its population, and global integration of its economy. China outpaces India, in sectors where the two compete for third country markets. Sino-Indian competition for these markets is bound to further intensify in the coming years.

Though some argue that the long term economic prospects of India are much better than China 's, China remains the undisputed economic powerhouse of the moment driving the Asian and global economy with India somewhere far behind. The fact of the matter is so long as India does not place its own economic house in order; it will remain a second-rate power even in Asia. And China will remain the Asian power that the world will look up to when trying to manage problems in Asia.

What should be equally, if not more, significant for India is the fact that it is China's economic transformation that has given it the capability to become a military power with China spending as much as $65 billion a year on its military. China's military may or may not be able to challenge US supremacy in the next few years but it will surely become the most dominant force in Asia. According to authoritative sources, China is set to overtake

Japan in the next decade to become Asia 's major regional military power. The US involvement in the global war on terror has put the "containment" of China on the backburner and China has seized on this opportunity to strengthen its armed forces further.

China imbibed the lessons of US military undertakings such as the 1991 Gulf War, war in Afghanistan and the recent operation Iraqi Freedom. These have spurred China's pursuit of the latest Revolution in Military affairs (RMA) manifested in the buying, adopting of latest technologies and weapons systems (particularly from Russia) along with concomitant changes in doctrine and organizational structures. The People's Liberation Army (PLA) has been shedding its manpower since late 1990s to save funds so as to be able to focus on high tech. Despite a western embargo on China preventing transfer of military technologies, China has been able to deftly use US corporations to garner and apply dual-use technologies. China is simultaneously pursuing a qualitative and quantitative transformation of its nuclear infrastructure. China plans to deploy new road-mobile, solid-fuelled, long-range missiles over the next several years possibly to counter US ballistic missile defence.

Overtime, China 's enhanced military prowess will lead it to assert its interests more forcefully, thereby, adversely affecting Indian interests. As China becomes more reliant on imported oil for its rapidly growing industrial economy, China will develop and exercise military power projection capabilities to protect the shipping that transports oil from the Persian Gulf to China. The capability to project power would require access to advanced naval bases along the sea lines of communication and forces capable of gaining and sustaining naval and air superiority.

China 's assistance to Myanmar in constructing and improving port facilities on two islands in the Bay of Bengal and the Andaman Sea is the first step to securing military base privileges in the Indian Ocean. This can be used as a listening post to gather intelligence on Indian naval operations and a potential forward base for future Chinese naval operations in the Indian Ocean. India 's traditional geographic advantages in the Indian Ocean are also increasingly at risk with deepening Chinese involvement in Myanmar. China 's increasing naval presence in the Indian Ocean is of tremendous strategic consequence for India. There are also suggestions that the balance of air power in the China-India theatre has shifted in China 's favour with it acquiring an inventory of about 1500 modern combat aircraft for deployment in the theatre.

China remains the only major power in the world that refuses to discuss nuclear issues with India for fear that this might imply a de facto recognition of India 's status as a nuclear power. It continues to insist on the sanctity of the UN resolution 1172 which calls for India (and Pakistan) to give up its nuclear weapons program and join the Nuclear Non-Proliferation Treaty (NPT) as a non-nuclear weapon state. This was reflected in China 's lack of response to the Indian Foreign Minister's proposal of a common nuclear doctrine for China, India, and Pakistan. China would not like to get into any sort of nuclear dialogue with India that might give the impression of China recognizing India as a nuclear power. Moreover, while both India and China have a "no first use" nuclear doctrine, China 's doctrine is not applicable to India as it is not a party to the NPT.

China has done its best to maintain a rough balance of power in Indian Subcontinent by preventing India from gaining an upper hand over Pakistan. It has consistently assisted Pakistan 's nuclear weapons and ballistic missile programs to counterbalance India 's development of new weapons systems. India 's preoccupation with Pakistan reduces India to the level of a regional power while China can claim the status of an Asian and world power. China signed a charter to step up bilateral defence cooperation with Pakistan "to help maintain peace and stability in South Asia " even as it professes to improve its relations with India. Moreover, even as India and China share similar concerns regarding Islamic terrorism in Kashmir and Xinjiang respectively, China has been rather unwilling to make a common cause with India against Pakistan. China 's use of India 's neighbours to curtail Indian influence has not been restricted to Pakistan. China has actively sought to contain India all around its periphery by engaging Nepal, Bangladesh and Myanmar.

Despite resolving most of its border disputes with other countries, China is reluctant to move ahead with India on border issues. India 's discussion of border issues with China is seen as a concession. India remains satisfied with the "positive" and "satisfactory" Joint Working Group negotiations on the boundary issue. Despite the need for an expeditious demarcation of the Line of Actual Control, the talks seem to be continuing endlessly and the momentum of the talks itself seems to have flagged.

The momentum of the issue of Tibet seems to have been lost. Tibet has become a platform for the projection of Chinese military power. India 's tacit support to Dalai Lama's government-in-exile has failed to have much of an impact either on China or on the international community. Today even Dalai Lama seems ready to talk to the Chinese as he realizes that in a few years Tibet might get overwhelmed with the Han population and Tibetans themselves might become a minority. The proposed opening up of the Nathula trade route that connects Tibet and Sikkim has been much trumpeted by the Indian government as a major achievement of Indian diplomacy. However, this step is fraught with dangers as there is no certainty that internal security threat posed by Chinese infiltration would not get worse with the opening of Nathula. This has probably led to some rethinking in India on this issue.

There were disturbing reports during the Indian Prime Minister's visit to China, that Chinese troops had intruded into the Indian territory along a stretch of the unfenced border with Arunachal Pradesh. China refuses to recognize Arunachal Pradesh as part of the Indian territory, laying claim to 90, 000 sq. km. of its land. If recent reports are to be believed after a two-decade gap, China has resumed the supply of weapons to various insurgent groups fighting in northeastern India. China seems to be getting successful in hemming India in from both, the eastern and the western flanks.

China and India: Different Approaches, Different Outcomes

What the above discussion of the divergence and convergence between Sino-Indian interests reveals is the success of China in attaining its foreign policy objectives and the failure of India to preserve its vital interests vis-à-vis China. This cannot simply be attributed to China 's economic and military strength. While China is definitely the bigger player in the region and the world at large but its success vis-à-vis India owes as much to its power as to the way that power has been cultivated and used. While realizing fully well that it would take China decades to seriously compete with the US, it has focused strategic energy on Asia. Its foreign policy is aimed at enhancing its economic and military prowess to achieve hegemony in Asia. China 's recent emphasis on projecting itself as peaceful power is merely aimed at allaying the concerns of neighbours lest they try to counterbalance it. China's readiness to negotiate with other regional states and to be an economically "responsible" nation is also a signal to other states that there are greater benefits in bandwagoning to China's growing regional weight rather than opposing its rise in any manner.

However, while declaring that it will be focusing on internal socio-economic development for the next decade or so, China has actively pursued policies of preventing the rise of other regional powers. In case of India, this manifests itself in its cultivation of Pakistan as a close ally. From supplying it nuclear and missile technologies to building its military infrastructure, China has done all it can to build Pakistan as a counterweight to India. This policy has largely succeeded as India no longer enjoys its earlier conventional superiority vis-à-vis Pakistan possession of nuclear weapons by both nations ensures that any step that India takes to strengthen its nuclear weapons profile is viewed by the international community as highly destabilizing in the context of the "nuclear flashpoint" that South Asia has become for the world at large. China has thereby been successful in emerging as a "responsible" global player, despite its abysmal nuclear and missile proliferation record while the international community rails at India for making the world much more dangerous.

China's attempts to increase its influence in Nepal, Bangladesh, and Myanmar, its persistent refusal to recognize parts of India such as Arunachal Pradesh, its lack of support for India's membership to the United Nations Security Council and other regional and global organizations, all point towards China's attempts at preventing the rise of India as a regional and global player of major import. It is this strategy that China has consistently and successfully pursued without any apologies. In fact, this strategy has been so successful that today China no longer believes that India can be a serious rival for Asian hegemony and some have pointed out, India is off of China 's diplomatic radar.

In contrast to China 's well-laid out policy vis-à-vis India, India has from time to time oscillated from one extreme to another. George Tanham has famously pointed out that India has shown little ability to think strategically on national security. In the case of India 's China policy, it needs to be realized that there is nothing really sinister about China 's attempts to expand its own influence and curtail India 's. China is a rising power in Asia and the world and as such will do its utmost to prevent the rise of other power centres around its periphery like India that might in the future prevent it from taking its rightful place as a global player. This is not much different than the stated US policy of preventing the rise of other powers that might threaten its position as a global hegemon. Just as the US is working towards achieving its strategic objective, China is pursuing its own strategic agenda.

There is also nothing extraordinarily benign in China 's attempts to improve its bilateral relations with India in recent times. After working to curtail India 's influence in various ways, China would not like to see India coming close to the US in order to contain China. In this geopolitical chessboard, both the US and China are using India towards their own strategic ends. India must resist the tendency of reacting to the actions of other. India 's attempt to come up a coherent strategy towards China based on identified strategic objectives is of paramount importance. Prime Minister Manmohan Singh declared that it wants to have friendly relations with China, a reasonable foreign policy objective. However, without a clear articulation of India 's national security objectives, pursuit of friendly relations with China should not become an end in itself. It should be a means towards achieving India 's larger strategic objective of emerging as a major regional and global player.

India 's China policy is also symptomatic of a larger misunderstanding in the Indian and political establishment with regard to a nation's foreign policy. For the left-liberal strand in the Indian polity, foreign policy is merely an extension of domestic policy. As such since India is a secular, democratic, and peace-loving nation, India 's pursuit of its relations with other states should merely be a reflection of these virtues. This has given rise to much of the moral rhetoric in foreign affairs. On the other hand, the Indian right, because of its preoccupation with establishing a "Hindu" nation and minority bashing, have extended its narrow sectarian view to foreign policy. The consequence has been its obsession with Pakistan as evil incarnate in its foreign policy agenda and its inclination to view the world in black and white, friends and enemies, evil and noble. Shaped by these forces, Indian foreign policy has merely been one of responding to events around it rather than anticipating them and evolving long-term strategies to deal with them. India's China policy is a casualty of this reactionary approach.

India needs to develop its economic and military might without being apologetic. It needs to clearly articulate its national interests and engage China on a host of issues, from the border problem to the alleged dumping of cheap Chinese goods in the Indian market. India needs to recognize that appeasing China is neither desirable nor necessary even as a direct confrontation with China is not something India can afford, at least in the near future. It must also be recognized that while for India, managing its relations with China is at the top of its foreign policy agenda, China does not view India as a significant global player and is largely indifferent to India's growing profile.

India is a rising power in Asia and there is nothing wrong in demanding its rightful place in the interstate hierarchy. Simply put India and China are two major powers in Asia with global aspirations and some significant conflicting interests. As a result, some amount of friction in their bilateral relationship is inevitable. The geopolitical reality of Asia makes sure that it will be extremely difficult, if not impossible, for *Hindi-Chini* to be *bhai-bhai* (brothers) in the foreseeable future. This reality should be accepted by the Indian policy makers, rather than wished away. India should make a serious attempt to manage this friction by expanding the zone of cooperation with China even as it tries to steadfastly pursue its national interests. India should display the confidence to craft a foreign policy that best serves its national security interests without always looking over the shoulders to make sure that China is not displeased. Again, India can learn a lot by examining how China has managed its relationship with the US in the last few years.

While India certainly needs to engage China in an effort at reconciling security and political perspectives, it is naïve to assert, as many do, that India should first be sensitive to China's concerns, real or imaginary, before defining its foreign policy goals and strategic agenda. Does China consult India in its pursuit of its own strategic objectives? It does not and neither should India expect it to. In a similar vein, India should define its foreign policy agenda in view of its own national security imperatives.

But for this to happen, the government of India will have to formulate a clear China policy and, more importantly, a broader national security strategy. Ad-hocism just won't do. This should be the top foreign policy priority of the Indian government if it wants India to emerge as a global power of any reckoning. India should heed to Sun Tzu's advice and recognize that a merely tactical foreign policy approach without the backing of a sound strategy will only lead to nowhere.

4

Doklam Standoff, Another War and Conflict between India, China and Bhutan

HISTORICAL PERSPECTIVE

Touching India's Sikkim state to the west, the region has been depicted as part of Bhutan in the Bhutanese maps since 1961, which in turn is also claimed by China. Till date the dispute has not been resolved after around 24 rounds of border negotiations between Bhutan and China. It is said that the China cites maps from before 1912 as part of its "ancient" frontier — Chinese maps, claims and dates of maps and to stake its claim over Doklam. China's claim of the border includes the entire Doklam area within the Chumbi Valley, ending at the Zornpelri ridge on the south and the joining point of the Doklam River on the east.

GEOGRAPHY OF THE CONFLICT

Chumbi valley has served as a trade route from Sikkim's capital Gangtok through Yadong and Gyantse to Dalai Lama's court at Lhasa, the enclave for a long time did not fall to the Chinese. The valley holds strategic significance for India, China as well as Bhutan. India sees it as a dagger pointed towards its so-called 'chicken's neck' sector in the North East and rapid Chinese road construction in Tibet could make things difficult for India.

According to the Bhutanese government, China attempted to extend a road that previously terminated at Doka La towards the Bhutan Army camp at Zornpelri near the Jampheri Ridge, two km to the south; that ridge, viewed as the border by China but as wholly within Bhutan by both Bhutan and India, extends eastward approaching India's highly-strategic Siliguri corridor.

The Bhutanese Foreign Ministry released a statement in late June clarifying its position and did not mention India at all. It offered the following assessment of what transpired in mid-June: "On 16th June 2017, the Chinese Army started constructing a motorable road from Dokola in the Doklam area towards the Bhutan Army camp at Zompelri."

Since the Chinese soldiers were in Bhutan's territory, it was Bhutanese soldiers who confronted them and asked them to return to normal positions. The Chinese pushed back the Bhutanese troops. It was apparent they were planning to build roads on Bhutanese territory, close to a strategically critical Indian location, and change the status quo on the ground.

INDIA'S STAKE

For India, the presence of its soldiers on the Doklam Plateau is a signal of its commitment to the independence of Bhutan, a test of its willingness to take on Chinese bullying in the region, and a security imperative – given that the defence of Doklam is virtually the defence of India, so close as it is to a vital Indian choke point. The construction 'would represent a significant change of status quo with serious security implications for India.' India underlined that the two governments had agreed in 2012 that the tri-junction boundary points between India, China and third countries will be finalised in consultation with the countries concerned. "Any attempt, therefore, to unilaterally determine tri-junction points is in violation of this understanding," it said.

In response to which Chinese Ministry of Foreign Affairs (MFA) spokesperson, Geng Shuang said, "In order to cover up the illegal entry by Indian troops into the Chinese territory, Indian side wants to infringe upon Bhutan's sovereignty and they try to confuse right from wrong. This is futile. We have no objection to normal bilateral relations between India and Bhutan but are firmly opposed to the Indian side infringing on Chinese territory using Bhutan as an excuse."

THE BONE OF CONTENTION

The Chinese official spokesman's claim was- "The so-called tri-junction, as the name suggests, is a point. It is not a line, much less an area. India misinterprets tri-junction point as an area, from ulterior motives. This time, the trespassing point of India army, is on the Sikkim-China border, which is 2000 metres away from the tri-junction point, Mount Gipmochi, by the 1890 Treaty." In a 15 page statement released on August 1, 2017, the Foreign Ministry in Beijing accused India of using Bhutan as "a pretext" to interfere and impede the boundary talks between China and Bhutan. The report referred to India's "trespassing" into Doklam as a violation of the territorial sovereignty of China as well as a challenge to the sovereignty and independence of Bhutan.

Boundary talks are ongoing between Bhutan and China and we have written agreements of 1988 and 1998 stating that the two sides agree to maintain peace and tranquillity in their border areas pending a final settlement on the boundary question, and to maintain status quo on the boundary as before March 1959. The agreements also state that the two sides will refrain from taking unilateral action or use of force, to change the status quo of the boundary." said the Ministry of Foreign Affairs, Royal Government of Bhutan.

On both sides, suggestions of a new war between the two nuclear-enabled neighbours, both with population of over a billion, are slowly becoming less unlikely, highlighting the potential for serious tussle between India and China.

STRATEGIC TRIANGULAR RELATIONSHIP BETWEEN BHUTAN, INDIA, AND CHINA

This section aims to analyse the relationship between Bhutan, India, and China with the concept of strategic triangle. The concept of strategic triangle has been widely applied by the academic circle since early 1970s in the analysis of the relationship between USA, Soviet Union, and PRC. Professor Lowell Dittmer of USA and Professor Wu Yu-shan of Taiwan have used the concept to form a theoretical structure for analysis of international relations and have applied it to the study of strategic triangular relationships of USA-Soviet Union-PRC and Taiwan-USA-PRC. Professor Dittmer classifies strategic triangular relationships into three types, namely menage a trois, romantic triangle, and stable marriage. Menage a trois refers to symmetrical amity between 3 action-takers. Romantic triangle refers to the state in which amity is shared between an action-taker in the pivot and two other action-takers in the wings, while there is enmity between the two action-takers in the wings. Stable marriage refers to a situation in which amity exists between two action-takers, and there is enmity between the two and a third action-taker. In his analysis of strategic triangular relationships, Professor Wu pointed out that in a triangular relationship, the relationship between any two action-takers are determined by external factors and internal factors. Internal factors refer to the interplay of security, economy, and ideology between two action-takers which causes effect on the relationship.

External factors refer to the influence of the two action-takers' individual relationships with the third party on their mutual relationships. The level of impact of internal and external factors varies from case to case, and there is no universal standard. Six roles exist in a strategic triangular relationship: pivot, friend, partner, wing, foe, and outcast. Pivot is the best position to be in. It shares amity with the other two action-takers and holds out enmity with two wings. If there is amity between two action-takers, and their relationship with the third action-taker is that of enmity, then the two which share amity are called "partners," and the one hated by them is called "outcast." In a strategic triangular relationship, the role with the most amity relationships stands in the best position. As such, the outcast is the worst position to be in, as it has to erase enmity with at least one partner to break free from isolation and break down the alliance of opponents. It would be difficult to change the status quo if enmity between the outcast and partners are based on long-standing internal reasons. Flexibility in the outcast's attitude would be the key in shattering the state of isolation.

Bhutan is a landlocked buffer state located between China and India, and is of strategic importance as it controls several important passes of the Himalayas. Since the British invasion to Bhutan in the 18th century, Bhutan has been in the hands of the British Empire and post-independence India. Bhutan has been acting on the "advice" of Britain and India with regard to foreign relations since early 20th century. Even now, Bhutan still depends on India for national defense and security. In addition to historical background, religious belief also ties India and Bhutan closer. Being a Buddhist kingdom, Bhutan is under heavy influence from religion, and it's only natural that it has a closer relationship to India than to the atheist PRC. India has been the biggest provider of economic assistance to Bhutan and the major force behind Bhutan's eight five-year projects. In a way, India is the "big brother," and Bhutan is the "little kid," together they form a close alliance. Alliance is one of the many ways in international politics to maintain the balance of power. In the case of Bhutan-India alliance, it is obvious that they are uniting against China.

India established formal diplomatic ties with the PRC in 1950, and became the first non-socialist country to do so. India was well received by the PRC. PRC Premier Zhou Enlai's 4 visits to India resulted in the signing of "Agreement on Trade and Transportation between India and the Tibet Region of China" in 1954 which established 5 principles of peaceful coexistence.

The signing of agreement and mutual visits between premiers and prime ministers deepen the bilateral relationship. Mutual visits between officials were frequent in 1950s. While border issue almost became a threat to the relationship, both sides had been toeing the line. Generally speaking, the bilateral relationship had been seeing rapid progress.

As for Bhutan-India relationship, based on the Treaty of Permanent Peace and Friendly Relationship signed by Bhutan and India in 1949, Bhutan agrees to follow the advice of India with regard to foreign relations. As there is no formal diplomatic relation between Bhutan and China, turmoil in the Tibet region in late 1950s sounded the alarm across Bhutan. Anti-violence movement in the Tibet region forced Bhutan to shut down its border trade activities with China completely in 1959.

India's relationship with China and Bhutan had been friendly during this time, with Bhutan accepting economic assistance, foreign relations advice, and protection from India based on the treaty. In this triangular relationship, China and Bhutan are the wings of India. The relationship between India and Bhutan was that of partner, and India was in desirable pivot position.

While the relationship between China and India had been friendly in 1950s, there existed serious differences in the MacMahon line introduced in early 19th century, and either was willing to give in. India, seeing that the PRC had yet to occupy the whole Tibet region, sent troops to occupy the Xikang and Tibet region south of the MacMahon line. It was time when border disputes between the two started to surface. By the time of the Korean War in 1951, the Indian troops had entered Tawang.

In 1954, India introduced a revision of its official map, incorporating the MacMahon line in the east, and 2,000 square kilometres of land in southern Ngari Prefecture in the centre, and Parigas in the west into its own territory. China renovated the Xinjiang-Tibet Highway in 1956-1957, which travels through Xinjiang to undetermined territories of Tibet. Large-scale anti-violence movement broke out in Tibet in 1959, the troops sent by PRC successfully removed Indian forces out of Tibet. In August of the same year, armed conflict broke out for the first time in the China-India border region. On the other hand, the fact that India provided asylum to the exile Dalai Lama after joining the anti-violence forces in Tibet certainly does not help in improving Sino-India relations. In May 1962, China and Pakistan issued separate communiqués claiming that both would reopen talks on border issues and sign a treaty after the Kashmir disputes between India and Pakistan are settle. (The Sino-Pakistan Border Agreement was signed later in March 1963.) This sent shockwaves across India, which refused to accept the Sino-Pakistan border agreement which hands Kashmir to Pakistan, creating even more tension between itself and China. The tensions eventually led to full-scale border war between China and India in October 1962, which ended in defeat for India. All these create severe damage to the development of Sino-India relationships. Hatred between the two led to 14 years of "cold war." Not until 1976 did signs of improvement begin to surface.

During this time, Bhutan shut down all border trade activities with China following anti-violence movement in Tibet and China's occupation of Tibet. There was no interaction between Bhutan and China. In the year that follows (1960), India dispatched military officers to Bhutan, and in 1961 the base for the Indian Military Training Team was set up in Bhutan. In addition to conducting scouting missions in Bhutan, India provided military training and defense equipment, and generously provided funds and technical staffs for Bhutan's five-year projects. India also exercised influence over Bhutan's foreign relations through its protection and economic assistance. In this triangular relationship, as China and India entered the phase of cold war, Bhutan, being an ally of India, naturally took India's side. The relationship between India and Bhutan was still that of partnership, and China assumed the worst position of outcast in the triangular relationship.

In 1976, China and India resumed the exchange of ambassadors. In 1979, India Minister of Foreign Affairs Atal Behari Vajpayee visited China, officially breaking 17 years of ice during which there had been no visit between the leaders of both sides. Beijing and New Delhi have been taking turns to host Sino-India border talks since 1981, with little progress.

Prior to 1980s, diplomatic contacts between China and Bhutan had been hindered by the fluctuating Sino-India relationship. India remained an obstacle in Sino-Bhutan relations. At the same time, the most controversial region in the east in Sino-India border talks, the Doklam highlands under the control of Bhutan, had direct effect on the Chumbi valley of India. Tawang was another touchy issue. Bhutan, being close to Tawang in the east and Sikkim in the west, became a hotcake in the eyes of China and India. China proposed the idea of "east for the west" in border talks with India, namely acknowledging the MacMahon line as the border line in exchange for control over Aksai Chin in the west. In talks with Bhutan, China offered the 495 square kilometre in the northern borders of Bhutan in exchange for the 269 square kilometre in northwest Bhutan. In its attempt of break down the Bhutan-India alliance, China tried to separate the Sino-Bhutan border issues from Sino-India border talks in order to talk to Bhutan separately and extend diplomatic relations. The attempts had not been successful until 1984.

During the period, Bhutan did not develop independent relationship with China and maintained the close and important relationship of partnership with India. As Sino-India relationship began to unfreeze, India was back to its favorable pivot position, with China and Bhutan being in the wings.

As for China-India relationship, in February 1987 India upgraded the status of Arunachal from union territory to pradesh, making the Arunachal Pradesh India's 24th pradesh and providing legal status to this controversial region. The action sparked strong protest from China, and relationship between the two was still under the influence of border issues. In December of the following year (1988), India Prime Minister Rajiv Gandhi visited China, setting a turning point for Sino-India relationship. In 1992, Burang County of China and Kungri of India opened to each other, resuming border trade activities after 30-year hiatus. The two countries went on to sign the "Agreement on Maintaining Peace and Stability in the Line of Control Region of China-India Borders" in 1993 and "Agreement on Establishing Mutual Trust in Military Affairs in the Line of Control Region of China-India Borders" in 1996. With both sides exercising restrain in border issues, Sino-India relationship took a turn for the better. While the Bharatiya Janata Party-led coalition government of India came up with the "argument of China threat" in 1998 for the purpose of conducting nuclear tests, relationship between the two soon recovered after a while of unpleasant ripples. Up to October 2004, officials from China and India had conducted 15 rounds of border talk and 12 meetings of specialists, with no final solution accepted by both sides. The current relationship is the best since 1960s. Following the visit of former India Prime Minister Vajpayee to China from June 22 to 27, 2003, China and India signed the "Statement of Guiding Principles for Relations and Full-Scale Cooperation between the People's Republic of China and the Republic of India" and 10 other major documents on the subjects of justice, education, culture, technology, energy, quarantine, and simplification of visa procedures as well as extension of border trade. In the joint statement, India acknowledges for the first time that the Tibetan Autonomous Region is part of the PRC territory and reiterates that ant-China political activities launched by the Tibetan people are strictly banned in India. As for the most important factor in Sino-India relations—border issues, 4 rounds of talks have been conducted between representatives of both sides, with no positive progress.

This period sees more frequent mutual visits between Bhutanese and Chinese officials, though mostly of lower positions. China proposed establishment of formal diplomatic ties and economic assistance to Bhutan, only to be replied that as usual, Bhutan needs to seek the "advice" from India first. While there is domestic approval for China's proposition, Bhutan is refrained from establishing diplomatic ties with China before securing the go-ahead from India.

In a strategic triangular relationship, if the relationship between two allies is not symmetrical, the third party can persuade or lure the weaker one to establish a more beneficial balanced relationship with it. In this triangular relationship, India is still in the favorable position of pivot. The relationship between China and Bhutan improved after 17 rounds of border talks and numerous mutual visits, but China needs to break down the partnership between India and Bhutan and establish independent formal diplomatic ties with the latter if it is to strengthen its relationship with Bhutan. China still has a long way to go to achieve the purpose. Despite India's pivot position, it still has to deal with the possibility of Bhutan being lured away by China's offers. If this becomes reality, a new triangular relationship would be formed, with China being in the pivot and India and Bhutan becoming wings. This would be the situation China loves.

INDIA AND CHINA AGREE TO END BORDER STANDOFF

India and China have agreed to an "expeditious disengagement" of troops in a disputed border area where their soldiers have been locked in a stand-off for more than two months, India's foreign ministry said on Monday. The decision comes ahead of a summit of the BRICS nations - a grouping that also includes Brazil, Russia and South Africa - in China beginning on Sunday, which Indian Prime Minister Narendra Modi is expected to attend.

Indian and Chinese troops have been confronting each other at the Doklam plateau near the borders of India, its ally Bhutan, and China, in the most serious and prolonged standoff in decades along their disputed Himalayan border. The Indian ministry said the two sides had agreed to defuse the crisis following diplomatic talks.

"In recent weeks, India and China have maintained diplomatic communication in respect of the incident at Doklam," the ministry said in a statement.

"On this basis, expeditious disengagement of border personnel at the face-off site at Doklam has been agreed to and is on-going," it said in a statement. It did not offer more details of the terms of disengagement from the area which had raised fears of a wider conflict between the Asian giants who fought a brief border war in 1962. China said Indian troops had withdrawn from the remote area in the eastern Himalayas. Chinese foreign ministry spokeswoman Hua Chunying said Chinese troops would continue to patrol the Doklam region.

"China will continue to exercise sovereignty rights to protect territorial sovereignty in accordance with the rules of the historical boundary," she said. The Chinese defense ministry said troops would remain on a state of alert. "We remind the Indian side to learn the lesson from this incident, earnestly respect the historical boundary and the basic principles of international law, meet China half way and jointly protect the peace and tranquillity of the border region," spokesman Wu Qian said in a statement.

"The world is not peaceful, and peace needs to be safeguarded. The Chinese military has the confidence and the ability to protect the country's sovereignty, security and development interests," Wu added.

SMOOTH SUMMIT

The trouble started in June when India sent troops to stop China building a road in the Doklam area, which is remote, uninhabited territory claimed by both China and Bhutan. India said it sent its troops because Chinese military activity there was a threat to the security of its own northeast region.

But China has said India had no role to play in the area and insisted it withdraw unilaterally or face the prospect of an escalation. Chinese state media had warned India of a fate worse than its crushing defeat in the war in 1962. Indian political commentator Shekhar Gupta said there was too much at stake for the two countries to fight over a small piece of territory.

"Hopefully, Doklam is a new chapter in India-China relations. Too much at stake for both big powers to let legacy real-estate issues linger," he said in a Twitter post. India and China have been unable to settle their 3,500-km (2,175-mile) frontier and large parts of territory are claimed by both sides.

THE INDIA-CHINA DIVIDE

The Chinese Communist Party's (CCP) dislike for the 'hardline Hindu nationalist' Bharatiya Janata Party (BJP) is no secret. The shifts in India's China policy since May 1998, as evidenced in the nuclear and missile arena, military spending, and pro-Tibet and pro-Taiwan views expressed by some ministers, are said to have undermined the key assumptions underlying China's India policy. Conversations with officials and strategic analysts reveal that the Chinese are concerned over the rise of BJP as a major political force in Indian politics and its implications for China's strategic objective of supremacy in Asia. Before Pokhran II, China's India-watchers had convinced themselves that there would be 'no significant or fundamental changes' in the BJP-led Government's nuclear policy and that BJP-led India would not take any major strategic initiative (such as overt nuclearisation, strategic alliance with the United States, or support to Tibetan independence).

Although the aspirations for major power status are held by almost all Indian political parties (barring the Communists who fear provoking their Chinese masters), the BJP covets that status most ardently and is the most willing to assert it through military policy. Beijing would prefer a non-BJP weak government like the left-dominated United Front (UF) government before Pokhran II, and the successive Congress governments that preceded it, which had fine-tuned Sino-Indian bilateral relations by playing second fiddle to an assertive China. A policy paper prepared for the Chinese leadership has recommended 'targeting the BJP' as its policies have eroded Beijing's leverage against New Delhi. One analyst compared India with Nazi Germany and Iraq arguing that since the end of the Cold War, India had become too powerful and ambitious (for example, demanding a permanent seat on the UN Security Council) and warned that if India does not wish to suffer the fate of Japan in the 1940s or Iraq in the 1990s, it should give up its ambition for regional hegemony and take concrete steps to improve relations with China.

The main objective of China's Asia policy has always been to prevent the rise of an Asian rival or peer competitor to challenge its status as the Asia-Pacific's sole 'Middle Kingdom'. As an old Chinese saying goes, 'one mountain cannot accommodate two tigers'. That China does not want India to emerge as an equal is evident from its staunch opposition to India's membership of the P-5 (UN Security Council), N-5 (Nuclear Club), ASEM (Asia-Europe Summit), and APEC (Asia-Pacific Economic Cooperation). (India was made the ARF (ASEAN Regional Forum) member in December 1995 despite Beijing's opposition to it.) Speaking at the Munich Security Conference in February 1999, India's National Security Advisor, Brajesh Mishra, hinted at the BJP government's much broader political ambition by predicting that 'in the 21st century a new security order is likely to arise in the Asia-Pacific region in which India should be granted as much respect and deference by the United States and others as is China today.' Beijing's India-watchers believe that only a firm policy based on absolute strength and proactive containment of India will force the BJP-led government to act soberly towards China. Beijing knows that while China's emergence as a great power has been accepted by Western and Asian nations, India's claim to great power is yet to be accepted. So it is in the CCP's interests to keep the BJP out of power. Beijing has been blamed by India's intelligence agencies, media and some politicians for the overthrow of the BJP-led government in April 1999. Strange as it may seem, the CCP has more in common with its bete noire, BJP, than its counterpart in India, the Communist Party of India-Marxist (CPM). In the BJP, the CCP has met its match, the latter's 'communist' pretensions notwithstanding. Contrary to the popular conception of the CCP and the BJP occupying opposite ends of the political spectrum, the BJP is the CCP's mirror image. Just as the CCP believes in the superiority of the Han race, Han civilisation and the Han culture while displaying patronising and condescending attitude towards minorities such as Tibetans, Mongols and Muslims and downplaying the repeated colonisation of the Han race first by Inner Asian tribes such as Mongols, Manchus and Hsingnus and then by the Europeans, the BJP believes in the superiority of the Hindu race, Hindu civilisation and Hindu culture while downplaying the repeated colonisation of India by Greek, Muslim and European invaders as a result of Hindu disunity and their contributions to Indian culture. What is more, the CCP's goal of a unified 'Greater China' is not much different from the RSS/BJP's dream of 'Akhand Bharat' (United India).

Just as the Chinese Communists lay claim to territories annexed by non-Chinese Mongol and Manchu empires (such as Tibet, Eastern Turkestan, Mongolia), the 'Akhand Bharat' concept includes territories (such as Burma and Sri Lanka) brought under control by the British. Much like the CCP, the BJP wants India to be an economic and military superpower in order to 'stand up' to great powers' bullying and coercion. Both have long nurtured the belief that as the two oldest civilisations and once great powers which were subjected to centuries of foreign domination, they must acquire the full spectrum of economic, technological and military (conventional, nuclear and information warfare) capabilities in order to be dominant regionally and influential globally.

Furthermore, the BJP's slogan of 'prosperous and powerful country' bears remarkable resemblance to the CCP's national goal: 'rich country, strong military' (fuguo qiangbing). Interestingly, both are courting the United States to help balance their relationships with each other until they are strong enough to do so on their own. Both want a new international status that is commensurate with their size, strength and potential. Historically and civilisationally, while China was the 'Middle Kingdom' of eastern Asia, India was the 'Middle Kingdom' of southern Asia.

The two parties are thus manifestation of the growing nationalism in India and China. Both also share remarkable similarity in economic outlooks and rhetorical excess. The BJP-led government is as aggressive in the pursuit of national interests as the CCP. Nor is it shy of flexing muscles and warning neighbours with 'serious consequences' if they don't behave-just as the Chinese Communists have always done! Although both the CCP and BJP have been labelled 'fascist', 'militarist' and 'ultra-natonalist' parties by their critics, the reality is that both are nationalist parties deeply conscious of their countries' history, culture and civilisational heritage to humankind and committed to restoring their countries' great power status. Both China after a century and India after a millenium of decline are keen to assume the great power roles they believe to be their historical and civilisational right. Both remain suspicious of each other's long-term agenda and intentions, and are attempting to fill any perceived power vacuum or block the other from doing so.

At the heart of Sino-Indian antagonism is the familiar Indian suspicion, which has now matured into a certainty, that China is seeking to deny India its proper stakes in the game of international politics. Both see themselves as newly rising great Asian powers whose time has finally come. This means that BJP's resurgent India will face CCP's rising China which will ensure a conflict of interests between the two giants unless their power competition is managed carefully. Their underlying power rivalry and their self-images as natural great powers and centres of civilisation and culture will continue to drive them to support different countries and causes. India versus China, not India versus Pakistan, has always been the main game in Asia. However, post-colonial Asia has not experienced both a strong China and a strong India at the same time. The BJP-CCP clash is borne not out of conflicting, but complementary, visions for their respective countries.

INDIA AND CHINA TELL TROOPS TO STAND DOWN IN DISPUTED DOKLAM PLATEAU

India and China have agreed to an "expeditious disengagement" of troops in a disputed border area where their soldiers have been locked in a stand-off for more than two months, India's foreign ministry said on Monday. The decision comes ahead of a summit of the BRICS nations - a grouping that also includes Brazil, Russia and South Africa - in China next month, which Indian Prime Minister Narendra Modi is expected to attend.

Indian and Chinese troops have been confronting each other at the Doklam plateau near the borders of India, its ally Bhutan and China, in the most serious and prolonged standoff in decades along their disputed Himalayan border. The Indian ministry said the two sides had agreed to defuse the crisis following diplomatic talks. India-China tensions escalate as soldiers hurl stones at each other in "In recent weeks, India and China have maintained diplomatic communication in respect of the incident at Doklam," the ministry said in a statement. "On this basis, expeditious disengagement of border personnel at the face-off site at Doklam has been agreed to and is on-going," it said in a statement. It did not offer more details of the terms of disengagement from the area which had raised fears of a wider conflict between the Asian giants who fought a brief border war in 1962. China said Indian troops had withdrawn from the remote area in the eastern Himalayas. Chinese foreign ministry spokeswoman Hua Chunying said Chinese troops would continue to patrol the Doklam region. "China will continue to exercise sovereignty rights to protect territorial sovereignty in accordance with the rules of the historical boundary," she said. India and China have been unable to settle their 3,500-km (2,175-mile) frontier and large parts of territory are claimed by both sides.

"China hopes India respects the historical boundary and works with China to protect peace along the border on the basis of mutual respect of each other's sovereignty," Hua added. The trouble started in June when India sent troops to stop China building a road in the Doklam area, which is remote, uninhabited territory claimed by both China and Bhutan. India said it sent its troops because Chinese military activity there was a threat to the security of its own northeast region.

But China has said India had no role to play in the area and insisted it withdraw unilaterally or face the prospect of an escalation. Chinese state media had warned India of a fate worse than its crushing defeat in the war in 1962. Indian political commentator Shekhar Gupta said there was too much at stake for the two countries to fight over a small piece of territory. "Hopefully, Doklam is a new chapter in India-China relations. Too much at stake for both big powers to let legacy real-estate issues linger," he said in a Twitter post.

EUROPE IS DIVIDED OVER THE INDIA-CHINA BORDER DISPUTE

Indian and Chinese troops have lined up against one another for months between a literal rock and a hard place — that being two remote Himalayan parts of a border each nation contests. But European leaders have found themselves in a more figurative dilemma. If Europe sides with Delhi, it will infuriate the economic powerhouse that is China, which is now the European Union's second-biggest trading partner. Side with Beijing, however, and Europe would denigrate the world's largest democracy, and one that wants to build better ties with the continent.

So since both nations are important strategic partners for the EU, "it is likely reluctant to take sides in the territorial dispute," said Bart Gaens, a senior research fellow at the Finnish Institute of International Affairs. "The EU will condemn the violence," if it breaks out, he added, "but it can do little more than to call for dialogue and a peaceful resolution to the dispute."

Tensions rise

Tensions started in June when a few dozen Indian and Chinese soldiers tussled over the Doklam plateau, which lies just within the border of Bhutan, India's friendly neighbor. Delhi says it's defending Bhutan's sovereignty from Chinese aggression on the disputed border: China reportedly began extending a road near the border in June and Indian troops moved in to stop the construction. China, however, says India illegally entered its borders. Then, in mid-August, sticks and stones were hurled as the two nations' armed forces squared off near Pangong Tso, a small desert lake that stretches between the Indian region of Ladakh and Tibet, an autonomous Chinese region. So far, no-one has been seriously harmed during the relatively uneventful border dispute.

Winter is coming

Tensions are partly to do with to historic disagreements over borders demarcations drawn by past colonial authorities. But Beijing and Delhi have typically adopted an "agree-to-disagree" policy over their 3,500 kilometer border, much of which each nation contests. Now, however, Indian hawks are calling on Delhi to "contain" an allegedly expansionist China, which many say successive Indian governments have failed to do.

A jingoistic Chinese media, meanwhile, has sought to remind India of what happened when the two countries last went to war in 1962, another conflict over a remote Himalayan border. China won that month-long war and almost 3,000 Indian troops were killed. Still, "India in 2017 is different from India in 1962," Indian Defense Minister Arun Jaitley retorted.

There are signs, however, that tensions are calming. On August 28, both nations agreed to pull back their soldiers, which the Indian government described as "expeditious disengagement." Just as important, winter is coming and when it does "all but a few stretches of the high-altitude border become impassable anyway," *The Economist*recently stated. But while it now appears that any serious conflict is unlikely to come from the recent standoff, some say it is inevitable that Asia's two newest superpowers will continue sparing in the future, perhaps someday violently. This ought to motivate European leaders to come up with a position on possible China-India disputes sooner rather than later.

Europe keeps quiet

There is scant evidence of coherent stance yet, however. As noted earlier, both China and India are strategic allies of Europe so taking sides would come as a detriment in some fashion. "The European embassies in New Delhi are still in a wait-and-watch mode, and unlike the U.S., have not spoken at all so far," Shairee Malhotra, associate researcher at the European Institute for Asian Studies, told me last week before the two nations agreed to pull back their troops.

Still, there are indications of who Europeans might favor — if push comes to shove. Ryszard Czarnecki, vice president of the European Parliament, penned an article for the parliament's magazine in July that warned of changes in Chinese foreign policy, which included infringements on "internationally accepted norms."

Another possible reason for European reticence so far is the fact that the three countries — Germany, France and the UK — that have the best relations with China and India are currently weighed down with domestic concerns, said May-Britt Stumbaum, director of the research group "Asian Perceptions of the EU" at the Freie Universität Berlin.

German federal elections will take place this month and the German electorate tends not to favor interventionist leaders. Emmanuel Macron, who became the French president in May, is still getting used to power and remains dogged by domestic disputes (and tumbling popularity that has hit near-historic lows). And Britain is waylaid by Brexit negotiations, which includes trying to improve trade relations with both India and China.

The web of geopolitics

One other explanation for Europe's tepid response is that the dispute between India and China has little to with each's domestic concerns. The border tensions in the Doklam plateau largely center on geopolitical matters, namely Delhi's support of Bhutan's territorial sovereignty. Bhutan, which has been mostly silent on the matter, still does not have direct diplomatic relations with Beijing. This is either out of solidarity for Tibetan independence activists, or because of "deference" to Delhi, as *The Economist* asserted.

Beijing, however, has long seduced India's main geopolitical opponent, Pakistan, which it has furnished with aid and military equipment for decades. More recently, China has used trade and aid to try to bring India's more amiable neighbors — Bangladesh and Sri Lanka, for example — into its orbit, to varying success. China also sees India as attempting to undermine its One Belt, One Road initiative, which will bring Beijing greater hegemony within

Eurasia. India's ascension this year to the Shanghai Cooperation Organization, a Beijing-backed Eurasian organization, was reportedly proposed by Russia as a way of constraining China's influence in Eurasia.

For European leaders to wade into this geopolitical web without a bloc-wide consensus and a functional plan would mean entangling itself, perhaps also exacerbating the situation in the process instead of quietening tensions.

MANCHU INVASION OF TIBET/CHINA'S FORWARD POLICY

The Younghusband expedition destroyed the military strength of Tibet and exposed its inner weaknesses. At the same time, China witnessed vacillation of Great Britain. Moreover, Tibet developed inner conflict. Relations between Lhasa and Kham were not smooth. Incidentally, the Khampas exhibited the same contempt for Lhasa even in 1950 after four decades, which helped China to "liberate" Tibet smoothly.

Under such circumstances China decided upon a new Tibet policy. General Zhao Erfeng, the Chinese warlord and Governor of Sinning, was appointed the new Army Commander for Tibet. Zhao (known in Tibet as Butcher Zhao) started advancing in the Tibetan territory as soon as Younghusband departed from the plateau.

His brother Zhao Erxun was responsible for Sichuan. The Zhao brothers aimed to integrate Tibet into the Chinese empire. They began by dividing Tibet into different administrative divisions; Amdo became the new administrative province of Qinghai. Parts of it were integrated into South of Gansu and northwest of Sichuan.

Kham became Xikang, Zhao invaded Kham in 1905. He began meticulously "razing monasteries, killing monks and beheading Tibetan officials, who were immediately replaced by Chinese officers in his effort to cinicize Kham." As French explorer Jacques Bacot has described: "Zhao was a truly terrible man, extraordinarily energetic and hard; he could coldly do things, after reflection, which would surprise us even when we knew that he was a maniac of cruelty." As Charles Bell has written: "The memory of Chao Erfeng's (Zhao Erfeng) ruthless invasion in Eastern Tibet, his destruction of the monasteries and killing of monks has established a memory of bitterness that is still alive in Tibet" While the Empress continued to reassure Dalai Lama, the ground situation was just the opposite.

Slight protests or old grudge resulted in mass killings. As many as 1,210 monks and laymen were butchered in Chating, and-more than 300 in Bating. Even the Dalai Lama was sacked. The Tibetan government sent an emissary to Calcutta with a request for sending a telegram to Beijing as the Amban did not forward their case earlier to Beijing. The Tibetan government treaded cautiously as the Dalai Lama was still in China. When he arrived, the news of arrival of the Manchu army led him to decide to seek political asylum in India. (Similarly, 50 years later, the 14th Dalai Lama had to flee to India after PLA's invasion of Tibet.) There was unprecedented revolt and uprising in Tibet against the Chinese, who were ousted from Tibet. The 13th Dalai Lama left Kalimpong for Tibet in June 1912. Tibet remained free for nearly 40 years till it was recaptured by the Chinese army.

The Simla Convention

Simla Convention was held between Great Britain, China and Tibet in 1914. In the convention, "Tibetans had come so well prepared with volumes and volumes of original documents, while Chinese had no documents to prove their allegations" The meeting was not fruitful due to the delaying tactics of the Chinese delegates. As Hugh Richardson has observed: "It was to ensure the reality of Tibetan autonomy but still to leave the Chinese with a position of sufficient dignity." In an agreement signed on April 27, China pledged not to convert Tibet into a Chinese province; on the other hand, Great Britain was not to annex any portion of the country. The boundary between Tibet and Arunachal Pradesh (then NEFA) was initialed by British and Tibetan representatives, to which McMahon gave his name. The problem cropped up as China did not want to surrender newly conquered areas of Kham (Eastern Tibet) by Zhao Erfeng, while Tibet insisted on them. The final document, of course, was signed on July 3, 1914 only by Great Britain and Tibet.

Chinese Claim Over Tibet

Tibet was an independent country when China's PLA invaded it in 1949. The International Commission of Jurists' Legal Enquiry Committee on Tibet thus reported in its study on its legal status: "Tibet demonstrated from 1913 to 1950 the conditions of statehood as generally accepted under international law. In 1950, there was a people and a territory, and a government that functioned in that territory, conducting its own domestic affairs free from any outside authority. From 1913-1950, foreign relations of Tibet were conducted exclusively by the Government of Tibet, and countries with whom Tibet had foreign relations are shown by official documents to have treated Tibet in practice as an independent State."

Chinese suzerainty claim over Tibet rests on the assertion that the area was conquered by the Mongol rulers of China. Basing on such queer logic, any country of the world may claim suzerainty over the other. For example,

Greece over Iran, Afghanistan and parts of India and Central Asia; and Mongolia over China, Central Asia and parts of West Asia; and so on. (Arpi, p. 265) Moreover, for Tibet, the relationship was based on the personal relationship between the Mongol and Manchu monarchs and the Tibetan Lamas as patrons and priests. It was never a suzerain-vassal relationship between China and Tibet. Such relationship was initiated and flourished during non-Han dynasties of Yuans and Manchus.

Lord Curzon, the Viceroy of India, referring to the suzerainty of China over Tibet observed: "Chinese suzerainty oyer Tibet is a constitutional fiction, a political affectation, which has only been maintained because of its convenience to both parties .... As a matter of facts the two Chinese (i.e. Manchus) Ambans at Lhasa are there not as Viceroys, but as Ambassadors."

The status of the Amban can be gauged from the fact that Younghusband refused the former's offer of mediation between him and the Tibetans and instead decided to deal directly with the Tibetan government. The explanation Amban Yu Tai gave to Mortimer Durnad, the then Foreign Secretary to the Government of British India, amply illustrates the status of Amban: "He was only a guest in Lhasa – not a master – and he could not put aside the real masters, and as such he had no force to speak of.?"

The Chinese suzerainty claim over Tibet ignores the fact that its neighbouring countries – Nepal, Bhutan, Mongolia – had their diplomatic missions in Tibet before the occupation of that country by the PLA. India's special interests in Tibet were recognized and the world community supported their cause in the U.N. The Chinese "suzerainty" claim was recognized by the colonial powers only due to compulsions of their "Great Game". Incidentally, even Mao Zedong accepted Tibetans as foreigners. After he was given food and shelter during his Long March through Tibetan region, he remarked: "This is our only foreign debt, and we must pay the Mantzu (sic) and Tibetans for the provisions we were obliged to take from them."

Militarisation of Tibet

Tibetan plateau is the most militarized zone in the world today. As against India's permanent deployment of 7-8 military divisions in the Himalayas, China has 5,00,000 soldiers stationed on the plateau. China has also 300 to 400 ready to fire nuclear warheads, and about 1,000 others that may be assembled at short notice, based on the Tibetan plateau. Chinese missiles bases are located at Serkhog (Datong) armed with DF-3 missiles, Terlenkha (Delingha) with DF-4 missiles and at other places to strike targets in Russia 'and India."

Development of Security Infrastructure in Tibet

China, right from early 1950s, planned and acted to provide and maintain its security infrastructure on the Tibetan plateau. Beijing built a 22,000-km highway network comprising 15 main highways and 315 subsidiary roads radiating from Lhasa within five decades. Railways construction took slightly more time.

The Southwest Bureau of the Chinese Communist Party's Central Committee, the Southwest Military Region Command, and the Command Headquarters of the 2nd Field Army of China jointly issued a 'Political Mobilisation Directive' on November 8, 1950 on China's armed invasion of Tibet. It read: "The task of marching into Tibet was to liberate Tibetan people, to complete the important mission of unifying the motherland, to prevent imperialism from encroaching on even one inch of our sovereign territory, and to protect and build the frontier of the motherland."

It also directed every officer and man of the PLO to "take every care in their march forward to preserve and save manpower and materials, actively repair and build roads to develop communication and transportation, immediately after the cessation of military action".

The 2,400-km Chengdu-Lhasa road to link Tibet with China and 2,100-km Siling-Lhasa road not only secured PLA occupation of Tibet, but also brought Chinese troops and armaments at India's doorsteps. A network of highways helped China plug all entry points of Tibet from India within seven years of its entry into Tibet.

India's Poor Handling of Tibetan Affairs

It is a well-known fact that India did not handle the Tibetan affair properly. This cost our country immensely. India was spending about Rs 5-6 crore per day about 12-13 years ago for its protection. The Chinese are spending many times more. The expenditure on both sides is far greater now.

As mentioned earlier, Nehru was shocked and psychologically shattered after the humiliation suffered at the Chinese hands in 1962. He realized, though late, that he had been taken for a ride by the Chinese leaders. But was that really the case? Did China really betray India? Or what is dubbed as Chinese betrayal and deception is a myth? Was it not a case of India's self-deception?

Nehru had a romantic view of the Indo-Chinese relations, as he was thoroughly incapable of understanding the Chinese behaviour and communist mindset of Mao and his followers. That's why he ignored the sage advice and words of caution of his colleagues. Nehru's remark about China, during his wartime visit to that country in 1939, is worth quoting: "I found, to my joy, that my desire that China and India should draw closer to each other was fully reciprocated by China's leaders, and more especially by that great man who has become the symbol of China's unity and her determination to be free. I met Marshal Chiang Kai-shek and Madame Chiang many times and we discussed the present and the future of our respective countries. I returned to India an even greater admirer of China than I had been previously, and I could not imagine that any adverse fate could break the spirit of these ancient people, who have grown so young again."

Nehru further wrote: "In my mind the problem of India was tied up with other world problems. More and more I came to think that these separate problems, political or economic, in China, Abyssinia, Spain, Central Europe, India, or elsewhere, were facets of one and the same world problem ... The challenge of fascism and Nazism was in essence the challenge of imperialism."

The solidarity with China's cause and struggle was not limited to words; it found active support in India. The Congress organised "thousand of meetings and demonstrations all over the country in sympathy with the people of China" and even other victims. Nehru continued to talk of Sino-Indian friendship even after October 1950 Chinese invasion of Tibet, as is evident by his noting dated January 12, 1951:

"Great nations have arisen in Asia with long memories of the past they have lived through and their eyes fixed on a future of promise... China has taken a new shape and a new form but whether we like that shape or form or not, we have to recognize that a great nation has been reborn and is conscious of her new strength. China in her newfound strength, has acted some times in a manner which I deeply regret. But we have to remember the background of China ... We, in India, have had two thousand years of friendship with China. We have differences of opinion and even small conflicts but when we hark back to that long past something of the wisdom of that past also helps us to understand each ether."

It is amply clear that Nehru had very high opinion about China, but the latter did not reciprocate. Chinese Communist journal *World Culture* described him as "a rebel against the movement for national independence, a blackguard who undermines the progress of the peoples' movement, a loyal slave of imperialism into (whose) slavish and bourgeois reactionary character has now been instilled the beastly ambition of aggression." The mismatch between Nehru's idealism and naivety and Mao's real politic, and their perceptions about each other proved costly for Tibet and India; the Himalayas became a zone of tension and instability. As mentioned above, while Nehru had a very high opinion about China, the Chinese leaders were full of contempt for him and other Indian leaders, including Mahatma Gandhi."

Sardar Vallabhbhai Patel was not happy over the PLA entry in Tibet but India's concerns were discourteously dismissed by the Chinese government. Patel wrote to Nehru: "It looks as though it is not a friend speaking in that language but a potential enemy". He suggested: "We have to consider what new situation now faces us as a result of disappearance of Tibet as we know it and the expansion of China up to our gates." He further noted prophetically:

"Chinese irredentism and Communist imperialism are different from the imperialism of the Western powers. The former has a cloak of ideology which makes it 10 times more dangerous. In the guise of ideological expansion lie concealed racial, national and historical claims ... While our Western and North-Western threats to security are still as prominent as before, a new threat has developed from the North and the North-East. Thus, for the first time, after centuries, India's defence has to concentrate itself on two fronts simultaneously. Our defence measures have so far been based on the calculations of superiority over Pakistan."

5

Sino-Bhutanese Border Dispute at Doklam

Authoritative depictions of historical Chinese maps by the People's Republic of China show Sikkim and Bhutan as part of Tibet or China for a period of 1800 years, starting from the second century B.C. From 1958, Chinese maps started showing large parts of Bhutanese territory as part of China. In 1960, China issued a statement claiming that Bhutan, Sikkim and Ladakh were part of a unified family in Tibet and had always been subject to the "great motherland of China". Alarmed, Bhutan closed off its border with China and shut all trade and diplomatic contacts. It also established formal defense arrangements with India.

1960s

Starting August 1965, China and India traded accusations regarding intrusions into Doklam. China alleged that Indian troops were crossing into Doklam (which they called "Dognan") from Doka La, and were carrying out reconnaissance and intimidating Chinese herders. At first, the Indians paid no attention to the complaint. However, after several rounds of exchanges, on 30 September 1966, they forwarded a protest from the Bhutanese government which stated that Tibetan grazers were entering the pastures near the Doklam plateau accompanied by Chinese patrols. The letter asserted that the Doklam area was to the "south of the traditional boundary between Bhutan and the Tibet region" in the southern Chumbi area. On 3 October, the Government of Bhutan issued a press statement in which it said, "this area is traditionally part of Bhutan and no assertion has been made by the Government of the People's Republic of China disputing the traditional frontier which runs along recognizable natural features." In response, the Chinese government replied that Bhutan was a sovereign country and that China did not recognize any role for the Indian government in the matter. It also asserted that the Doklam area had "always been under Chinese jurisdiction", that the Chinese herdsmen had "grazed cattle there for generations" and that the Bhutanese herdsmen had to pay pasturage to the Chinese side to graze cattle there.

China later formally extended claims to 300 sq. miles of territory in northern Bhutan and areas north of Punakha, but apparently not in Doklam. Bhutan requested the Indian government to raise the matter with China. However, China rejected India's initiatives stating that the issue concerned China and Bhutan alone. Indian commentators state that the Chinese troops withdrew after a month and that the fracas over Doklam brought Bhutan even closer to India, resulting in the appointment of 3,400 Indian defence personnel in Bhutan for training the Bhutanese Army.

Border negotiations

Border negotiations between Bhutan and China began in 1972 with India playing a supporting role. However, China sought the exclusion of India. Bhutan commenced its own border negotiations with China in 1984. Prior to putting forward its claim line, it carried out its own surveys and produced maps that were approved by the National Assembly in 1989. Strategic expert Manoj Joshi states that the Bhutanese voluntarily shed territory in the process. Other scholars noted a reduction of 8,606 km area in the official Bhutanese maps. The Kula Kangri mountain, touted as the tallest peak in Bhutan, has apparently been ceded to China.

Bhutan said that, through the course of border talks, it had reduced 1,128 km of disputed border areas to 269 km by 1999. In 1996, the Chinese negotiators offered a "package deal" to Bhutan, offering to give up claims on 495 km^2 in the central region in exchange for 269 km^2 in the "northwest", i.e., adjacent to the Chumbi valley, including Doklam, Sinchulumpa, Dramana and Shakhatoe. These areas would offer strategic depth to Chinese defences and access to the strategic Siliguri Corridor of India. Bhutan turned down the offer, allegedly under Indian persuasion.

Having turned down China's package deal, in 2000, Bhutanese government put forward its original claim line of 1989. The talks could make no progress afterwards. The government reported that, in 2004, China started building roads in the border areas, leading to repeated protests by the Bhutanese government based on the 1998 Peace and Tranquility Agreement.

According to a Bhutanese reporter, the most contested area has been the Doklam plateau. Chinese built a road up the Sinchela pass (in undisputed territory) and then over the plateau (in disputed territory), leading up to the Doka La pass, until reaching within 68 metres to the Indian border post on the Sikkim border. Here, they constructed a turn-around facilitating vehicles to turn back. This road has been in existence at least since 2005. In 2007, there were reports of the Chinese having destroyed unmanned Indian forward posts on the Doklam plateau.

Current position

"Boundary talks are ongoing between Bhutan and China and we have written agreements of 1988 and 1998 stating that the two sides agree to maintain peace and tranquility in their border areas pending a final settlement on the boundary question, and to maintain status quo on the boundary as before March 1959. The agreements also state that the two sides will refrain from taking unilateral action, or use of force, to change the status quo of the boundary." —*Ministry of Foreign Affairs, Royal Government of Bhutan.*

Notwithstanding the agreement, the PLA crossed into Bhutan in 1988 and took control of the Chumbi Valley near the Doklam plateau. There were reports of the PLA troops threatening the Bhutanese guards, declaring it to be Chinese soil, and seizing and occupying Bhutanese posts for extended periods. Again, after 2000, numerous intrusions, grazing and road and infrastructure construction by the Chinese were reported as reported in the Bhutanese National Assembly.

FACTOR IN BORDER DISPUTE

This is perhaps the most militarized Buddhist enclave in the world. Perched above 10,000 feet in the icy reaches of the eastern Himalayas, the town of Tawang is not only home to one of Tibetan Buddhism's most sacred monasteries but also the site of a massive Indian military buildup. Convoys of army trucks haul howitzers along rutted mountain roads. Soldiers drill in muddy fields. Military bases appear every half-mile in the countryside, with watchtowers rising behind concertina wire.

A road sign on the northern edge of town helps explain the reason for all the fear and the fury: The border with China is just 23 miles away; Lhasa, the Tibetan capital, 316 miles; and Beijing 2,676 miles. "The Chinese army has a big deployment at the border, at Bumla," said Madan Singh, a junior commissioned officer who sat with a half-dozen soldiers one afternoon sipping tea beside a fog-cloaked road. "That's why we're here." Though little known to the outside world, Tawang is a flashpoint in relations between the world's two most populous nations. It is the focus of China's most delicate land-border dispute, a conflict rooted in Chinese claims of sovereignty over all of historical Tibet.

In recent months, both countries have stepped up efforts to secure their rights over this rugged patch of land. China tried to block a $2.9 billion loan to India from the Asian Development Bank on the grounds that part of the loan was slated for water projects in Arunachal Pradesh, the state that includes Tawang. It was the first time China had sought to influence the territorial dispute through a multilateral institution. Then an Indian general announced that the Indian military was deploying extra troops and fighter jets in the area. The growing belligerence has soured relations between the two Asian giants and has prompted one Indian military leader to declare that China has replaced Pakistan as India's biggest threat.

Economic progress might be expected to bring the countries closer. China and India did $52 billion of trade last year, a 34 percent increase over 2007. But businesspeople say that border tensions have infused official deliberations over business deals, dampening the willingness of Chinese and Indian companies to invest in each other's countries. "Officials start taking more time, scrutinizing things more carefully, and all that means more delays and ultimately more denials," said Ravi Bhoothalingam, a former president of the Oberoi Group, the luxury hotel chain, and a member of the Institute of Chinese Studies in New Delhi. "That's not good for business."

The roots of the conflict go back to China's territorial claims to Tibet. Not only does the Dalai Lama, the exiled spiritual leader of the Tibetans, live in the foothills of the western Himalayas with the blessing of the Indian government, but China insists that this swath of northeast India has historically been part of Tibet, and thus should be part of China. Tawang is a thickly forested area of white stupas and steep, terraced hillsides that is home to the ethnic Monpa people, who practice Tibetan Buddhism, speak a language similar to Tibetan and once paid tribute to rulers in Lhasa. The 6th Dalai Lama was born here in the 17th century.

The Chinese army occupied Tawang briefly in 1962, during a war with India fought over this and other territories along the 2,521-mile border. More than 3,100 Indian soldiers and 700 Chinese soldiers were killed and thousands wounded in the border war. War memorials highlighting China's aggressions in Tawang here are big draws for Indian tourists. "The entire border is disputed," said Ma Jiali, an India scholar at the China Institutes of

Contemporary International Relations, a government-supported think tank in Beijing. "This problem hasn't been solved, and it's a huge barrier to China-India relations."

In some ways, Tawang has become a proxy battleground, too, between China and the Dalai Lama, who passed through this valley when he fled into exile in 1959. From his home in the distant hill town of Dharamsala, he wields enormous influence over Tawang. He appoints the abbot of the powerful monastery and gives financial support to institutions throughout the area. Last year, the Dalai Lama announced for the first time that Tawang is a part of India, bolstering the Indian government's territorial claims and infuriating China.

Traditional Tibetan culture runs strong in Tawang. At the Tawang monastery, an important centre of Tibetan learning, monks express apprehension about China's rule over Tibet, which the Chinese army seized in 1951. "I hate the Chinese government," said Gombu Tsering, 70, a senior monk who watches over the monastery's museum. "Tibet wasn't even a part of China. Lhasa wasn't a part of China." Few expect China to try to forcefully annex Tawang, but military skirmishes are a real danger, analysts say. The Indian military recorded 270 border violations and nearly 2,300 instances of "aggressive border patrolling" by Chinese soldiers last year, said Brahma Chellaney, a professor of strategic studies at the Centre for Policy Research, a research organization in New Delhi. Mr. Chellaney has advised the Indian government's National Security Council.

"The India-China frontier has become more 'hot' than the India-Pakistan border," he said in an e-mail. China has grown increasingly hostile to the Dalai Lama after a severe outbreak of ethnic unrest in Tibet. This year, it turned its diplomatic guns on India. China moved in March to block a $2.9 billion loan to India from the Asian Development Bank, a multi-nation group based in Manila that has China on its board, because $60 million of the loan had been earmarked for flood-control projects in Arunachal Pradesh, the state that includes Tawang. The loan was approved in mid-June over China's heated objections. Weeks after China first tried to block the loan, the chief of the Indian air force, now retired, told a prominent Indian newspaper that China posed a greater threat than Pakistan. Another official, J.J. Singh, the governor of Arunachal Pradesh and retired chief of the Indian army, said the next month that the Indian military was adding two divisions of troops, totalling 50,000 to 60,000 soldiers, to the border region over the next several years. Four Sukhoi fighter jets were immediately deployed to a nearby air base. Since 2005, when Chinese Prime Minister Wen Jiabao visited India, the two countries have gone through 13 rounds of bilateral negotiations over the issue. A last round was just held last month, with no results. Though China has actually resolved many of its border disputes in recent years, India remains a glaring exception.

The Government of Tibet in Exile

From July 20 to 23, 1994, Beijing staged the Third Forum on Work in Tibet which recommended the total destruction of an entire civilization flourishing on the Tibetan Plateau for thousands of years. This cultural "empire" once encompassed far-flung areas like Buryatia, Tuva and Kalmykia in Russia; Mongolia; Laddakh, Lahaul-Spiti, Sikkim, and Arunachal Pradesh in India; Mustang, Dolpo and Solo Khumbu in Nepal; Bhutan and parts of western China.

The policy formulated in 1994 in Beijing-and these days pursued with Cultural Revolutionary zeal in Tibet-will mean the annihilation of the spiritual homeland of this shared culture. Implementation of the Third Work Forum is thus having a crippling impact on the traditional culture of millions of non-Tibetans as the well-spring of their cultural inspiration is forcibly drained and there is nothing to replenish the continuous growth and development of this distinct and highly evolved civilization.

Losing Hearts and Minds

The decisions made at the Third Forum rest on two fundamental conclusions which Beijing drew. It realized it was losing out in two vital fields-ideology and propaganda. For a state whose existence is justified by its ideological superiority and the power of its propaganda to shape the thinking of the masses, the implications of this for the future was at best uncertain, at worst dangerous. Beijing concluded it was losing the ideological war because, despite the unrelenting assault on Tibetan Buddhism, Tibetans were as devoted to their traditional beliefs as ever. Beijing has succeeded in physically enslaving the country but it has not won over the hearts, minds and loyalty of the Tibetan populace.

Communist ideology, enforced by the military might of China, had failed to dent the heart of Buddhism. Added to this was the communist authorities' total bafflement at the non-violent policy underpinning the Middle Way Approach advocated by His Holiness the Dalai Lama to resolve the issue of Tibet's future status. For a regime which is based on Mao's dictum that political power grows out of the barrel of a gun, this supposedly eccentric philosophy which says victory lies in capturing the hearts and minds of people by the power of ideas rather than killing by the power of the gun comes as a bolt from the blue. Much of Beijing's knee-jerk reaction to, and its bafflement at, His Holiness the Dalai Lama's new policy of rapprochement lies at the heart of its new hardline policy.

Beijing considered it was losing the propaganda war because, for one reason or the other, the world's media and its pop culture considered-at least for the moment-Tibet and Tibetan Buddhism their very own cuddly pandas. Despite its financial might China found it extremely difficult to exterminate this image of Tibet and get its voice heard on the Tibetan issue in the court of the international media. In order to address these weaknesses the Third Forum concentrated on two issues. One was to focus on Tibet's economic development in the hope that this would keep Tibetan demonstrations off the streets. This was tantamount to bribing the Tibetans with promises of riches to come if they toed the party line. The other concern was to win the coming and new generations of Tibetans over to the Chinese viewpoint.

Beijing has given up on the present generation of Tibetans as a lost cause. If the coming generations of Tibetans were also lost to the 'Dalai Clique' this, the Chinese concluded, would have dangerous consequences for Chinese rule in Tibet. The 15-year-old Gyalwa Karmapa's dramatic escape from Tibet in January 2000 was a warning to the Beijing authorities of the erosion of loyalty to China. The Karmapa's flight, and the earlier escape of Agya Rinpoche, the abbot of Kumbum Monastery, came as a huge embarrassment for China, because retaining these high lamas gave China a degree of legitimacy for its rule in Tibet. This is the reason why Beijing is enforcing with greater strictness its 1993 instruction of recalling young Tibetans studying in schools and monasteries run by Dharmasala in India. This is also the rationale for Beijing closing down schools in Tibet which are privately run by Tibetans.

For these reasons Tibet today is in the throes of a second Cultural Revolution as the Chinese authorities step up their long-term strategy to exterminate Tibet's distinct cultural and ethnic identity. The authorities are pursuing a four-pronged strategy to achieve their final objective. They have stepped up repression while employing their huge propaganda machine to paint a rosy picture of Tibet. They have quickened the pace of economic development to dampen Tibetan nationalism and are simultaneously moving more Chinese settlers onto the Tibetan Plateau to change Tibet's demographic composition and to ease social unrest because of mounting unemployment back in China.

The Third Work Forum on Tibet was convened by the top Chinese leadership and was presided over by President Jiang Zemin. The authorities have now enshrined this Work Forum as the most "important strategic policy to rejuvenate Tibet" and have hailed its directives as the new manifesto for party work on the plateau. The significance of the Third Work Forum lies in the fact that it overturned the more liberal policies laid out for Tibet's "development" by the First and Second Work Forums held in 1980 and 1984. The first two work forums were initiated by the late Hu Yaobang, then Secretary General of the Chinese Communist Party.

This liberal and somewhat maverick leader is credited with masterminding a series of measures to improve the social, economic and political conditions in Tibet. The brief spell of liberalization markedly improved the living conditions of the majority of Tibetans and contributed to a more relaxed intellectual and social climate.

The Third Work Forum reversed these policies and reinstated hardline measures under which Tibet is still reeling today. The Tibetans in Tibet perceive the current repressive policies as a second Cultural Revolution. The question is why did China choose to jettison its earlier more liberal policies and adopt a manifesto which is leading to the systematic destruction of Tibet's distinct culture. The answer lies in domestic and international events which forced China to formulate a series of hardline policies on Tibet which eventually crystallized into the Third Work Forum for Tibet. The world which confronted China in the late 1980s and early 1990s was a frightening one.

Starting from 1987, Tibet was rocked by a string of protest demonstrations, which called for Tibetan independence. One of the largest demonstrations which erupted on March 5, 1989 in Lhasa, forced the authorities to impose martial law on the city. These demonstrations are now seen to have been an inspiration behind the outburst of Chinese students' pro-democracy uprisings. The authorities saw the series of Tiananmen Square demonstrations as a sign of their Central Government losing control, and in an attempt to regain supremacy, the authorities slaughtered-perhaps hundreds if not thousands of students on June 4, 1989. These demonstrations were a chilling replay to the authorities of the May 4, 1919 student demonstrations in Beijing which signalled a political and cultural awakening across the erstwhile Middle Kingdom.

Bejing's fears of losing control were exacerbated by external events which saw the unraveling of the communist world. The Solidarity Movement in Poland, the fall of the Berlin Wall, and the implosion of the Soviet Union fed Beijing's paranoia over threats to the Chinese Communist Party hold on power. Official China's fears were further inflamed by the rapidly changing attitude of the broad masses as they turned back from communism to traditional beliefs like Confucionism, Buddhism, Islam, Christianity and indigenous folk cults.

In the eyes of ordinary citizens communism was becoming totally discredited and this, more than anything else, was the biggest nightmare for China's leadership. The leadership's justification for staying in power was being disavowed by the masses. For a one-party dictatorship this historically indicates the first step along the slippery road to dissolution and removal of power.

For these reasons the Chinese leadership then reverted to its earlier view that traditional beliefs were its real enemy. In competing with Buddhism, Confucionism, Islam, Christianity and other isms, communism was losing out in terms of its ability to retain the loyalty and allegiance of the masses. The leadership revived the old aphorisms once served up to the Tibetan people to justify their policies to destroy Tibetan Buddhism during the Cultural Revolution. Bewildered Tibetans were then told that just as there cannot be two suns in the sky, so there cannot be both Buddhism and socialism in Tibet. Inevitably Buddhism then had to give way to socialism. And again, today, religion is being blatantly sublimated to Chinese state power.

These were the fears of the Chinese leaders when they met in Beijing in 1994 to hammer out their new Tibet initiatives. For the Chinese authorities Tibet is an especially sensitive issue because of their conviction that hostile Western forces are using the issue of Tibet to "westernize" China and to lead to its territorial fragmentation. The third generation Chinese leaders came to the conclusion that stability in Tibet was vital to the stability of China as a whole. Earlier, Tibet was merely of peripheral concern to the vital interests of China's sprawling communist empire. Now, with the Third Work Forum, the authorities were saying, "We must clearly understand that we must do our work in Tibet not only for the sake our of own region's stability and development, not only for the interests of our people, but also for the sake of the whole nation's stability and development."

In Tibet, China faced peculiar problems because of the inherent strength of Tibetan Buddhism and the depth of devotion of the populace to His Holiness the Dalai Lama. The sustained burst of religious revival that followed in the wake of the brief spell of liberalization in Tibet confirmed the leadership's worst fears that decades of concerted assault on Tibetan culture and religion had not extinguished the people's traditional beliefs and values. From merely nuisance value, the Chinese leadership now viewed Tibetan Buddhism as a very real and imminent threat to the stability of Chinese rule in Tibet.

At the same time the Chinese leadership's attitude towards His Holiness the Dalai Lama changed. From being an uncertain ally in the peace process in Tibet, the current Chinese leadership now saw him as a full-blown "enemy". A top-level conclave held in Beijing on March 10, 1993 concluded that, "There are different factions within the Dalai Clique; they are, however, unanimous in their political nature and position. They differ from each other in ideological viewpoints and ways of expressing them. Different strategies must be adopted to use their differences, to deal with them differently in order to divide and destroy them."

Repeated statements by high-level officials describe the struggle against "splittism", the official term for Tibetan independence, as a "life-and-death struggle". At the 1994 annual meeting of the "TAR" Communist Party Committee to brief members on the policy thrust of the Third Work Forum on Tibet, Raidi, deputy Secretary of the Committee said, "Up to now, his (the Dalai Lama's) standpoint on Tibet's independence has never changed, and we must reveal his double-faced true colour. The focal point in our region in the struggle against splittism is to oppose the Dalai Clique. As the saying goes, to kill a serpent, one must first cut off its head."

In short, the Third Work Forum decided that Beijing was in a position to solve the Tibet issue without the Dalai Lama's involvement. It abandoned the earlier liberal policy of including His Holiness the Dalai Lama in any future settlement of Tibet's status. His Holiness the Dalai Lama was clearly singled out as the cause of China's "Tibet problem".

The Third Work Forum also abandoned the policy of granting concessions to Tibet because of the plateau's "special characteristics". This policy had been the cornerstone of recommendations made by the First and Second Tibet Work Forums.

To carry out its new hardline policies in Tibet, Beijing appointed Chen Kuiyuan as the "TAR" Party Secretary in 1992. Chen Kuiyuan's appointment is significant because he had a track record for being a tough and ruthless administrator. He had already served as the First Secretary of the Chinese Communist Party in Inner Mongolia and is credited with repressing the rebellious Mongols, many of whom refer to him as "the butcher". Chen

Kuiyuan was especially recommended to the post by Hu Jintao, the current Vice-President of China, who was then the First Secretary of the Chinese Communist Party in Tibet.

Tackling Tibetan Nationalism

The Third Work Forum policies chalked out for Tibet contained four key elements. China stepped up the scale of repression in Tibet. External propaganda work was escalated. The pace of economic development in Tibet-and its corollary of encouraging more Chinese settlers and businessmen to take advantage of the economic boom on the "roof of the world"-was also increased. In short, Beijing had decided to tackle Tibetan nationalism head-on and observers are still assessing the consequences on both Chinese rule in Tibet and on the populace.

Beijing remains convinced that these key components of its current policy will stabilize Chinese rule over Tibet and solve once and for all, the vexed problem of its negative image over the way Tibet has been handled. One main target of the current policy of repression is Tibetan Buddhism. Chinese leaders are increasingly alarmed by the proliferation of monasteries and temples which the period of liberalization spawned throughout Tibet: they are seen as the bastions of Tibetan nationalism. The authorities have set up "Democratic Management Committees" to control monasteries and nunneries and created "Work Inspection Teams" to supervise the "education" of monks and nuns.

A major thrust is underway to break the bond of loyalty between the clergy in Tibet and His Holiness the Dalai Lama in India. Campaigns like "Strike Hard" and "Patriotic Re-education", unleashed in 1996, are aimed at crippling the rise of Tibetan Buddhism which the authorities suspect is weaning the loyalty of the Tibetan people away from the communist party and towards His Holiness the Dalai Lama. One salient feature of the "Strike Hard" campaign is how differently it is interpreted in China and Tibet. China's "Strike Hard" campaign was started to weed out corruption. Tibet's version is used as a political tool to eliminate those whom the authorities label "splittists". In Tibet, rather than striking at corruption, the authorities turn a blind eye to this social disease in the hope that it will erode the traditional morality of Tibetans and undermine Tibetan Buddhism.

In fact, at a secret meeting held in December 1999 in Chengdu, capital of Sichuan province, Chen Kuiyuan, the hardline Party Secretary of "TAR" recommended to the Central Chinese Government that an all-out effort must be made to eradicate Tibetan Buddhism and culture from the face of the earth so that no memory of them will be left in the minds of coming generations of Tibetans-except as museum pieces.

Chen Kuiyuan stated that the main cause of instability is the existence of the Dalai Lama and his Government-in-Exile in Dharamsala and these must be "uprooted". He recommended that Tibet, Tibetan people and Tibetan Buddhism-in other words the very name of Tibet-must be destroyed and the "Tibet Autonomous Region" be merged with provinces like Sichuan. While treating Tibetans to boot-heel subjugation at home, internationally China was on an overdrive propaganda blitz. At a brainstorming conclave held on March 10, 1993, Zeng Jian-hui, Vice-Minister of the Propaganda Ministry, told participants, "The propaganda work on the question of Tibet is one of the focal points of the entire external propaganda work...With regard to attacks by the West and the Dalai Clique and their frequent activities, our external propaganda should launch offensive. We should expand our spheres of influence; in particular, we should infiltrate our propaganda into the mainstream life of the West.

"Firstly we should continue to send Tibetan scholars and Tibetan singing and dancing troupes abroad to lecture and perform. Secondly, relevant embassies and consulates should aim at the public opinion and the activities of the Dalai Clique in the countries where they are stationed and utilize speeches, picture exhibitions, special articles and other forms to carry out propaganda work, so as to win over officials and people of those countries... We should reinforce the work of utilizing the power of foreign propaganda. A few years ago, in the light of the situation of that time, we made arrangements for foreign journalists to visit Tibet."

The September 3, 2000 edition of *People's Daily* carried a story headlined "Tibet Welcomes Foreign Journalists for Objective Reporting". It stated that "A senior Tibetan official said Sunday that Tibet welcomes foreign journalists to come for objective and just reporting, but not those who take distorted views. Raidi, Deputy Secretary of the Tibet Autonomous Regional Committee of the Communist Party of China and Chairman of the Standing Committee of the Tibetan Autonomous Regional People's Congress, made the remarks at a meeting here with a press delegation of Thailand." In this context, it is interesting to note that N. Ram, the editor of India's *Frontline* magazine, devoted 36 pages of the September 15, 2000 issue to promote the Chinese line and recommended that the Indian Government expel the Central Tibetan Administration from Indian soil for being the main stumbling block to normal relations between India and China. It is difficult to assess to what extent the views contained in his stupendous reporting marathon are his own.

These editorial outbursts are in line with policy decisions outlined in the early nineties. During a two-day secret conclave in March 1993 in Chengdu, Vice-Minister Zeng Jian-hui, told participants, "All foreigners that we entertain and send to Tibet must have a relatively objective opinion of Tibet. We should use people from abroad to carry out the propaganda on Tibet for us, which is more powerful than if we do it."

Along with its external public relations strategy, China is presently carrying out a potentially much more dangerous policy of speeding up the pace of Tibet's economic development and its related drive to bring more Chinese settlers onto the Tibetan Plateau.

Beijing's Western China Development Programme, which incorporates Tibet in its ambit, is devised to shift the focus of China's economic activities from Coastal China to the interior-both to narrow the imbalance in the level of economic development between the two regions and to ease population pressure on the coastal areas which attract millions of migrant workers.

The focus of Beijing's Western China Economic Development Programme in Tibet is to exploit the plateau's still untapped minerals and other natural resources and to upgrade Tibet's infrastructure-like roads and telecommunications-to facilitate transportation of these resources to China. The other purpose of the heightened level of economic activity is to divert the Tibetans' attention from their political fate to focus on their livelihood-thus undermining Tibetan nationalism. The Chinese authorities aim to manipulate the situation in Tibet still further by bringing in more Chinese settlers who would then demographically cement Chinese rule once and for all. These current hardline policies and their implementation in Tibet are impacting the stalled Sino-Tibetan Dialogue and will vitally affect the ability of Tibetans to survive as a distinct people and culture.

Beijing's Flawed Perceptions

The basic flaws in China's new policy in its search to resolve the problem of Tibet is thinking the solution can exclude the involvement of His Holiness the Dalai Lama. The other is in attempting to solve the problem over the heads of Tibet's citizens.

These two fundamental mistakes will exacerbate China's Tibet problem, not solve it. The reason lies in the history of Tibet and in the sentiments of the people. The institution of the Dalai Lamas of Tibet is more than 600 years old, if we start from the birth of the first Dalai Lama in 1391. In the course of its growth and development, the very institution itself came to symbolize fundamental beliefs and the political destiny of the nation. The bond between the Dalai Lamas and the Tibetan people is fundamental and unbreakable; any attempt, however sustained, will never succeed in driving a wedge between the two.

Consequently, China's current policy of forcing Tibetans-especially monks and nuns-to denounce His Holiness the Dalai Lama and pledge loyalty to the Chinese Communist Party will prove counterproductive.

In view of this the Third Work Forum's basic assumption that in the case of Tibet time is on the side of China, and that Beijing can stall the problem of Tibet till the demise of the present Dalai Lama whereupon the issue of Tibet will solve itself, is fatally flawed-based as it is on a mistaken perception of the role played by the institution of the Dalai Lamas in the development of Tibetan history.

This assumption, if not reviewed, revised and abandoned, will prove catastrophic for the Chinese leadership and for those who chose to turn their whimsical personal analysis into state policy.

The reason is simple. The Chinese Communist Party was founded in the 1920s and came to power in 1949. Within this short span of time the masses have lost faith in communist ideology, and members of the party these days pay mere lip service to the ideological justifications of the party. Conversely, the institution of the Dalai Lamas as a political force is more than 300 years old.

These days the Dalai Lama is recognized by Tibetans throughout the world as the heart of Tibetan nationalism. How can a party which has lost its soul outlast an institution which symbolizes the very soul of a people? For these reasons it is imperative for China to review and re-assess its current hardline stance towards Tibet.

China must re-start its stalled peace process over Tibet and consider His Holiness the Dalai Lama as a vital and active partner in the procedures. If China does this it will have won a powerful ally and companion along the road to peace, stability and continued prosperity.

THE SINO/INDIAN DISPUTE

Ever since its establishment in 1949, the attitude of the Communist Chinese Government towards India has been bound up with the Tibetan issue. India had, on gaining independence in 1947, inherited the British "special position" in Tibet, along with the Mission in Lhasa and trade agencies in larger towns. It had retained the services of British officials stationed in Tibet. When, in 1949, Tibetan leaders made their bid to contact foreign Governments, they first contacted these officials, and it was only a short step for the suspicious minded Chinese to regard this as evidence of Indian collusion with the British.

The Communist Chinese also had ideological reasons for believing that such collusion existed. At the time of their coming to power, Moscow was propagating the line of a world divided into two camps, with the Indian Government depicted as a tool of British imperialism and firmly situated in the opposing camp. The Communist Chinese leaders, who previously had had little contact with the outside world, faithfully repeated these accusations against Nehru and his Government.

Following the Chinese occupation of Tibet in late 1950, Peking's suspicions of the Indians were further aroused when Nehru, in notes to the Chinese Government, expressed the "surprise and regret" of his Government at the Chinese action. He described as "deplorable" the Chinese use of force in Tibet.

Standard diplomatic practice stipulates that a state does not criticise the behaviour of another state acting within its own territorial boundaries unless there are special reasons for so doing. The Indians justified their criticism of the Chinese on the ground of their special interest in Tibet, from which the Chinese inferred that the Indians were implying some restriction on Chinese sovereignty. A sharp reply was received from the Chinese accusing the Indians of unwarranted interference and claiming that the policy of the Indian Government was "affected by foreign influences hostile to China in Tibet".

Nevertheless, whatever suspicions the Chinese may have felt about the Indians in 1949-50 must to some extent have been allayed by subsequent developments. India opposed the 1950 Tibetan appeal to the United Nations; it was one of the few non-communist countries not to condemn China's intervention in the Korean War; it sought to have China seated an the United Nations. The culmination of these moves to improve relations with China was the signing, in April 1954, of an agreement by which India recognised without qualification China's sovereignty over Tibet and conceded many of India's former rights there. A few months later the Chinese Premier, Chou En-lai, paid a successful visit to India, and in October of the same year Nehru visited Peking.

The very considerable improvement in Sino/Indian relations from 1950 to 1954 was on the Indian side almost entirely the result of efforts by Nehru, who saw friendship between China and India as the starting point of a new order in world affairs. It must have been obvious to the Chinese that considerable opposition to Nehru's pro-China policies, at least as far as Tibet was concerned, existed both within and outside the Indian Government. It should also have been clear that problems were going to arise over wide discrepancies in the claimed Sino/Indian border, as shown in maps published by both sides.

However, as long as Nehru's China policy appeared to produce results, his opposition in India remained silent. It was important for both Nehru and the Chinese that this policy continued to appear to give results, and hence the efforts made by both sides to keep intact the edifice of good relations. The Chinese, under the 1954 agreement, allowed India to maintain certain trade and pilgrimage rights in Tibet.

They sought to play down the significance of border differences, stating that they had simply inherited their claimed Sino/Indian frontier from the pre-1949 Nationalist Government and that it would be "revised" in due course. Nehru, for his part, avoided public mention of the reality and extent of border differences, and it seemed that both sides were moving towards a compromise settlement of the question.

What were these differences, and what evidence was there that both sides were in fact prepared to compromise?

The Sino/Indian border can be divided into three sectors:

(i) an eastern sector where 99,000 square kilometres of territory described by the Indians as the Northeast Frontier Agency, or N.E.F.A is in dispute: (ii) a middle sector where some 2.000 square kilometres of territory on either side of the main Himalayan passes is disputed: and (iii) a western sector where the Indian province of Ladakh borders on Tibet and Sinkiang and where both the Indian/Tibet and Indian/Sinkiang borders are disputed, in particular the ownership of some 30,000 square kilometres of high plateau country known as the Aksai Chin.

To an outside observer looking at the frontier as it stands, an apparent basis for a compromise settlement would be for China to drop its claim to the N.E.F.A. in exchange for India dropping its claim to the Aksai Chin, with both sides making concessions over the middle sector and the Ladakh/ Tibetan border. Such a settlement accords with the realities of both geography and administrative control two important criteria in the settlement of border disputes. The N.E.F.A. lies to the south of the Himalayan watershed and is controlled by India. The Aksai Chin, for the most part, lies to the north of the main range, and the Chinese claim to have controlled the area since 1950. In 1956-7, they built a strategic road across the Aksai Chin, linking Sinkiang with Tibet. That the Indians learnt about the road only from a map published by the Chinese in 1958 is substantial evidence that India was not in control of the area.

The historical basis of the border is more confused. The Indian claim to the N.E.F.A. rests almost entirely on acceptance of the McMahon Line, a line agreed to by the Tibetans and British in 1914 as the border in this area. In the Aksai Chin area no agreement has ever been reached on the alignment of the border. Nevertheless, if both sides were to take a generous view of the historical data, a basis for a N.E.F.A./Aksai Chin exchange could be found.

During the post-1954 honeymoon period of Sino/Indian relations, both sides did in fact seem prepared to take a generous view of the situation and to move towards a compromise settlement. In 1956, Chou En-lai admitted privately to Nehru that, although lie thought the McMahon line "was not fair", nevertheless China would accept the line as the border with India after they had "consulted with the Tibetan authorities". Chinese recognition of the McMahon Line was also implied when its eastern extension was accepted as a basis for border negotiations with Burma, and by Chinese de facto acceptance of the line as the dividing line between Chinese and Indian forces in the area.

Nehru, for his part, appeared willing to play down the Indian claims to the Aksai Chin. He tried to delay disclosure if the news that the Chinese had built a road in the area. After the news had been revealed, he sought to play down the economic significance of the area, describing it as a "barren tundra". He even went so far as to cast doubt on the validity of the Indian claim to the area. In statements to the Indian Parliament during early 1959, Nehru pointed out that "during British rule, this area was neither inhabited: nor were there any outposts", adding that "this place, Aksai Chin area, is distinguish completely from other areas. It is a matter for argument which part belongs to us and which part belongs to somebody else. It is not clear".

Nehru's efforts to take the heat out of the Aksai Chin question were not entirely successful. (One of his critics even suggested building an atomic reactor in the area to promote its economic development.) News of the Chinese road in the area appeared to trigger off long-suppressed Indian sensitivity over the border issue, and, in August 1958, the Indian Government made a formal claim to the disputed territory in all three sectors. In a letter to Nehru of January 1959, Chou En-lai claimed that the Aksai Chin was Chinese territory and added that the McMahon Line was a "product of British aggression", illegal, and had "never been recognised by the Chinese Central Government". He proposed that the existing status quo he maintained, however, pending a negotiated settlement of the dispute, and added that China would take a "realistic attitude" over the McMahon Line.*

The Tibetan uprising of March 1959 upset the delicate balance of Sino/Indian relations. Reports of Chinese military action to suppress the uprising, together with the sight of thousands of Tibetan refugees crossing into Indian territory, quickly aroused feelings of alarm and anger in India, particularly among those who believed their country had an historic interest in Tibet. Nehru's Right-Wing critics charged that India should never have allowed the Chinese into Tibet in the first place. Nehru, influenced possibly both by Indian public opinion and his own feelings on the question, came out in open condemnation of Chinese behaviour in Tibet.

The Chinese reacted even more strongly than they had in 1950. Nehru, in addition to condemning the Chinese, had spoken of his sympathy with "the aspirations of the Tibetans for autonomy". He had given asylum to the Dalai Lama, who was also allowed facilities to make his 1959 appeal for U. N. action over Tibet. And finally, the Chinese had reason to believe that the Tibetan guerrillas were receiving arms from across the Indian border.

In May 1959 the Chinese published a long article urging, almost begging, Nehru not to be swayed by his reactionary Right-Wing critics and to return to the path of Sino/Indian friendship. With a frankness and detail probably unmatched by any other Chinese statement on foreign policy, the article set out the Chinese case over Tibet, and accused the Indians of unjustified interference. Indian trade with Tibet was greatly restricted. Clashes involving casualties occurred at several points along the disputed border as the Chinese Army extended its control over border areas in an effort to restrict the move-court of Tibetans across the frontier.

These border clashes, following in the wake of the Tibetan uprising, appeared to put an end to Nehru's willingness to compromise over the border dispute. Having earlier in 1959 cast doubt on the Indian claim to the Aksai Chin, in September he stated before the Indian Parliament that the Chinese claims were "absurd" and would mean "handing over the Himalayas to them as a gift". A Chinese call in November 1959 for negotiations and a twenty-kilometre military withdrawal from the McMahon Line in the east and the "line of actual control" in the west to prevent a recurrence of border clashes was met with an Indian demand for a prior Chinese withdrawal from the Aksai Chin. A Chinese reply pointing out that this should also be paralleled by an Indian withdrawal from the NE.F.A. was ignored. In the end the Chinese appeared to settle for a freezing of the existing status quo - without negotiations or a twenty-kilometre withdrawal.

However, if the Chinese were happy to keep things as they were (keeping also their road across the Aksai Chin), Nehru and his Government were not. Throughout 1960-61 Indian opinion progressively hardened, and demands for the Government to do something about Tibet and the disputed border increased. The army was given full control over the frontier districts and it proceeded to build up its strength in these areas.

During the summer (northern) of 1962, Indian military patrols repeatedly crossed the Chinese-claimed line of actual control in the western sector of the frontier. Posts were established well behind the Chinese forward positions in territory claimed and occupied by the Chinese. Frequent and insistent Chinese protests were met with the bald statement that the Indians were merely operating in Indian territory. By August 14, Nehru was able to announce that India had three times as many posts in the western sector as the Chinese. He asked for a free hand to continue the build-up of Indian strength in the area.

The Chinese had repeatedly warned that a continuation of such activity would end in hostilities. On July 9, they had warned the Indians "to rein in on the brink of the precipice". On August 4, they called for immediate negotiations on the border. The Indians replied that negotiations could not be held until the Chinese had ceased their occupation of "every square inch of sacred Indian territory", and that the Chinese must first "vacate their aggression" in the Aksai Chin. The Chinese replied on September 13 proposing talks to begin on October 15 "without preconditions", that is, without a Chinese withdrawal from the Aksai Chin. The Indians refused the offer.

While Indian military pressure was building up along the Chinese-claimed border in the western sector, a curious situation was developing along the McMahon Line in the eastern sector. The Indians claim that at its western end the McMahon Line was not accurately drawn: that it was meant to have followed the crest of a line of hills known as the Thag La ridge. The Chinese claim, and have produced the original McMahon Line from the Tibetan archives to prove their point, that the line as originally drawn lies approximately twelve miles south of this ridge along the southern side of a small river valley. (Western maps show the McMahon Line in conformity with the Chinese claim.) The area between the Indian and Chinese versions of the McMahon Line is described by the Indians as the Dho La strip.

This was not the only unilateral revision of the McMahon Line carried out by the Indians. In his letter to Chou En-lai of September 29, 1959, Nehru admitted that in the Migyitun area (to the east of the Dho La strip) the border shown on Indian maps "differs slightly from the boundary shown in the Treaty map". He claimed that when the McMahon line was drawn, "the exact topographical features in this area were not known". The Indians have also now come to admit that "blind adherence" to the original McMahon Line would leave the Dho La strip on the Chinese side at the border.

It is not clear who first occupied the Dho La strip. The Chinese claim that the area had always been under their control and that Indian troops moved in during 1962. The Indians claim they had long occupied the area and that the Chinese began a to establish posts in the area after September 8, 1962. What is clear is that on October 12, 1962, Nehru announced in the Indian Parliament that he had given the order to drive the Chinese out of the Dho La strip.

Eight days later, on October 20, the Chinese attacked in force across the Thagla La ridge and into the disputed strip, while advancing their troops into the Chinese-claimed territory in the western sector where the Indians had earlier established posts. Four days later, the Chinese called for a ceasefire to be followed by a withdrawal of both sides from the line that separated them at that moment (the so-called October 24 line of actual control). Failing to get a satisfactory response from the Indians, they advanced troops south of the Dho La strip into the N.E.F.A., defeating Indian military forces in the area. Two weeks later, they withdrew to the positions occupied on October 24. The main point of contention between the Chinese and Indians ever since has been whether the Chinese should maintain their October 24 positions or withdraw further to the positions they occupied before fighting broke out.

The Chinese attack of October 1962 has led to an almost complete breakdown in relations between China and India. The level of each country's diplomatic representation in the other has been greatly reduced. Many thousands of Chinese nationals have been expelled from India. The few Indian nationals living in China have, in one way or another, been forced to leave. Border incidents have continued. Both sides have launched extreme propaganda campaigns against each other, the Chinese denouncing Nehru as a representative of the "big bourgeoisie" and a tool for U. S. aggressive designs against Tibet, while the Indians denounce the Chinese for having aggressive, imperialist designs against Indian territory. Both sides have gone to great lengths to discredit each other inter- nationally. Both sides have increased their military preparedness along the Himalayan frontier, particularly India, which has doubled its military budget to a level it cannot afford.

The question thus arises: Who is primarily to blame for the hostility in Sino/Indian relations? From the account already given, the primary cause of the hostility was the post-1959 dispute over the Sino/Indian border leading to the Chinese attack of October 20. But why the sudden emergence of such a dispute between two countries previously enjoying good relations?

Reverting to the terminology of our previous discussion on hostility between states, both sides see the breakdown in relations as being caused by the active hostility of the other side. This hostility, they claim, is both ideologically and national- interest based. The Chinese are accused of having acted in a hostile manner out of a desire to acquire territory and out of strong ideological dislike for the Indian Government. The Chinese claim the Indians have designs against Chinese territory and that their Government is under the influence of anti-Chinese and pro-U. S. reactionary elements.

Both sides realise that they have somehow or other to explain why the other side suddenly, in 1959, decided that its interests were no longer served by the maintenance of normal relations. The Indian explanation is that Chinese pre-1959 policy was designed to lull India into a false sense of security and so facilitate Chinese ambitions. The Chinese explanation was that reactionary elements began to gain the upper hand in the Indian Government in 1959, and point to the post-1959 increase in U. S. aid to India as evidence.

In fact there is good reason to believe that the hostility shown by each side towards the other was reactive rather than active: that each side was reacting to the believed hostility of the other. To take the Chinese side of things first.

In terms of the account already given, it seems likely that the Chinese attack of October 20, 1962, was primarily a reaction to Indian military pressure along the disputed frontier during preceding months. It could be argued, however. that the behaviour of the Chinese before October 20, and in particular their propaganda attacks against the Indians from 1960 onwards, cannot be explained simply as a reaction to previous events: that overall Chinese behaviour must therefore include some aggressive component.

The Chinese had in fact made their first hostile move against the Indians back in 1959 when they restricted Indian trading and other rights in Tibet. The Chinese had also, according to the Indians, extended somewhat the area they claimed in the western sector. And they had, according to the Indians, been responsible for the 1959 border clashes already mentioned. The Indian charge is based on alleged differences between the frontier claimed by the Chinese to 1956 and that shown on a map of the claimed Sino/Indian frontier handed to the Indians by the Chinese in 1960. The Chinese deny any difference between the two lines.

Unless these apparently hostile acts of the Chinese can be explained in reactive terms., in terms of their reacting to previous Indian actions, then it would seem that the Chinese had taken the initiative in hostility towards India and were largely responsible for the eventual breakdown in relations.

The hardening of the Chinese attitude towards India in 1959 was clearly related to Tibetan developments in that year. In judging the behaviour of the Chinese, we need, in effect, to ask whether their sensitivity over Tibet was sufficient to explain this hardening of attitude.

To accept that the Communist Chinese are, in fact extremely sensitive toward Tibet does not necessarily imply a simple acceptance of Chinese propaganda. What we know of Chinese thinking and behaviour, strongly suggests that this sensitivity does exist. If all non-communist Chinese believe that China has the right to consider Tibet as an integral part of her territory, we should accept that Communist Chinese are equally convinced. If many non-communist Chinese believe (as they do) that Britain had designs against Tibet, we should accept that Communist Chinese, educated to believe in the evils of US Western imperialism, will be at least equally fearful. We do not need accept that these views are correct; we may even consider they are absurd. But if we are going to get anywhere in trying to understand China's behaviour, we should start from the assumption that these views may be sincerely hold in Peking.

Nor may it be so absurd for the Communist Chinese to think along these lines. The Chinese legal claim to Tibet, it has been argued, appears difficult to refute. As for fears of foreign designs, if the British had earlier convinced themselves that the activities of one Russian agent in Lhasa could lead the politically unstable Tibetans to ally themselves with Tsarist Russia, the Chinese could be excused for thinking that the presence of a British Mission in Lhasa dealing directly with the independent-minded Tibetans and arranging on occasion for the supply of arms from India was evidence of British ambitions eventually to detach Tibet from China, and that India may have inherited these ambitions.

Similarly, it would not be entirely surprising if the Chinese viewed the supply of foreign arms to Tibetan guerrillas from northern India in 1959 as confirmation that such ambitions existed. Finally, the Chinese were hound to be impressed by the demands of the Indian Right Wing for action against the Chinese in Tibet.

For example: some weight could be attached to the fact that the then Chief of the Indian Army Staff wrote a not unenthusiastic foreword for a book published in 1961 entitled The Chinese Aggression. The author of the hook, a Dr. Satyanarayan Sinha, predicted that the "clash of the Indochinese weapons for the possession of the Himalayas will lead to making Tibet an independent country again", and suggested ways in which this could be done.

These, then, are the reasons for believing the Chinese may he sensitive about Tibet. Chinese behaviour provides further confirmation. British officials captured in Tibet in 1950 were subjected to long imprisonment and continual interrogation - treatment far more severe than that meted out to British nationals who fell into communist hands elsewhere in China. And there was Nehru's sad admission to the Indian Parliament in 1959 after talks with Chou En-Iai, of the Chinese having "some sort of kink in their minds... of foreign countries, United Kingdom or America, somehow making incursions into Tibet".

In sum, therefore, it does not seem unreasonable to conclude that the Communist Chinese sincerely believed they had a right to Tibet and that their position in the area was threatened from the direction of India. In which case they would have interpreted Indian behaviour in 1959 as an indication of hostility to which they felt compelled, or entitled, to react.

However, if Chinese behaviour in 1959 can be explained in reactive terms, can the same be said about the Chinese attack of October 1962? Even if the Indian claim to the Dho La strip was doubtful, does not the violence and intensity of the 1962 attack suggest that China was doing more than retaliate for any wrongs she may have believed the Indians to base committed?

By 1962, the Chinese were confronted not only by Indian agitation over Tibet, but also by two further aspects of Indian behaviour which would even more easily have been misunderstood. They were: (i) the Indian military build-up along the Sino/Indian border in 1961-2 and (ii) rigid Indian insistence that, as a precondition to border negotiations, the Chinese must first evacuate the whole of the Aksai Chin.

At the time, the Indians justified their position on negotiations and their military build up in terms of the correctness of their border claims. Indeed, the official Indian position was that the line claimed by India as a border had already been defined historically, and that the only purpose of negotiations was to demarcate on the ground the exact alignment of this border. From this it followed that they were justified (a) in regarding rival Chinese claims, and the occupation of the Aksai Chin, as evidence of Chinese hostility, and (b) in insisting that occupied territory had to be vacated before there could be negotiations. In the meantime the Indians had no alternative but to use military means to counter the Chinese "aggression".

If India was in fact the injured party in the territorial dispute, the Indian attitude over the disputed border would have been explicable at least to an impartial observer, and possibly even to the less impartial Chinese. There would be less justification for the Chinese reacting in the way they did. But was this the case? To answer this question we need to take a closer look at the historical background to the Sino /Indian frontier, and shall begin with the eastern sector, or N.E.F.A.

Until the 1920's, the region now known as the N.E.F.A. was largely unexplored. It was, and still is, inhabited by tribes of Tibeto-Burmese origin, some of which enjoyed trade and tributary relations with Tibet. Certain areas in the north of the region, the Tawang district for example, were inhabited by Tibetans and were under administrative control from Tibet.

The McMahon Line was negotiated with the Tibetans in 1914 at the time of the Simla Conference. It was drawn as far to the north as possible, since the British at the time sought to forestall a feared Chinese expansion into the foothills bordering the Assam plains. The McMahon Line as part of a bargain whereby the British would press the Chinese to concede territory elsewhere to Tibet.

Even so, the Tibetans were not entirely happy about losing territory south of the McMahon Line, the Tawang district in particular. Their acceptance of the line was conditional on possible future adjustments in their favour. No such adjustments, were ever made. The British also failed to extract the promised concessions from the Chinese, since the latter refused to accept the Convention produced at the Simla Conference. Thus, even as a Tibetan/ British frontier, the McMahon Line does not have full validity, particularly as the Tibetans subsequently, in 1936, made a formal request to the British for revision of the line in their favour a request which the British ignored. As late as 1946, the Tibetans were still collecting taxes in the Tawang area.

And, in 1947, the Tibetans approached the newly established Indian Government, seeking the "return" of "Tibetan territories" from Assam to Ladakh.

The Indian reply to this approach may be of interest in the light of complaints to be voiced later by the Indians over the manner in which the Chinese spoke of their border claims being inherited from previous Chinese Governments "The Government of India should be glad to have an assurance that it is the intention of the Tibetan Government to continue relations an the existing basis until new Agreements are any reached... This is the procedure adopted by all other countries with which India has inherited Treaty relations from His Majesty's Government".

The validity of the McMahon Line as a Chinese/Indian frontier is considerably more doubtful. True, in rejecting the draft Simla Contention, the Chinese did not specifically object to the McMahon Line as drawn on the map of Tibet attached to the Convention. But, as the Chinese point out, the then Chinese Government had no way of knowing what this line was supposed to represent, since the terms of the McMahon Line agreement were for some reason kept secret by the British and Tibetans until 1929. It could, in theory, have been a border between Tibet and a Chinese-owned N.E.F.A. Moreover, Chiang Kaishek's Government was later to make it clear to the British (and the Indians after 1947) that it did not accept the McMahon Line. The Chinese have also pointed out that, since neither the British nor the Chinese regarded Tibet as a sovereign entity, the Tibetans were obliged to obtain Chinese approval for any frontier negotiated with a foreign power. * Failure to obtain this approval, both at the Simla Conference and later, meant that the McMahon Line never at any stage enjoyed international legality. And finally, as the Chinese never tire of pointing out, many Western and Indian maps, including one reproduced in a book by Nehru himself, Discovery of India, have, even in recent years., shown the Sino/Indian border as running along the edge of the Assam plain in conformity with the traditional Chinese claim.

The 1906 Convention between Britain and China (see page 95) had required China to accept responsibility for Tibet's foreign relations. "The 1907 Anglo/Russian Convention required Britain 'not to enter into negotiations with Tibet except through the intermediary of the Chinese Government". Negotiations with the Tibetans over the McMahon Line were thus a breach of both conventions - a possible reason why the terms of the McMahon Line agreement were kept secret.

For the Communist Chinese to appear to be willing to drop their N.E.F.A. claim is no small concession in view of the very considerable doubts as to the validity of the McMahon Line. Indeed, the Nationalist Government in Taiwan feels so strongly shout the justice of the Chinese clams that its official newspapers have accused Peking of being willing to abandon "sacred" Chinese territory. They have predicted that the present Communist Chinese leaders will be condemned by future generations of Chinese for their betrayal of China's interests.

Nevertheless, the Indian position was that the Chinese should not only drop their claim to the N.E.F.A. but to the Aksai Chin also. How strong is the Indian claim in the western sector of the disputed frontier?

The province of Ladakh, which lies on the Indian side of the disputed western sector, was originally a semi-independent state with a complex tributary relationship with Tibet. It was far from being clearly defined Indian territory. These links with Tibet were severed as a result of the 1841 invasion of Tibet from Kashmir, and Ladakh was incorporated into India. In the agreement which followed the invasion, the Ladakh/Tibet border was defined simply as following "the old established frontier", and it was only subsequently that British cartographers decided where this frontier should lie. A small area lying between the Chinese-claimed and Indian-claimed frontiers is in dispute.

By far the larger area in dispute, the Aksai Chin, lies for the most part north of the Ladakh/Tibet frontier, and its ownership depends on a definition of the Ladakh/Sinkiang border. At the end of the nineteenth century, the British decided an effort should be made to define this border, and in 1899 a note was delivered to the Chinese suggesting a possible alignment. This alignment is shown on the map above, and it will be seen that it leaves with China much of the territory at present in dispute. The Chinese never replied to the note. Shortly afterwards, the British attitude changed. Alarmed by growing Chinese weakness in Central Asia, and fearing Russian expansion into the area (fears similar to those being entertained in connection with Tibet), the British felt they should establish the border as far north as possible to forestall any southward advance by the Russians. British maps began to show the border as lying far to the north along the Kun Lun mountains. Chinese agreement was never sought for this claimed border (despite the fact that the British recognised Chinese sovereignty in Sinkiang) ; presumably it was only being put forward as an emergency measure in case the Russians attempted to seize Sinkiang. By the 1920's the Russian threat had disappeared, and it was deemed safe to drop this particular claim.

In subsequent years, British and Indian maps showed a variety of claim lines some coinciding with the present Chinese claim line, some the claim line along the Kun Lun mountains, and some an in-between claim line which ran south of the Kun Lun mountains but which included the Aksai Chin as Indian territory. Maps showing this last claim line were in general use at the time of the 1947 transfer of power, and appear to constitute the basis of the present Indian claim to the Aksai Chin. However, the only border to have ever been officially proposed to the Chinese by the British in this area was that of 1899, and, as already mentioned, this border left most of the Aksai Chin with China.

Whatever the merits of rival Chinese and Indian claims to the Aksai Chin area, it does seem clear that the Indians can hardly speak of the frontier they claim in this area as being already defined by history and therefore subject only to demarcation. In this connection a rather curious aspect of the Indian position should be mentioned - an aspect which has been overlooked by most students of the Sino/Indian dispute. Numerous Indian authorities, including Nehru himself, have claimed historical validity for their version of the Indian! Sinkiang frontier on the ground that the line proposed by the British in 1899 "ran along the Kun Lun range to a point east of 80° longitude, where it met the eastern boundary of Ladakh". In fact, the 1899 line ran well to the south of the Kun Lun mountains, and the text of the proposal speaks only of the tine meeting "the spur running south from the Kun Lun range, which [the spur] has hitherto been shown on our maps as the eastern boundary of Ladakh. This is a little east of 80° east longitude".* A misquotation of these dimensions is rather serious, particularly when it is used to justify an official claim to some 30,000 square kilometres of territory, and when, on the basis of this claim, negotiations are refused in favour of a military solution of a complex border dispute.

The only observer who appears to have noted this misquotation is Alastair Lamb. In his book, *The China-India Border,* he gives the full text of the British note of 1899 and lists some of the Indian authorities who have misquoted the 1899 proposal. Distribution of his book within India has been banned.

It would seem, therefore, that an impartial observer who takes into account not only the historical background of the border dispute, but also the equally relevant criteria of geography and administrative control, would agree that the Chinese are not being unreasonable when they call for border negotiations on the basis of the present status quo. If, as seems to be the case, the Chinese are prepared to do a N.E.F.A./Aksai Chin exchange leaving India in control of far the largest and most valuable of the territories in dispute, he may even feel that the Chinese are being quite generous. And if our impartial observer were to reach such a conclusion, it seems highly likely that the Chinese would be convinced of the reasonableness of their position and the unreasonableness of the Indian demand for a unilateral Chinese withdrawal from the Aksai Chin.

If the Chinese were in fact convinced that they were in the right over the border dispute, they would in all probability have interpreted the Indian military build-up along the disputed border in 1961-2 as evidence of active hostility. Striking confirmation that this was the case is contained in the "Tibetan Documents" - official Chinese documents which were captured by Tibetan rebels in 1961 and which subsequently found their way to the U.S., where they have been translated and published. These documents were intended as background briefing to senior Chinese military commanders stationed along the Sino/ Indian border. As such, their contents cannot be dismissed simply as propaganda. The documents warned of U.S./Indian collusion to build up pressure along the Tibetan frontier as a prelude to a joint attack against Tibet. Military commanders were instructed to observe strictly the twenty-kilometre troop withdrawal from the line of actual control and to avoid clashes with advancing Indian patrols since this would provide the "imperialists" with the pretext they needed to justify their planned attack.

BORDER CONFLICT MORPHS INTO BROADER DIPLOMATIC JUJITSU

New Delhi has experienced diplomatic stare-downs over other issues such as Beijing's decision to issue stapled visas to Indians residing in certain parts of Jammu and Kashmir, Assam, and Arunachal Pradesh; states that border the contested Sino-Indian boundary. Stapled visas are not stamped on passport pages, but they are separately stapled on to the Indian passports. The message that the Chinese government is trying to deliver is that such visas are only issued to residents of Indian regions that are claimed by Beijing. In September 2010, General B.S. Jaswal of the Indian Army, who was based in the Indian-administered state of Jammu and Kashmir, was denied a Chinese visa. General Jaswal was to join an Indian army delegation visiting China as a part of bilateral dialogue. In response, India cancelled the military exchange with China that year.

Again in January 2012, India cancelled a 30-member military delegation's visit to China because a visa was denied to a delegation member belonging to the Indian Air Officer from Arunachal Pradesh, a state that borders Tibet. In November 2012, Indian along with several Asian countries reacted alarmingly to the new design of the Chinese passport watermarks that show nearly "90 percent of the South China Sea, Arunachal Pradesh and Aksai Chin, as well as famous tourist attractions in Taiwan" as part of People's Republic of China."

India countered sharply by "stamping a round seal of the map of India" depicting the "correct external boundaries on visas stamped on such passports." Beijing's move was intended to be a clever ploy to force rest of the Asian states with which China has outstanding territorial disputes to acknowledge Beijing's territorial claim by stamping such passports with entry and exit stamps. In a testy exchange in New Delhi, the Former Chinese Ambassador to India, Zhang Yan, told an Indian journalist to "shut-up" at an official reception, when he was repeatedly questioned about Indian territory being depicted as belonging to China in a map enclosed in a folder that was included along with a bilateral business agreement.

India is not the only state that has felt the power of coercive and clever strategies employed by Beijing; several other Asian states, particularly Japan, Vietnam, and the Philippines, have been impacted by these aggressive strategies. Japan in its Annual Defense White Paper has pointed out that the People's Republic of China is using aggressive strategies to change the status-quo of the territorial disputes with Japan and other countries in the Asian sphere. Japan has identified specific activities such as intrusion into Japanese territorial waters, violation of its airspace, and instances when the Chinese Navy has locked its weapons radar on Japanese vessels in East China Sea. Even the United States has not been immune to Chinese military assertiveness. In April 2001, Chinese Air Force forced an American EP-3 spy plane to force land in the island of Hainan. The plane and the crew were only released after sustained negotiations between both countries. In 2009, Chinese warships forced an Indian submarine that was trailing them in the Gulf of Aden to surface. In August 2011 an Indian Warship *INS Airavat* that was completing a scheduled port call in Vietnam was challenged by the Chinese Navy and asked to identify itself when it was about 45 nautical miles from the Vietnamese coast.

New Delhi and Beijing's competition is not limited to the border issue; both have also become serious competitors in the economic and diplomatic arena. Beijing has engaged in diplomatic moves to keep India out of ASEAN, the UN Security Council, Shanghai Cooperation Group (SCO), Nuclear Suppliers Group (NSG), and sought to deny bank loans from Asian

Development Bank (ADB) that was targeted for projects in Arunachal Pradesh that the Chinese claim as their own.

BORDER AND TERRITORIAL ISSUES REMAIN DOMINANT

Fifty years since Chairman Mao's decision to teach India a lesson during the 1962 war, India and China's position on the border issue has significantly hardened and become more unyielding. India also become highly reluctant to cede to China any bit of pride or territory already in its possession; it has decided to challenge China at multiple levels despite the enormous asymmetry in power between them. Mutual unwillingness to compromise on certain core territorial claims and particularly the inability of the Indian government to sell any such compromise to its domestic audience, PLA's acceleration of the military budget, and the growing Sino-Pakistan military collaboration has elevated the fear of Chinese invasion and increased the real probability of sudden military thrust by China across the border.

In an effort to counter China's growing assertiveness, India has started to engage in multipronged diplomatic and military strategy. It has started making big-ticket military purchases from the United States, Israel, France, United Kingdom, and Russia (which still remains India's largest military benefactor). More recently, India has embarked on a diplomacy campaign to engage with Japan, Vietnam, Philippines, and even Mongolia operating on the principle of potential *enemy of my enemy is my friend* as a part of its "Look East" policy. All of these moves by India are aimed at deterring Beijing from engaging in actions, including the use of force, to alter the status quo on the border in such a manner that it is irreversible.

India's moves haven't gone unnoticed in Beijing, which for a long time ignored its equally populous neighbor. A highly influential article published in the official English news outlet—Xinhua—argued that India should pause its Look East policy and not seek to "estrange and antagonize its neighbor by taking it as an imaginary enemy and get unwisely involved in affairs which fall within others' backyards, it would hold its national strategies as hostage and put at stake its own national interests." Li Hongmei's article warns India against unwisely getting entangled in the foreign policies of other East Asian states in the hopes of deterring China.

Although India has managed to defend the status quo on the border despite repeated parries by the PLA, it has also ominously heighted Indian insecurities of large-scale military action across the border by the People's Republic. Now China looms as a larger threat across the horizon than India's primordial adversary—Pakistan. This is not beyond the realm of imagination when viewed in the context of 1962 war for which India was poorly prepared and completely surprised. The scars from the loss of 1962 war initiated by Chairman Mao's diktat of teaching "India a lesson" and the fear and awe (or power asymmetry) produced by China's breathtaking growth, infrastructural development, soft power, and the expansion of military capacity in all areas (land, sea, air, cyber, and space) has made India extraordinarily weary and wary.

New Delhi has struggled to define its relations with China and it is shying away from treating China as "enemy number one," but clearly China is not a frenemy either; it is less than an enemy, but surely more than a frenemy. Or more simply, to India, China represents a regional power and a very real security threat and in the near future a superpower that it has to be perpetually concerned about because of the outstanding territorial dispute and economic power differentials. What China has done through this regular border incursions is establish that the undemarcated border areas are disputed and more importantly the Chinese have defined the shape and structure of the border all that is left to do for India is to politically agree to that boundary. All of this neatly fits with the three core objectives of the Chinese grand strategy.

The long history of repeated border clashes or border intrusions or transgressions as India has chosen to describe them since the Sumdorong Chu Valley Incident in 1986 to the latest incidents in Ladakh shows that the border dispute has been a major flashpoint in Sino-Indian Relations that has carried over from the days of British India. According to the Union Ministry of India (which is responsible for internal security and border management) there have been over 600 border incursions by the PLA since 2010. Moreover, the Chinese have successfully managed to prevent India from building any major infrastructure on the Indian side of the border, while they have built extensive array of military infrastructure (railway lines for troop movements, fortified bunkers, airfields positioned with modern Sukhoi-27 fighter jets) on the Chinese side. Enormously concerned about Chinese military capabilities, India's "Cabinet Committee on Security's (CCS) has given the final nod for raising a new mountain strike corps (50,000 soldiers), apart from two "independent" infantry brigades and two "independent" armoured brigades, to plug operational gaps along the LAC as well as to acquire "some ground offensive capabilities" against China." The Indian army has also agreed to secure 145 ultra-light 155mm howitzers from the American firm BAE Systems in a deal worth $660 million; these howitzers are to be positioned along the rugged Indo-Tibetan mountain terrain.

GROWING PRO-CHINA SENTIMENT IN BHUTAN

Increased Chinese assertiveness is not India's only headache in Bhutan, which has also seen a surge in the number of people, especially younger ones, who want closer economic ties with China. "The younger generation see economic merit in having closer economic relations with China, as compared to the older people who are more disposed towards India's view," Haran, who served as India's envoy to Bhutan between 2012 and 2014, said.

"Even the current king Jigme Khesar and the prime minister are in favour of closer relations with China. It is just his father, the fourth king Jigme Singye, who are more cautious in opening up to China," the former envoy said.

Under the Bhutanese constitution, the king oversees national security and foreign affairs. "There is an understanding between the father and the son, under which Singye still looks after defence and foreign relations, while the son takes care of domestic politics," Haran noted.

"While there are no direct trade relations between Bhutan and China, 75 to 80% of goods in Bhutanese market are Chinese-made," Haran said. "Most of these goods are routed through India and south-east Asian countries," he added.

Haran mentioned that last year's standoff in Doklam witnessed a further growth of the anti-India lobby in the Himalayan kingdom, which until then kept a low-profile. He said, "Before, people raising anti-India voices in the media and public space kept a low profile. They have started to come out in the open and have become more brazen since Doklam happened.

PRIME MINISTER MODI'S VISIT TO CHINA

Beijing pays especially close attention to border issues and bilateral ties, both of which it regards as sensitive. The Chinese realise that settlement of the border issue is central to any improvement in India-China relations, but have kept it unsettled over the decades to pressure India. China has simultaneously sought to weaken India's stand in the border negotiations by promoting doubts regarding the actual alignment and even legitimacy of the McMahon Line.

The Chinese are meticulous record keepers and the Chinese Communist Party (CCP)'s increasingly powerful Propaganda Department keeps tight control to ensure a narrative approved by the Party. It controls appointments and removals of senior editorial personnel in the state-owned audiovisual and print media nationwide. It additionally approves and closely supervises content by issuing instructions thrice a day detailing which topics should be covered, ignored or downplayed, and the prominence that each should be given. China's communist regime is adept at harmonising records with the Party's approved narrative and the predictably selective reporting by China's official media, including Xinhua, of important bilateral events and discussions is, therefore, important. Dr. SidharthIn the context of Prime Minister Modi's visit (May 14-16, 2015) to China, there have been an unusual number of comments and articles by China's normally reticent officials and media, including on the disputed India-China border. Bilateral relations and border issues are subjects that are usually off-limits for the Chinese media where only authorised officials are permitted to voice "views".

On April 18, 2015, China's authoritative official news agency 'Xinhua', reported the arrival in India on a 4-day (April 15-18, 2015) visit of a CCP delegation led by Politburo Member and Party Secretary of Shaanxi, Zhao Zhengyong. Zhao Zhengyong was quoted as saying that India and China were both "implementing the outcomes of Xi Jinping's visit to India, the momentum in development of China-India relations is good, and that there is positive progress in inter-party exchanges and regional cooperation". He said "China expects that Indian PM Modi's visit to China will give a new impetus to China-India relations". Hinting at the inequality in the two economies, Xinhua observed that the "Indian side admired the leadership of the CCP and China's economic and social achievements, and said that India is willing to learn from China's successful experiences and further deepen China-India pragmatic cooperation. Both sides hope that the Indian PM Modi's visit to China is an opportunity for both the countries and it will take bilateral relations to a new height".

A week later, the Chinese-language Meijiang Network, an economic news service established in December 2004 and owned by the State Financial Daily Press and Publication Administration, commented on the upcoming visit. It quoted China's Ambassador to India as remarking that in case ongoing discussions concluded successfully then agreements totalling US$ 10 billion could be signed during Prime Minister Modi's visit. The chapter included explicit references to the New Silk Economic Road and, referring to Modi's itinerary, said his "first stop in China will be Xian, the historical city from where the Silk route begins". It sought to lure India into supporting the 'One Road, One Belt' by hinting at the potential for Chinese investments and pointing to the investments worth US$ 46 billion announced by Xi Jinping while on his recent state visit to Pakistan. It added that as "China-India are the two large developing countries in Asia, so trade and economic cooperation will be the main agenda of Modi's visit to China". Wu Tiaoli, an Assistant Researcher at the Institute of Asia-Pacific and Global Strategy in the Chinese Academy of Social Sciences (CASS), described the Modi government's policy towards China as "reflecting a "double track policy". He said "India wants to expand economic, trade and investment cooperation with China and wants to decrease the balance of trade gap with China and, therefore, the deepening of China-India Trade will create new opportunities". Trying to put the gloss of economic development on China's relations with Pakistan, he reasoned that "construction of the China-Pakistan Economic Belt will eliminate the Indian doubts, moreover, it will help India to understand the project". He added that "China is also promoting the BCIM Economic corridor as part of the 21st Century Maritime Silk Route Project, which also requires India's support and participation". Wu Tiaoli assessed that as the world's two largest developing nations "China-India relations have gone beyond the bilateral context, and now have global and strategic significance". He described the bilateral trade volume of almost US$ 70 billion in 2014, as "modest".

The Deputy Director of the South Asia Research Institute of the Yunnan Academy of Social Sciences, Yang Siling, recalled Chinese President Xi Jinping's suggestion in New Delhi in September 2014, that India "converge" its 'Mausam Project' with the 'One Road, One Belt' and the observation of Chinese Ambassador Le Yucheng that this would "make India a natural and significant cooperative partner of China". He conceded that "in comparison to China's enthusiastic attitude, India seems to be ambiguous about the initiatives of China's 'One Belt, One Road" and attributed this to its feeling "limited by the geopolitical competition".

Four questions relating to Prime Minister Modi's visit to China were raised in Chinese at the regular weekly briefing by China's Ministry of National Defence (MND) held on April 30, 2015. The fourth and last question sought clarification whether China's decision to invite India's Northern Army Commander indicated a change in its position on Kashmir. The MND spokesman's reply was categoric. Reiterating China's claim on J&K, the spokesman stated: "China has a consistent and clear stance on the issue of Kashmir. And on the specific arrangements of border defence exchanges, discussions between the two sides are still going on".

The reply to the second question was also interesting. Asserting that "the China-Indian boundary issue is a problem left over from history", the spokesperson added "joining hands to maintain peace and tranquility in areas along the China-Indian border is the important consensus reached by both sides. The Chinese defence troops have always been strictly abiding by the agreements reached by the two governments, and we hope the Indian side can meet China half way".

A Chinese-language Xinhua dispatch of May 7, 2015, which officially announced Modi's visit to China from May 14-16, went viral on China's social media. The dispatch listed Modi's itinerary and said "China has done its homework for the visit of powerful and popular Modi. Ten days before his visit, he opened Chinese Weibo to play the emotional card, and the blog posts are full of 'friendship', 'blessing' and other words. He is ready to embark on the road to the East. Modi expects a lot from China, and in the economic aspect his main focus is investment and the projects under negotiations, and political dialogue involving the Sino-Indian border dispute". Saying "It is foreseeable that Modi's pragmatic China policy will continue — cooperation on economic and trade and balance in diplomacy" it pointedly asked whether "Modi can have both—the fish and bear's paw?"

Comments of the spokesperson of the Chinese Ministry of Foreign Affairs (MFA) at the regular briefing a day earlier (May 6) were carefully worded. Important was the Chinese Foreign Ministry spokesperson's statement that "The bilateral relationship boasts strategic significance and global influence. Over the past years, China and India have kept their relationship developing in a sound and steady manner and figured out a way to get along with each other that focuses on mutual benefit and cooperative development, accommodates each other's concerns and properly handles differences". The spokesperson added "President Xi Jinping paid a successful state visit to India last September when he mapped out the development of China-India strategic cooperative partnership for the next five to ten years together with Indian leaders". Stating that both sides are closely coordinating the visit and "It is believed that efforts by the two sides will ensure the success of Prime Minister Modi's visit and showcase the importance attached by the Chinese side to China-India relations and to the visit", the spokesperson said in conclusion that "We expect and believe that the visit will help enhance mutual understanding and mutual trust between the two countries, step up bilateral cooperation across the board and enable the bilateral relations to make bigger strides at a faster pace and in a more stable manner."

In the span of a week till May 15, 2015, the state-run 'Global Times', a subsidiary owned by the CCP's official newspaper People's Daily, published at least six articles on the visit. All underlined the mutual lack of trust and emphasised that China was far ahead of India in economic terms.

Particularly acerbic and critical was the article on May 11, 2015, by Hu Zhiyong, a research fellow with the Institute of International Relations at the

Shanghai Academy of Social Sciences. Hu Zhiyong is reputedly close to the CCP leadership and articulates their views. Describing Modi as a "pragmatist, rather than a visionary," he said Modi had "been busy strengthening India's ties with neighboring countries to compete with China, while trying to take advantage of the tremendous opportunities for economic development created by China". It accused him of "also playing little tricks over border disputes and security issues, hoping to boost his domestic prestige while increasing his leverage in negotiations with China". Saying that "the ball is in India's court to deepen the bilateral relations" he added that "for China, developing friendly cooperation with surrounding countries has always been the foothold of its diplomacy" and that "close ties with India, China's largest neighbour in South Asia, is of great importance to China's perimeter security and stability". He added that improvement in Sino-Indian relations are "severely constrained" by the views of a number of Indian elites who "deem the rise of Beijing as a threat to New Delhi's development".

Asserting that the "two sides have never established real strategic trust" he listed steps that Modi should take, namely (i) "he should no longer visit the disputed border region in pursuit of his own political interests"; (ii) he should "not deliver any remarks that infringe on the consensus on bilateral ties"; and (iii) "the Indian government should completely stop supporting the Dalai Lama, and stop making the Tibetan issue a stumbling block to the Sino-Indian relationship".

Hu Zhiyong was equally uncompromising on issues of economy and trade, saying that "New Delhi is reluctant to admit the widening trade gap is its own fault, nor is it willing to examine its own economic structure and the quality of its exports to China", but instead repeatedly accuses or directs its anger at China. Scathing was the observation that "due to the Indian elites' blind arrogance and confidence in their democracy, and the inferiority of its ordinary people, very few Indians are able to treat Sino-Indian relations accurately, objectively and rationally". He accused some Indian media of "irresponsibly exaggerating the conflicts between the two sides, adding fuel to the hostility among the public". Hu Zhiyong concluded with the comment that "Modi should seize the chance of his China visit to enhance bilateral cooperation" and "political mutual trust between leaders".

Ding Gang, a Senior Editor of the CCP's authoritative mouthpiece People's Daily, apparently voiced the Party's views on May 13, 2015, in a column in the Global Times. He wrote that if India and China join hands they could change Asia's geopolitical and economic landscape, but "there seems always to be a lack of mutual trust between the dragon and the elephant". He added that "there is more competition than complementarity" between India and China leading directly "to a zero-sum game. In other words, one side moving up on the supply chain will likely squeeze the domain of the other".

Stating that there are many "unsustainable factors in the trade structure of China and India", he said if China invests more in India's infrastructure this may prove counter-productive as it could "cause more concerns for India about the flooding of Chinese commodities" and that involvement of Chinese enterprises could entangle them in "India's perplexing land system". He recommended that China "make well-planned and targeted industrial transfers in accordance with the development and investment ability of its enterprises and set up production bases in India to make use of its cheaper labour force and invest in training selected Indian workers through the Asian Infrastructure Investment Bank. He asked India to draw upon China's strength in technology and funding. He urged more access to local markets for Chinese telecommunication enterprises, saying China could do likewise for India's pharmaceutical companies and forecast that the two countries could "ultimately create a common market of 2.6 billion people".

Global Times on May 13, 2015, published an article by Swaran Singh, an Indian scholar in JNU, Delhi, which said that the PMO's last-minute decision to cancel BJP President Amit Shah's meeting with the Dalai Lama at Dharamsala on May 2, 2015, "showed the cost that the Modi government was willing to take to please Chinese leaders." Stating that the RSS has had a negative view on China since 1962, it referred to an article in the RSS' official paper Organiser, which said that "the well-calibrated symbolism of Modi and Chinese President Xi Jinping shows the duo has a better chance in achieving breakthroughs and bringing down negativity over political questions." The author said "the story compares Modi to the Buddha and the poet Tagore in having left a deep impression on China's popular consciousness". Stating that the "ruling establishment of India does not wish to leave any stone unturned to ensure the positive environment for the Xi-Modi summit, which is expected to usher in a subtle "reset" in China-India relations", it commented that "their summit should mark an important but first step in their long journey together into building, not just theirs, but Asia's future".

The article in the Global Times on May 14, 2015, by Liu Zongyi, an assistant research fellow of the Shanghai Institutes for International Studies (SIIS) and a visiting fellow of the Chongyang Institute for Financial Studies, Renmin University of China, was interesting. It blended veiled warnings with the potential promise of improved ties. Pertinent were the statements that "realizing regional security, including the stability in Afghanistan and the security in the Indian Ocean, requires concerted efforts from both China and India" and that "at present Washington is the major provider of security in the vast Indian Ocean, so if it exits, India will need the cooperation of other countries".

It candidly stated that "the boundary disputes are a conundrum in the bilateral relationship. If they can't be solved at an earlier date, the two sides should more closely stick to the code of conduct they reached before." It recalled the proposal by Xi Jinping made last September that "China and India should work together to establish a closer partnership of development rather than becoming rivals in competition" and said "Modi is considered as a state leader with strategic insights. He may become a Nixon-style statesman because of his pragmatism and capacity to resolve major contradictions between China and India and to tackle the common challenges of development". Acknowledging that "there is indeed competition and a lack of mutual strategic trust between the two rapidly emerging Asian powers" it said "over the past year, India, under the Modi administration, has become a star on the world stage." It cautioned, however, that "Modi's victory in the country's general elections last May has injected enormous confidence into India's economic development" but "had also offered hope to the US, Japan and other nations attempting to take advantage of New Delhi to contain China". It took note of India's ambiguous attitude towards China's 'One Belt, One Road', the 21st Century Maritime Silk Road initiatives, and the Asian Infrastructure Investment Bank (AIIB). In conclusion, the article observed that "India longs for economic integration in Asia. However, it is reluctant to see China acting as the single leader in the region but expects to share the role". A Xinhua editorial of May 14, 2015, was more balanced. It described the "exchange of visits by the leaders from the world's two largest emerging economies" as signaling "warming relations between the two oriental giants". The report played up the fact that Xi Jinping had travelled outside Beijing to receive Modi and said "Sino-Indian ties could be among the most important bilateral relationships". It said "if the "Chinese Dragon" and the "Indian Elephant" co-exist harmoniously and realize peaceful, cooperative development, it will bring benefit to not only their combined 2.5 billion people, but also those living beyond their borders." Emphasising that "China is an infrastructure powerhouse, while India has infrastructure deficits" it said "China can help India upgrade its railway stations and overhaul its high-speed rail networks" thereby giving both economies a big boost. It noted that

India has created world-class software and competitive pharmaceutical industries.

Another Global Times editorial on May 15, 2015, captioned 'Sino-Indian ties can conquer West's doubts' focused on the so-called attempts by the West to sow discord between India and China. It said "The dragon-elephant pas de deux has made headlines once again, but suspicions from the Western world soon poured in, saying the surface friendliness cannot cover the fact that Sino-Indian relations have irreconcilable maladies. No matter how much cooperation they can establish, border disputes will offset all progress".

Asserting "it is obvious that the Western elite doesn't want to see India and China drawing closer to each other", the editorial said "it will be a long-term test for China and India to get rid of distractions imposed by the West and stick to a path which can benefit the national interest of both countries". Admitting that "the bilateral relationship is still vulnerable to many sensitive issues", it said "although no bullets have been fired along the border for decades, tensions still remain". The editorial conceded that "lack of mutual trust still disturbs both sides" and "media reports raise concerns about each other from time to time", but stressed that "China and India should think out of the box where delusions of persecution prevail" otherwise cooperation will not be possible when "only distrust and hostility are rife". It underlined this theme saying that it "is hard for China and India to develop a strategic partnership, but it will be dreadful for both sides to vie with each other" and that mutual fundamental interests demand that "no side should look at the other with contempt or arrogance, and their problems should be addressed between the two with no need to introduce a third party".

China's authoritative official news agency Xinhua on May 15, 2015, reported on the meeting between India's Prime Minister Modi and Chinese Premier Li Keqiang.

Stating that the two met in the Great Hall of the People on May 15 morning, Xinhua quoted Li Keqiang as saying, based on the statement issued by the Chinese Ministry of Foreign Affairs (MFA), that "Last year, the Chairman Xi Jinping successfully visited India. Yesterday, Chairman Xi Jinping carried out a fruitful meeting with you at Xian. My first state visit as the Chinese Premier was India. China and India are not rivals and should become an important partner". Stating that "Both sides need to expand their relation from Asia to the world, and promote strategic mutual trust, economic cooperation.... and promote the common development of China and India" it said "Li Keqiang pointed out that China is willing to join hands with India to build a closer partnership for development".

Li Keqiang was reported as saying that the leaders of both countries should "make full use of wisdom to deal with sensitive issues such as borders, maintaining momentum in the negotiations to establish cooperation framework mechanism to ensure peace and tranquility in the border area, while focusing on promoting the bilateral strategic cooperation and common development, and promote the formation of a true "Asian Century". To complement their economic advantages and in a veiled reference to the 'One Road, One Belt', he said they should be "docking development strategies" and "pushing ahead BCIM Economic Corridor" etc. He pointed out that China is willing to participate in India's Industrial Corridor. The Xinhua report included no reference to Prime Minister Modi's comments on the need for China to reconsider its approach on the border and other issues which would otherwise restrict development of bilateral ties. The focus of China's official media in the days around Prime Minister Modi's visit to China was clearly on the promotion of bilateral economic ties.

There was a definite effort to push China's major economic initiative of 'One Road, One Belt' together with calls for enhanced access for Chinese companies. While authoritative articles and comments by senior CCP officials in the months leading up to the visit had emphasised China's unchanged stance on the issue of the border, in the days proximate to the visit the border issue found very brief mention.

Where it did, like in the Chinese Defence Ministry briefing, India was urged to meet China at least halfway. Hu Zhiyong's article in Global Times on May 11, 2015, was rather blunt in listing the steps that India needs to take to improve bilateral ties. All articles underscored the distrust in the relationship. Pertinently, Xinhua and China's official media blanked out Modi's remarks urging China to "reconsider its approach" on the border and other outstanding issues, made during meetings with Chinese President Xi Jinping, Premier Li Keqiang and in his address to students in Tsinghua University in Beijing.

6

Genesis of the Doklam Crisis

A series of talks were held and agreements were signed between Bhutan and China over the border dispute since 1984. Almost 24 boundary talks were held leading to agreements signed by both the sides in 1988 and 1998 with an agreement to maintain the status-quo in the disputed area. It was also agreed by both the parties to prohibit the use of force and to strictly adhere to the use of peaceful means for negotiation.

The present position of China, according to Bhutan, is a violation of the 1988 and 1998 border agreements and unilateral change of the disputed boundary in the Doklam area where China is constructing a road as part of its One Belt One Road Initiative. Therefore, the issue is not just limited to a border confrontation; rather it has implications far beyond this. It is in fact a hidden intent of the Chinese grand imperial design of making the 'Chinese Dream' a success in creating vassal states and to implement the colonial project of the One Belt One Road without any hindrance leading to the present state of affairs in the India-China border. This will be discussed later in detail.

How is India linked to the Issue?

Dok La became the site of a standoff between India and China since June 2017 following an attempt by Beijing to construct a road from Yadong on the Doklam plateau to which Bhutan has objected. Unlike China and Bhutan, India doesn't have any claim over the region in crisis. However, India supports the claim of Bhutan over the territory. As per the 1949 Treaty between India and Bhutan, Thimpu agreed to let New Delhi guide its foreign policy with border sovereignty. Furthering this agreement both Bhutan and India signed a Freindship Treaty in 2007 stating to abide close friendship and cooperation with each other on issues relating to their national interests. Since India holds Bhutan's sovereignty as sacred and inviolable on June 18 Indian troops crossed into the disputed territory between Bhutan and China in an attempt to prevent the illegal construction of the road leading to the longest standoff between New Delhi and Beijing since 1962.

THE CHINESE DESIGN

The present border crisis shouldn't be seen merely as a border skirmish; rather it is the product of an all-out Chinese strategy to dominate over Asia by creating vassal states through its policy of 'Chinese Dream' and 'Belt and Road Initiative' launched recently in May 2017 by Xi Jinping, the President of China. The highly ambitious Chinese Dream is a pet project of President Jinping and this he cannot allow to fail. Hence China cannot back off from Doklam.

Let's know about this Chinese Dream Project. This project unequivocally states that China should return to its imperial glory led by the son of heaven in Beijing. (Roy 2017) The implicit message is Chinese expansionism and creation of vassal states along its border. Until the arrival of the British, Nepal, Sikkim and Bhutan had been vassal states of the Qing Empire from 1644-1911. (San 2017) The Britishers then took over the control of these countries to expand its influence in Tibet and India wanted to inherit these assets. (*Global Times*, 2017) As part of its grand strategy, China is using the past to serve the present and trying to reconstruct the history by creating vassal states around its border. Like the way it cowed down its South China Sea neighbours, China attempted the same strategy in Bhutan as well without even imagining that India will jump in to protect the territorial sovereignty of Bhutan.

Hence after the trespassing of the Indian soldiers into the disputed area on June 19 China has renewed its call for India to withdraw its troops from Doklam and issued veiled threats through its state-controlled media by warning of repetition of the consequences of 1962.

It has further followed with fire drills, high altitude training programmes, tank rolling and gathering arms and ammunitions in Tibet and addressing the diplomats of different countries located in Beijing about the Chinese position literally threatening India by media warfare, psychological and legal warfare as well. While border skirmishes are a regular affair, why is this time China so enraged and adamant over the Doklam issue? The answer lies in Beijing's pet 'One Belt, One Road' project.

One Belt One Road (OBOR), also known as Belt and Road Initiative (BRI), is another pet project close to Jinping's heart. In May 2017 Beijing had hosted countries across the world to showcase the Chinese vision of Belt and Road which is also called as the New Silk Road project. (Pantucci 2017) The Belt and Road initiative, officially announced in 2013, is an attempt to revive the historic Eurasian Silk Road that is approximately 2000 years old with a vigour to reconnect Europe with Asia and Africa with the use of modern transportation, in order to boost trade, investments, and economic development, as well as to improve diplomatic relations, scientific progress and cultural exchange for all countries and regions across the Eurasian continent. (Magiri 2017)

India was also invited to this summit. In spite of persistent Chinese requests, New Delhi had prefered not to join the project apprehending Chinese hegemony in the region. The doubt came true when the flagship project, the China-Pakistan-Economic Corridor, (CPEC) was initiated through Pakistan Occupied Kashmir—a disputed territory which India claims as her own. The suspicion was further heightened when China transgressed in Doklam unilaterally defying the agreements it had inked with Bhutan over border disputes. With the protest in Balochistan and PoK over the CPEC and scathing criticism from the media and people of Pakistan, the way for China in BRI doesn't look as smooth as Beijing had expected. After the slow start of the CPEC, China is in no mood to afford another stumbling block in its way of OBOR. Hence, Beijing is hardening its stand in Doklam and trying to make its way anyhow. However, after India's firm stand on the Doklam issue China is surprised and planning a face-saving formula by waging war through the state-controlled media. It is trying to create a psychological fear in the minds of the Indian soldiers by telecasting the Army drills and training in high altitudes. It is also holding talks with the envoys of different countries placed in Beijing and advancing historical texts to argue the Chinese claims legally.

Reasons of Hardening its Stand

Although, the rhetoric of armed conflict and media gimmick of putting two Asian neighbours on the brink of war is recent, the disagreement and distrust between the two giant neighbours is age-old. Since 1962 both New Delhi and Beijing didn't have a normal relationship even though the relationship was slightly moderated under globalisation on economic terms. Nevertheless, the low political interaction between the two was unable able to solve the intricate political disputes. The recent standoff between New

Delhi and Beijing is the result of China's use of Pakistan as a proxy against India; New Delhi's boycott of the BRI International Forum Summit; China's objection to Dalai Lama's visit to Arunachal Pradesh; Beijing's opposition to New Delhi's aspirations for full membership of the Nuclear Suppliers Group (NSG); and Chinese open support to a Pakistan-backed terrorist, Masood Azhar, against the backdrop of UN blacklisting.

What does this mean for Neighbours?

The intention of China and the hidden agenda of the Belt and Road Initiative are not unknown to countries around China now. The doctrine of Chinese dream is the logic behind China's BRI project to create vassal states like Nepal, Bhutan and client states like Pakistan around its border. For countries like Myanmar, Sri Lanka and importantly Nepal, now the Belt and Road casts a shadow over its realisation. However, many of them are debt-trapped by China and may not be able to come out of the shackle. After the Doklam incident, one country which must be worried most is Nepal. Given the Himalayan state's geopolitical location between India and China and its feeble military might, Nepal is at the crossroads.

India's Position

While China is hyperactive in trying to appease Bhutan and hence engaged the Pakistani envoy to India, Abdul Basit, to negotiate with Thimpu with an agenda to dump New Delhi, India, in spite of the veiled threats by the Chinese media of irreparable consequences like 1962, increasing ceasefire violation on the India-Pakistan border by Islamabad at the instance of Beijing and the issuance of warnings from China of an armed conflict of massive scale, India has decided not to exacerbate the situation in Doklam. New Delhi is not wiiling to engage with China in a war. India has made it amply clear that diplomacy is the prefered choice. National Security Adviser Ajit Doval's visit to attend the BRICS summit in Beijing may help in breaking the ice. But the Chinses adamancy over troop withdrawal by India first and New Delhi's stand on Doklam may further complicate the issue.

THE CHINA-INDIA BORDER DISPUTE

The entire China-India boundary has never been formally delimited by any mutually-accepted treaty. There has existed a boundary line of actual control between the two countries. It took shape on the basis of the extent of each other's administrative jurisdiction over a long course of time. The entire boundary has been traditionally divided into three sectors—the eastern sector, the middle sector, and the western sector with all in dispute. The western sector involves the dispute over the Aksai Chin area India claims as part of Latah andChina claims as part of Xinjiang. The middle sector involves a dispute over various points between the Tibet-Kashmir- Punjab border junction and the Nepal-Tibet-Uttar Pradesh border junction. The eastern sector involves a dispute over the area between the pre-1914 Outer Line and the McMahon Line.

In the eastern sector, the British–Indian government had observed the foothills of the Himalayas as the "Outer Line" of its administrative jurisdiction by 1914. Although the Chinese-Tibetan authorities had claimed the tribal areas beyond the British Outer Line within the Tibetan jurisdiction, their administrative jurisdiction actually covered only Tawang tract, the Walong area along the Lohit valley, and some other scattered enclaves in the tribal areas.

Today the line of actual control observed by both sides conforms to the McMahon Line. The disputed area between the pre-1914 Outer Line and the McMahon Line covers a total area of 90,000 square kilometers. According to China, this area is composed of Tibet's three districts of Monyul, Loyul and lower Zayul. According to India, this area is its Arunachal Pradesh, formerly the North-East Frontier Agency of Assam State.

In the western sector, the line of actual control runs roughly along the Karakoram range, conforming to the Chinese claim. The Indian government claims that the boundary runs along the Kunlun range from theKarakoram Pass. The disputed Area is the Aksai Chin region between the two ranges, covering a total area of about 33,000 square kilometers. This area falls mainly in China's Xinjiang and part of it belongs to the Ari District of Tibet. India claims that it is part of its Ladakh area of the State of Jammu and Kashmir. This area, sparsely inhabited, serves as the traffic artery linking Xinjiang and Tibet.

Therefore, in terms of the general China-India border dispute, the McMahon Line in the eastern sector and Aksai Chin in the western sector have been central to the negotiations on the settlement of the border dispute.

The Mystery of the McMahan Line

After Russia successfully divided Mongolia into Outer and Inner Mogolia with the Outer Mongolia as a buffer zone between China and Russia, the British- Indian authorities dreamed the same dream and tried to divideTibet into Outer Tibet and Inner Tibet and made the Outer Tibet as a buffer zone between British India andChina. To achieve such a objective, the Simla conference was held in 1914,with British Henry McMahon, Chinese Chen

Ivan, and Tibetan Lonchen shatra as representatives. There were actually two parallel conferences at Simla, the tripartite conference focusing on the division ofTibet, and the other was the secret one, keeping Chen Ivan out of their negotiations on the Indian-Tibetan boundary. In early 1914, Henry McMahon and Lonchen Shatra secretly negotiated on the division of Tibet and the boundary between Assam and Tibet as a package deal. An agreement was reached through a secret exchange of notes in Delhi on March 24 and 25, 1914. This boundary line, later known as the McMahon line, was shown on a map in two sheets.

The tripartite conference focused on McMahon's proposal referring to China's suzerainty over Tibet and the outer-inner division of Tibet. On the map attached to the draft convention of the conference, two lines were drawn, one red and the other blue. The red line showed Tibet as a geographical and political unit, and the blue line divided Inner from Outer Tibet. In its southern extension, the red line curves around along the crest of theHimalayas, roughly conforming to the McMahon Line except in the Tawang tract where the McMahon Line reached short of the Tawang tract, implying that the Tawang tract remained part of Tibetan territory. On this map, the Tawang tract was not put within the British-Indian territory.

Without the consent of the Chinese government, Chen Ivan, under McMahon's threat and pressure, initiated the draft convention on April 27, 1914, but with the clear understanding that "to initial and to sign are two different actions," and that his initials would not bind his government, whose views he would immediately seek. The next day, the Chinese government instructed Chen Ivan that "The Chinese representative was forced to initial the draft convention. The Chinese government cannot accept it. You should declare it invalid." Since Chen Ivan refused to sign the draft convention, it was then amended and initialed by McMahon and Lonchen Shatra on July 3, 1914. On the map attached to the draft convention, the McMahon Line was marked just across the town of Tawang, indicating that the area to the north of Tawang would fall within the Tibetan territory.

The British-Indian government did not accept the Simla convention. Viceroy Hardinge forwarded McMahon's report on the Simla conference to London on July 23, 1914, stating that the Indian government recognized that a consideration of the northeastern frontier did not form part of the functions of the conference, and the views and proposal put forward might be regarded as personal to Henry McMahon, not carrying the endorsement of the Government of India. Chen was also instructed to declare that the Chinese government "would not recognize any treaty or similar document that might now or hereafter be signed between Great Britain and Tibet." The Tibetan authorities understood that without securing the Sino-Tibetan boundary, they could not accept the Indo-Tibetan boundary.

The Dalai Lama even recognized the logic relationship between the status of Tibet and the legality of the McMahon Line. In his 1959 address to the Indian Council of World Affairs, he contended that if Tibet had no sovereignty when the Simla convention laid down the McMahon Line, that line was invalid. He challenged Nehru that if you deny the sovereign status to Tibet, you deny the validity of the McMahon Line."

Three maps are related to the Simla conference. One is attached to the March 24 notes; one to the April 27 convention, and the third to the July 3 convention. As far as the Tawang Tract is concerned, the three maps show the McMahon line quite differently. On the first map, the McMahon Line was shown running alng south of the Thagla range far north of Tawang; on the second map, it is not shown in the Tawang tract; and on the third one, it is superimposed on the word " Tawang".

In 1936, Basil Gould, Political Officer in Sikkim, was dispatched to Lhasa and discussed the Tawang issue with the Tibetan government. The Tibetan attitude was Tawang had been Tibetan up to 1914 and they regarded the adjustment of the Tibet-Indian boundary as part and parcel of the general adjustment and determination of boundaries contemplated in the 1914 convention. If they could, with British help, secure a definite Sino-Tibetan boundary, they would observe the Indo-Tibetan border as defined in 1914.

In 1944, just before the British quit from India, basil Gould informed the Tibetan authorities that the Bitish-Indian government was willing to modify the McMahon Line soas to exclude Tawang from the territory it claimed.

He also proposed that the Se La range should be a new boundary line. However, The Tibetan authorities did not accepted it and continued to collect revenues in the Tawang tract and remained administrative control over the Tawang tract. It was in February1951 that the Indian government took over the Tawang tract by force before the PLA entered and liberated Tibet. The Tibetan authorities organized protest demonstrations in Tawang and Lhasaagainst India's occupation of the Tawang tract, but no avail.

As far as the objective of the Simla conference was concerned, it certainly aborted. The McMahon Line was not even accepted by the British-Indian government. After the Simla conference, from 1914 to 1935, on the official maps published by the Survey of India, the McMahon Line was not shown, but instead the Outer Line along the foothills of the Himalayas was shown.

The Tibetan authorities continued to exercise administrative jurisdiction in the tribal areas as they did before.

The Simla conference went down in history as an unaccomplished cause. As to the Simla conference, the first official record appeared in Volume XIV of the 1929 edition of Aichison's Treaties. It did not refer to the McMahon Line, but to the discussion on the Sino-Tibetan frontier. It was stated that a tripartite convention was drawn up and initialed in 1914, but the Chinese government refused to permit its representative to proceed to full signature.

In 1935, Olaf Caroe, deputy secretary of the Foreign and Political Department of the British-Indian Government discovered the secret documents of the Simla conference in dealing with a case involving the illegal entry into Tibet through the Tawang tract. He realized that the northeastern frontier might be a matter of dispute with the Chinese in the future. He proposed to revise the official record of the Simla conference in the Aichison's Treaties and show the McMahon Line on the official maps. The British government approved his proposal.

This original 1929 edition was soon withdrawn from circulation and replaced by a spurious edition, actually printed in 1938, but with an imprint of 1929. However, at least three copies of the original 1929 edition survived, one in Peking Library, one in Harvard University library, and one in the India Office. In the revised edition, it was stated that the Simla conference negotiated an agreement on the status of Tibet and the boundary of Tibet with both China and India. Such a revision was nothing but scandalous diplomatic forgery. Then the McMahon Line began to appear of the Indian official maps. However, it was still marked as "Undemarcated Boundary."

The Puzzle of Aksai Chin

In the western sector of the China-India border, the dispute has centred on the Aksai Chin area. The British left Aksai Chin area as "undefined" at the time of their transfer of power in 1947.nehru himself once stated that " it is a matter of argument as to what art of it (Aksai Chin) belongs to us and what part of it belongs to somebody else.... The point is, there has never been any delimitation there in that area and it has been a challenged area." Before the British left India, the British-Indian government had shown no boundary at all in that area on its official maps. In Volume XII of Aichison'd Treaties published in 1931, it was stated that"The northern as well as the eastern boundary of the Kashmir state is still undefined." The Survey of India maps published in the 1900s and 1930s did not indicate any boundary alignment or show any colour difference in this are, and wide spaces between Kashmir and Xinjiang and between Kashmir and Tibet were shown blank. Louis Dane, Indian Foreign Secretary, stated clearly in a letter to the Indian office that Aksai Chin was I Chinese Xinjiag. The neighbourhood of the Lanak Pass at the head of the Changchenmo valley was supposed to be the most northerly boundary point on the Kashmir-Tibet border.

In 1945, guided by Olaf Caroe, then foreign secretary of India, on new Survey of India maps the Aksai Chin area began to be shown by a colour-wash with the words "Boundary Undefined" marked on it. In 1947, the Indian Army in its "top secret" m submitted to the British Cabinet Mission accepted the Karakoram range as the northern boundary of India in the western sector.

However, after the signing of the trade agreement concerning Tibet in 1954, following Nehru's instructions, new Survey of India maps began to show an international boundary in the western sector running along the crest of the Kunlun range, which for the first time placed the whole Aksai Chin area within the Indian territory. According to Sir H.A.F. Rumbold, an official in the Indian Office, the Simon Commission wished to include a map of India in Volume I of their report in 1929. Rumbold found nothing in the India office to justify the line on the Kunlun range shown on some maps. The Commission accordingly adopted a line roughly along the crest of the Karakoram range, excluding the Aksai Chin area. Nehru, even on August 28, 1959, stated in the Lok Sabha that "This was the boundary of the old Kashmir state with Tibet and Chinese Turkestan. Nobody had marked it."

On the other hand, Chinese maps have shown the Karakoram range as its boundary in the western sector at least since the 1920s. There was no evidence that the British-Indian authorities ever disputed this with the Chinese government before they left India in 1947. The widely accepted modern concept of boundary marking involes three steps: delimitation, delineation and demarcation. Delimitation involves defining the boundary in written terms through treaties and agreements. Delineation involves sketching the boundary in maps through joint boundary surveys. Demarcation involves marking the boundary line on the ground through pillars, chains and other markers.

Reviewing the historic facts for the entire China-India border, such a China-India boundary has never existed, though each side has made its own territorial claims. Historical facts have also showed that, in the old days, wide desolate tracts in the remote high mountains between the two countries were physically inaccessible. Therefore, the China-India border dispute has been the dispute on the "zone" rather than the " line" in the eastern and western sectors. Mutual understanding and recognition of such historical evolution of the China-India border should become the starting point for the future border deliberations.

TERRITORIAL PROBLEMS BETWEEN SINO-INDIA

In terms of "the rise of China" and its "implications for India", the title of this book, the Sino-Indian territorial dispute represents an immediate arena in which India is having to face the uncomfortable implications from having an increasingly stronger neighbour. For India, the ability of China to deny India's hopes of territorial settlement on India's terms has become ever clearer in the wake of China's rise in military power in and around their disputed territory, which remains the biggest amount of land still in dispute in Asia.

As such, "the 4,056—kilometre (2,520 miles) frontier between India and China, one of the longest inter-state borders in the world, remains ... not defined, let alone demarcated, on maps or delineated on the ground". Here, the judgement over a century ago of Lord Curzon, British Viceroy of India 1898-1905 still seems relevant; the most urgent work of Foreign Ministers and Ambassadors ... is now the conclusion of Frontier Conventions in which sources of discord are removed by the adjustment of rival interests or ambitions at points where the territorial borders adjoin", for "frontiers are indeed the razor's edge on which hang suspended the modern issues of war or peace, of life or death to nations".

Admittedly, the territorial issue has been officially decoupled from the wider Sino-Indian relationship; as with the PRC rhetoric that "China and India have already reached consensus on the border issue. Before it is completely resolved, both countries will endeavour to maintain peace and stability in the border areas and will not let the border issue affect the general picture of China and India's cooperation". However, in reality their territorial issues do affect their wider relationship, in PRC terms "the existence of immense territorial disputes between China and India".

In dispute terms, this chapter argues that, in International Relations (IR) theory terms, the territorial disputes between India and China involve *classical geopolitics* entwined with *critical geopolitics*. Each strand of geopolitics, in their different ways, both involve the respective "position" that India and China hold for themselves and for each other in their immediate and extended neighbourhood.

Whilst each side argues from history, the chapter argues that in reality the evidence from history is rather ambiguous and inconclusive for both sides' territorial claims. Indeed, history is a sterile area to argue from, as one Indian commentator put it, "can we go beyond history to look at solutions which do not hark back to the past?"

The chapter argues that, from the outside, resolution of the issue seems feasible enough in terms of simple seeming territorial trade offs involving Arunachal Pradesh and Aksai Chin; but is complicated by smaller geographic issues surrounding Tawang, and wider geopolitical issues surrounding Tibet and indeed the balance of power in Asia between India and China.

The two main areas of dispute along this Himalayan frontier are the *Western Sector* (Aksai Chin, around 37,250 square kilometres/ 14,380 square miles); and the *Eastern Sector* (Arunachal Pradesh, around 83,740 square kilometres/ 32,330 square miles). On the one hand, Arunachal Pradesh is inhabited by over a million people, Indian citizens, and includes important Buddhist centres like Tawang. On the other hand, Aksai Chin is a virtually uninhabited bleak barren plateau with no permanent settlements. It is the place "where not a blade of grass grows" as Jawaharlal Nehru once dismissively said; but where China's National Highway 219 runs through Aksai Chin as a key geopolitical infrastructure link for the PRC between its provinces of Tibet and Xinjiang. One further complication is China's occupation of the Shaksgam valley; around 5,180 sq kilometres/1,930 square miles, to which Pakistan relinquished its Baltistan-related claims in 1963, but over which India maintains its own Kashmir-derived claims. Smaller pockets of disputed territory are found, the *Middle Sector* fringes of Himachal Pradesh and Uttar Pradesh. Elsewhere along the Himalayas, lingering uncertainty over China's recognition of Sikkim's incorporation into India in 1975 is entwined with continuing PRC claims to the "Finger Area" in the north of Sikkim, with 71 supposed incidents reported of Chinese troop "incursions" in 2008. Nearby territorial disputes between China and Bhutan around the Chumbi Valley triangulation point with India are of further concern to New Delhi, given the Chumbi Valley's location looking down onto the India's sensitive Siliguri corridor which links India's northeastern states with the rest of India.

Wider nuances arise with India's Foreign Secretary (2004—2006) Shyam Saran, and his comments about *the logic of geography*. In front of one audience, it was a question for Saran of "geopolitical reality" in which "I would like to focus particularly on Asia, where the interests of both India and China intersect. It is said that the logic of geography is unrelenting. Proximity is the most difficult and testing among diplomatic challenges a country faces", where "to those who harbour any skepticism about this fact, it would suffice to remind that we share one of the longest [and disputed] land borders in the world with China.

In front of another audience, it was again a question that "it is said that the logic of geography is unrelenting and proximity is the most difficult and testing among diplomatic challenges a country faces"; with the following gloss that "frontiers with neighbours are where domestic concerns intersect with external relationships. This is where domestic and foreign policies become inextricable and demand sensitive handling", and in which "it is important for us to look at the [disputed] boundary question from the long-term and strategic perspective of India-China relations, rather than as a mere territorial issue.

The territorial issues between India and China form one of the biggest land disputes in Asia, and are of significance not only for the size of area under dispute, but also because the two disputants are the big countries most evidently on the rise in Asia. Alongside this *logic of geography*, there is then what Neville Maxwell called "the logic of power"; a *logic of power* whereby powerful states "in their expansive phases push out their frontiers until they meet the resistance of a strong neighbour or reach a physical barrier which makes a natural point of rest". In geopolitical terms, the current point of rest is along the Himalayas/Karakoram range, but in the long term where exactly is the "natural" point of rest between them? Amidst talk of mutual IR *security dilemma* dynamics, China's strengthening of military forces and related infrastructure in Aksai Chin and Arunachal Pradesh zones is now a spur to India's own more halting augmentation of military forces and related infrastructure. Meanwhile, both countries are seeking to expand their wider strategic space at a time when their immediate mountain borders remain unresolved.

CHINA OCCUPIED DOKLAM

Prime Minister Narendra Modi and external affairs minister Sushma Swaraj of misleading the nation over Chinese troops occupying the Doklam plateau, saying Indian security and strategic interests have been compromised. "The satellite imagery and media reports suggest that China has established military establishments in Doklam near Indian borders which indicates that India's security and strategic interests have been compromised," said Congress spokesperson Randeep Singh Surjewala.

The Congress' reaction comes a day after media reports cited new satellite images to say that the infrastructure build-up in Doklam — the site of a tense standoff between the two countries last summer — included a "full-fledged" military base. ThePrint described one of the constructions as "concrete" and said that there was at least one complete mechanised regiment deployed. According to NDTV, the build-up was at two locations at the Doklam plateau and one of them was "a massive, full-fledged Chinese military complex".

"It seems that the government was snoozing while the Chinese troops occupied the Doklam plateau as suggested by satellite images. And it seems China is planning Doklam 2.0 like retreat near the Indian borders," said Surjewala. "The Prime Minister has mastered the art of electoral rhetoric as he has failed miserably to ensure the protection of our borders." Showing the satellite images, Surjewala said China had constructed a two-storey watch tower, seven helipads and several military establishments in Doklam.

"What is the government doing as China has occupied the entire Doklam plateau? Is the government, Prime Minister, defence minister aware of these constructions?" Slamming Swaraj, Surjewala said the ministry of external affairs had issued a statement after the end of the three-month Doklam standoff, saying the troops of both countries were doing expeditious disengagement. "Even Sushma Swarajji said (this) in Parliament. And when we asked about the details, she said the troops of both countries were returning to their posts. At that point, there was no reason to question her statement," he said. He said after the tensions at Doklam were resolved, the Chinese foreign ministry had said while it had withdrawn the troops, it shall keep on patrolling the area.

The Congress leader demanded to know how the issue of tri-junction at Doklam would be decided in future when the China had occupied the entire plateau. Surjewala said: "In October, Modiji announced at a public rally that Doklam issue as a victory. However, the satellite imagery released in media reports suggest that Chinese troops have constructed military establishments. On Wednesday, Indian army chief General Bipin Rawat said the Chinese military has carried out a "mostly temporary" buildup in Doklam. "They have carried out some infrastructure development, most of it is temporary in nature. But while their troops may have returned and the infrastructure remains, it is anybody's guess whether they would come back there, or it is because of the winter they could not take their equipment away," Rawat said during a session in the multi-lateral 'Raisina Dialogue'.

DOKLAM CHINESE TERRITORY, INDIA SHOULD HAVE LEARNT LESSONS: CHINA

China on Monday said Doklam is a "Chinese territory" and the question of changing the status quo does not arise after India's envoy Gautam

Bambawale warned Beijing against any attempt to change the present state of affairs on the plateau.

In an interview to Hong Kong-based *South China Morning Post*, Bambawale said any attempt to change the status quo in Doklam would lead to another stand-off.

The ambassador, however, said both the nations were well within their rights for an army build-up behind the point of the face-off – and the status quo in Doklam remained in place.

Regarding the border issue, China is committed to maintaining peace, stability and tranquillity there and Donglang (Doklam) belongs to China as we have historical conventions. So China's activity there is within its sovereign rights. There is no such thing as changing the status quo.

"Last year, thanks to our concerted efforts, our diplomatic efforts and wisdom that we properly resolved this issue," Hua added.

"We hope the Indian side could learn some lessons from this, stick to historical conventions and work with China to ensure the peace and stability in the border area as well as a good atmosphere for the development of bilateral ties," Hua said.

"China and India are exploring ways to resolve their territorial dispute through negotiations so that we can arrive at a mutually acceptable solution and pending the final solution, the two sides should work together and maintain peace and tranquillity in the area."

India and China were locked in a 73-day stand-off at Doklam in the eastern section of their border. The crisis erupted after Indian troops halted road construction at Doka La in the region, citing Bhutan's claim to the area.

Doka La is very close to India's artery which connects its Northeast with the rest of the country. The stand-off was resolved in August.

The ambassador also stressed the need to demarcate the 3,448-km-long disputed border, which is the root cause of friction between India and China.

Talking about the delimitation of the boundary, Hua said:

"China's position is clear and consistent. The east, middle and western side is yet to be officially demarcated. China is committed to resolving the relevant dispute through negotiations."

The long-winding India-China border has three sectors: The western sector between Ladakh and the Chinese-held Aksai Chin; the central sector ranges from Uttarakhand and Tibet; the eastern sector divides Sikkim and Arunachal Pradesh from Tibet.

Asked how China viewed Bambawale's remarks that India does not see China's growing engagement with the South Asian countries as a threat, Hua said: "I commend these positive remarks made by the Indian ambassador. As the two countries are growing at a fast pace, China and India present each other opportunities and also to the world.

We share similar national conditions, development goals as well as common interests". "We have every reason to be each other's partners. So we would like to work with India to enhance political trust and mutually beneficial cooperation under the guidance of two leaders (Indian Prime Minister Narendra Modi and Chinese President Xi Jinping) to achieve the common development," said Hua.

CHINA AND INDIA STAND READY TO FIRE AT EACH OTHER: WHAT'S NEXT

Hundreds of troops from China and India, Asia's two largest countries and hardly best friends, are locked in a standoff on the Doklam plateau, a region of the Himalayan mountain kingdom Bhutan where China was apparently building a highway. China fancies that plateau its own. As a protector of Bhutan, India has mobilized up to 10,000 troops "for any contingency," writes Brahma Chellany, professor of Strategic Studies at the New Delhi-based Center for Policy Research, in an opinion piece here. The highway project is off for now, but China's foreign ministry has demanded Indian forces leave before it can hold any talks. China calls the region administered by Bhutan traditional pastureland for Tibetans and controls Tibet itself as a Chinese territory.

It's easy to imagine the standoff since late June will lead to an actual battle between the two countries, who behave something like regional superpowers. Each side's leader has its reputation to defend at home. China figured its claim to the plateau was well established and saw as a "sign of arrogance" that India would marshal its forces given that it lags the Chinese in economic, military and social indices, says Mohan Malik, professor at the Asia-Pacific Center for Security Studies in Honolulu.

But each side will probably just hold tight to scope out the other from a distance until the governments can talk. "The track record for calming border tensions between China and India is normally quite good," says Sameer Lalwani, deputy director for The Stimson Center think tank's South Asia program. He cites a 1986 standoff that lasted 10 months until solved through high-level talks. Today's standoff could "peter out" as colder weather sets in, proceed to formal talks if Indian troops pull back or "deepen but remain stable with both sides digging in, making permanent their military positions and infrastructure," he says.

China and India are ominously used to these standoffs, reducing the odds of armed conflict. Both have learned to live with grey zones in the Himalayas dividing them, neither conceding nor pushing the other side out. They most obviously dispute two regions, Aksai Chin and part of Arunachal Pradesh, with China controlling the former and India holding the latter.

Still, the Doklam standoff in Bhutan, a country that called neighboring India for support this time, comes amid particularly virulent Chinese protests and as India pushes back more broadly against Chinese control in the region. It's helping Vietnam resist Beijing's hold in the disputed South China Sea even though it lacks a claim there and it's even building a north-south trade corridor that would rival China's "Silk Road" for economic co-development with other countries. There's always a chance of miscalculation or accident on the Doklam plateau, Lalwani notes.

But the two sides that fought a month-long border war in 1962 signed an agreement 31 years later to maintain harmony even as disputes fester. Troop standoffs in 2013 and 2014 were "pretty tense," Chellany tells Forbes. Yet they didn't go to war. This standoff probably won't either. Officials in New Delhi say it can be resolved without "muscle flexing," according to Indian media reports.

You hear a lot of vocal chord flexing, of course. China's Huanqiu.com news website reported in Chinese Sunday that India must withdraw "illegal" border troops and asked whether it was "really prepared" to fight a war with China at 10,000 feet above sea level. An Indian legislator was quoted on the Indian News Express Wednesday website saying China has planted a nuclear bomb in Pakistan with the intent to strike India.

But dialogue at least at the quiet, informal level is expected before those words translate to actions. Indian National Security Advisor Ajit Doval is already scheduled to visit Beijing by month's end. Ministers from both are meeting for regional trade talks in India, as well, despite the border bugaboo.

"The only possible solution to the current standoff is for the Chinese and Indian sides to withdraw from Bhutan's Doklam plateau," Chellany says. "It will also allow China to save face while safeguarding Bhutan's territorial interests." Eventually, he says, the two sides should hold "unpublicized negotiations…to defuse the current crisis and work out a mutual retreat."

7

Sino-Indian Standoff in Sikkim-Tibet-Bhutan Border

China has lodged a protest with India alleging that the Indian Army crossed the boundary in the Sikkim section and demanded their immediate withdrawal. It also released photographs which purportedly showed Indian soldiers crossing the boundary wall.

The face-off between the two armies have also affected the movement of pilgrims to Kailash Mansarovar Yatra in Tibet from the Nathula pass side.

Chinese defence ministry spokesman Ren Guoqiang had said that recently China has begun the construction of a road in Donglang region but was stopped by Indian troops crossing the Line of Actual Control (LAC).

LESSONS FOR INDIA AND CHINA FROM 1967 NATHU LA CLASH

The current India-China standoff along the frontier in Sikkim is similar to one in 1967 that led to four days of bloody clashes between the soldiers of the two countries.

The bloody clashes between Indian and Chinese troops nearly 50 years ago at Nathu La in Sikkim, the scene of an ongoing standoff, are a grim reminder of how the unsettled border of the two countries has triggered hostilities.

The fighting that erupted on September 11, 1967 was preceded by months of accusations from both sides about incursions and territorial intrusions. The language used by China at that time to warn Indian authorities was strikingly similar to the aggressive narrative emanating from Beijing five decades later. It even included references to the 1962 border war, which was fresh in the minds of military commanders on both sides at the time. "The Chinese Government must tell the Indian Government in all seriousness: You must draw lessons from your past experience, stop provocative activities along the China-Sikkim border and cease all your calumnies against China, otherwise you are bound to eat the bitter fruits of your own making," said a note handed over by China's foreign ministry to the Indian embassy in Beijing on April 11, 1967.

On September 10, a day before hostilities broke out, the foreign ministry issued another terse warning , calling Indian leaders "reactionaries" who were "component part of the worldwide anti-Chinese chorus currently struck up by US imperialism and Soviet Revisionism in league with the reactionaries of various countries".

The message, sent to New Delhi through the Indian embassy, said: "The Chinese Government sternly warns the Indian Government: the Chinese Border Defence Troops are closely watching the development of the situation along the China-Sikkim boundary. Should the Indian troops continue to make provocative intrusions, the Indian Government must be held responsible for all the grave consequences."

The external affairs ministry countered the Chinese allegations with its own version of events, saying China's troops had violated agreements. "The Chinese Government is well aware that the Sikkim-Tibet border is a well-defined international border and has been recognised as such by China. By launching an armed attack the Chinese Government is seeking to build up tension at a point on the border which has never been in dispute," the external affairs ministry told Beijing in a note.

The initial clashes in 1967 lasted four days. While the 1962 war was a debacle for New Delhi, the Indian Army proved more than a match for the Chinese five years later. According to an account of the clashes written by Maj Gen Sheru Thapliyal, who was posted in Sikkim at the time, the Indian side lost more than 70 soldiers while the Chinese casualties were more than 400.

"We gave them a bloody nose," a former Indian diplomat told Hindustan Times. A second round of clashes erupted at Cho La on October 1, 1967, leading to more casualties. But Indian troops stood their ground and forced the Chinese soldiers to withdraw at Cho La. Since then, the border in the Sikkim sector has remained free of violence. In 1967, Sikkim was a protectorate of India and it joined the Indian union as a state in 1975. China recognised the frontier in the Sikkim sector in 2003.

The last bullet fired along the China-India frontier was in the Arunachal Pradesh sector in October 1975 , when border patrols from the two sides accidentally came face-to-face amid dense fog at Tuhung La and an Indian soldier was killed. This is often cited by Indian politicians and diplomats to drive home how calm the boundary with China is, say, compared to that with Pakistan.

SIKKIM STANDOFF: INDIA MUST BRACE FOR CHINESE RHETORIC OBSERVE PATIENCE

China's Ambassador to India Luo Zhaohui expressed his belligerent stance that there can be "no compromise" and that the "ball is in India's court" in resolving the nearly three-week-old standoff at the Sikkim-Tibet-Bhutan borders. In the light of the G20 summit meeting at Hamburg this week and where Prime Minister Modi and President Xi Jinping are expected to meet, his comments appear to be part of a diplomatic hard-ball being played by China.

Since Chinese efforts to construct a road unilaterally in the Bhutanese-claimed area closer to Sikkim began, the situation is snowballing into a war of words, if not a war in reality. Both sides reportedly mobilised forces, since the incident on June 16, and represent quantitatively higher numbers than compared to those deployed in the stand-offs at Depsang Plains in 2013 and at Chumar in September/October 2014 and 2015. Yet, despite ratcheting up by the Chinese side, we can only expect some flashes in the pan.

First, while a British Indian-Qing Dynasty Convention of March 1890 outlines a border treaty between Sikkim and Tibet along the watershed principle, no demarcation of territories — writes GS Bajpai in a 1999 book on Sikkim — was made subsequently, given the British focus on trade and Sino-Tibetan differences and intransigence. The areas of the current stand-off in Sikkim-Bhutan areas were never formalised into treaties between Bhutan and China. Besides, as the area is at the tri-junction of three countries, Indian consent is necessary for finalising a border treaty in future.

The Chinese argument that Indian Army had "intruded" into its territory was contested by the Bhutanese government on June 20. The Bhutanese also countered that Beijing was violating the 1988 and 1998 understanding on status quo. China has also been selective by citing the 1890 treaty while terming the 1914 McMohan Line as "unequal". More recently, Beijng termed the Permanent Court of Arbitration at The Hague verdict on South China Sea dispute as "illegal"! Such selective arguments are bound to weaken Chinese positions in the short term.

Second, invoking the special relations between India and Bhutan since 1910 that were reiterated in 1947 and as recently as 2007, Indian troops stopped the Chinese from building the road in the contested territories of Bhutan and China. For India, the building of a Chinese road with military back-up in Chumbi valley has security consequences for the vulnerable Siliguri Corridor. Thus, the Chinese military construction activity in Bhutanese-claimed territory violates not only the Bhutanese sovereignty but also aggravates Indian national security concerns.

Such brazen actions by China are matched by the Indian resolve to protect its interests. Still, it is only expected that the current stand-off then will fizzle out with stiff Indian resistance. Third, citing the stand-off, China had cancelled the Mansarovar Yatra of Indian pilgrims through Nathu La and an Indian media delegation visit to Beijing.

Significantly, the rhetoric on the Chinese side has taken a sharp turn towards escalation. The Chinese foreign ministry spokesperson's comments on July 3rd suggested that Indian troops are "trespassing" into China's territory. The editorial in Global Times on July 4 went further by stating that India "will suffer worse losses than 1962" and that China's military should "expel Indian troops out of Chinese territory" and be "kicked out"!

China's recent statements on Singapore (after its Starlight exercises with Taiwan), Vietnam and Philippines (on South China Sea) and Japan (on Senkaku Islands) followed a similar pattern of psychological war and coercive diplomacy. In this backdrop, India needs to brace for more such rhetoric but to observe patience and perseverance.

Fourth, given the recent isolationist policies practised by the United States, as reflected in the withdrawal from the Trans-Pacific Partnership, climate change and the pivot, China's game plan in its drive to acquire a leadership position in Asia is to make inroads in all parts of the region including South Asia. While it tried to create fissures in Nepal, Bangladesh, Afghanistan, Sri Lanka and Maldives, the latest stand-off in Sikkim and the Chinese discourse officially and in the media, reflects its desire to break the age-old bonhomie between Bhutan and India.

At the multilateral level, Beijing intends to replicate the Southeast Asian formula to South Asia that is SAARC + China. Both at the bilateral and multilateral levels China wants to make further inroads in the region, displacing India

Not only does India need to further strengthen its ties with South Asian countries but also respond, not tactically as has been the case so far but strategically, in the larger region of Asia at the diplomatic, economic and military levels.

CHINA'S NEGOTIATIONS ON SIKKIM STANDOFF WITH INDIA

With no end in sight to the standoff in the Sikkim sector, China on Saturday said there is "no room" for negotiations to resolve the military face-off and the only solution is the withdrawal of Indian troops from the Donglang or Doklam region.

India will face "embarrassment" if it does not withdraw its border troops to its own side and the situation could get "worse", the official Xinhua news agency said in a commentary on Saturday night.

"China has made it clear that there is no room for negotiations on this incident, and India must withdraw its border-crossing troops from Doklam. For China, border line is the bottom line," the commentary said. The commentary sought to add yet another dimension to the face-off by bringing in the Ladakh region and linking it to Pakistan, China's "iron brother" ally.

"India should not regard the existing situation as the same as or even similar to the previous two standoffs in 2013 and 2014 near Ladakh, a disputed area between China, Pakistan and India in southeastern Kashmir. Diplomatic efforts led the troop's frictions there to a well-arranged end. But this time it is a totally different case," it added.

It is rare for China to call Ladakh a "disputed" region and make a reference to Kashmir. This is the first time that China has clearly articulated – through one of its primary official channels - that there is no room for parleys to resolve the weeks-long impasse in Donglang, which is under China's control but claimed by Bhutan.

Until now, the foreign ministry had listed the withdrawal of Indian troops hinted as a precondition for resolving the face-off but had hinted there is an ongoing effort to end it through diplomatic negotiations.

Xinhua is an organ of the Chinese government and is affiliated to the State Council, the Communist country's cabinet. Commentaries published by Xinhua and the People's Daily, the Communist Party of China (CPC) mouthpiece, are taken to be a reflection of the thoughts of the government and the all-powerful CPC.

"India has repeatedly ignored China's call for pulling its border-crossing troops from Doklam area back to its own territory. However, turning a deaf ear to China will but worsen the month-long standoff and put itself further into embarrassment," the commentary said.

It added that India had "lied" to the world by saying it dispatched troops to Donglang to help its ally Bhutan, whereas "apparently" Thimphu had extended no invitation to New Delhi to intervene.

"New Delhi claimed encroachment of its own territory by China before saying it sent troops to 'protect' its 'ally' Bhutan, a sovereign state which has apparently so far made no such an invitation for the sake of that boundary area," it said.

Bhutan and China don't have diplomatic ties but have held 24 rounds of talks to resolve a boundary dispute. The commentary, however, described foreign secretary S Jaishankar's remarks during a recent speech in Singapore as a "positive" sign.

"What China would like to see more are corresponding actions taken by India. "China has a will to solve the problem peacefully by diplomatic means, and China also cherishes the peace and serenity in the border areas, but the precondition is that the trespassers of India must withdraw unconditionally."

INDIA SHOULD REVISIT ITS TIBET POLICY

The Indian government's response to the protests in Tibet has been to merely state its "distress" about the situation and reaffirm its position that Tibet is an "internal" affair of China. New Delhi had assured Beijing that its position on the Tibet issue is "clear and consistent" and that this "would not change in the future." The Indian position is based on its traditional opposition to separatist movements and to foreign intervention in support of such movements. Also, given the present dynamics of India-China relations with greater synergy as the goal, New Delhi does not favour supporting the Tibetan cause. However, protests by Tibetans have implications for India as the Tibet issue is entangled with the India-China border dispute.

The Tibet issue is rooted in the histories of the three countries – India, China and Tibet. Tibet has existed throughout history as a distinct civilization with rich culture, language, religion, polity and identity. Through the centuries India and Tibet have maintained strong religious and trade ties, and have shared a peaceful border. But the advent of British power in the Indian sub-continent altered the nature of this relationship.

The British Raj's policy towards Tibet was shaped by the Great Game and the need to prevent Russia from posing a threat to India. It was against this backdrop that the Raj called for the tripartite Simla conference in October 1913, which was attended by representatives from British India (Henry

McMahon), Republican China (Chen Yifan) and Tibet (Lonchen Shatra). The goal was to settle the boundary between British India and Tibet on the one hand and between Tibet and China on the other. The result was the Simla Agreement of 1914, which the Chinese representative initialled but only under British pressure. The Agreement divided Tibet into Inner and Outer Tibet. China was given sovereignty over Inner Tibet but only suzerain control over Outer Tibet. And the boundary between India and Tibet was demarcated, with the Raj retaining trading and extra-territorial rights in Outer Tibet.

Independent India inherited this arrangement, which boiled down to sustaining Tibet as a buffer zone with de facto independent status under Chinese suzerainty. In the post-1949 period, when the People's Republic of China came into being, India urged China to let Tibet continue as an autonomous region in line with its historical status, religious, cultural and political identity. However, the entry of 20,000 PLA troops in 1950-51 into Tibet ended its independent status and eventually brought to the fore the India-China border issue.

During his 1954 visit to China, Jawaharlal Nehru had raised the issue of inaccurate border alignment as depicted in some Chinese maps. Premier Zhou Enlai responded that these maps were reproductions of old Kuomintang maps and that his government has had no time to revise them. However, Nehru's December 14, 1958 letter, in which he had once again raised the issue of Chinese maps depicting the border alignment inaccurately, elicited a different response from Zhou. The Chinese Premier wrote back on January 23, 1959 stating that the Sino-Indian border was never delimited and that China has never recognised the McMahon Line.

After the 1962 India-China war, China began to claim some 90,000 square kilometres of Indian territory in the eastern sector and 38,000 square kilometres in the Aksai Chin area. These claims flow directly from China's control over Tibet and its felt need to consolidate its rule over this rebellious territory.

Between 1947 and 1954, India's position on Tibet was based on recognising it as an independent nation. Tibet represented itself as an independent country at the Asian Relations Conference held in New Delhi in March-April 1947. But India subsequently gave up this position on April 29, 1954, when it signed an agreement with China on trade and intercourse between India and Tibet. Under the terms of the agreement, India gave up all extra-territorial rights and privileges that it had inherited from the British Raj and recognised Tibet as part of China. This, in effect, was a unilateral concession without the Indian government gaining anything in return. In subsequent decades, New Delhi has repeatedly reiterated that Tibet is a part of China, in spite of the latter's encroachment into and extravagant claims over Indian territory, the border war it imposed on India in 1962, and the unresolved border dispute at the centre of which lies Tibet. In effect, such reiteration has meant the dilution of a bargaining card in the border negotiations. In 2003, the Vajpayee government went further than any other government before by stating that the "Tibetan Autonomous Region of China is part of the territory of China." This has two critical implications for Indian security. First, it excluded Inner Tibet (present day Sichuan, Yunnan and Qinghai provinces) from the geographical notion of Tibet, thus recognising Inner Tibet as Chinese land. Second, it provided China a greater opening to advance its claims on Arunachal Pradesh. For, Outer Tibet or the Tibetan Autonomous Region (TAR), according to the Chinese definition, includes Arunachal Pradesh, which it refers to as its 'southern state'.

India has consistently failed to understand nuances in Chinese diplomatic practice and negotiating tactics. China is tackling the Tibet problem at two levels. One, it is involving the Dalai Lama's representatives in fruitless talks, while also disparaging him as a 'splittist' who aims to disintegrate China. Two, it is arm-twisting India by repeatedly claiming that Arunachal Pradesh is part of China. Here, it is worth noting that at the sixth round of talks with Tibetan representatives Chinese negotiators had conveyed that the Dalai Lama should accept Arunachal Pradesh as part of China, which the Dalai Lama has refused to accept. China is not seriously considering a resolution to the Tibet issue or the border dispute with India. It is simply buying time till the Dalai Lama passes away, after which, it hopes, the Tibetan movement would fizzle out. This would also further weaken India's bargaining position on the border negotiations while at the same time gaining for itself greater manoeuvrability.

The presence of the Dalai Lama in India along with 120,000 Tibetan refugees spread across 35 settlements is leverage for India. But India has so far steadfastly avoided using the Tibetan card. Given the intricate linkage between the Tibet issue and the border dispute, India needs to revise its policy on Tibet. Its present policy of appeasement and unilateral concessions has not stopped China from claiming Indian territory. Chinese maps continue to show Arunachal Pradesh as part of China, and Jammu and Kashmir as falling outside India. Some Chinese maps still do not represent Beijing's revised position on Sikkim.

The latest unrest among Tibetans provides an opportunity for India to revisit and revise its Tibet policy. First, India should make it clear to the Chinese government that developments in Tibet are a concern for India and that it cannot remain unaffected by developments there. Second, on the border issue, instead of merely restating that all of Arunachal Pradesh is an integral part of its territory, India should make it very clear that these are non-negotiable. Third, upholding its democratic principles as well as its cultural affinity with the Tibetans, India should impress upon the Chinese that while it does not support political activity by Tibetans in its soil, it also cannot suppress peaceful demonstrations by them. Fourth, India should move away from its 'over-cautious' and diffident policy on Tibet and adopt a more independent stand that takes into account its national interests.

CENTRAL GOVERNMENT'S POLICY AND DALAI LAMA

Starting from the point of maintaining the unification of the motherland and national unity, the central government adopted an attitude of patient waiting towards the Dalai Lama after he fled abroad. His position as a vice-chairman of the NPC Standing Committee was preserved until 1964. However, surrounded by foreign anti-China forces and Tibetan separatists, the Dalai Lama completely renounced the patriotic stand which he once expressed and engaged in numerous activities to split the motherland.

Publicly advocating that "Tibet is an independent state." In June 1959, the Dalai Lama issued a statement in Mussoorie, India which read "Tibet had actually been independent." In March 1991, during his visit to Britain, the Dalai Lama told the press that Tibet "is the biggest occupied country in the world today." He proclaimed on many occasions that "the task of realizing the independence of Tibet has fallen upon all Tibetans in and outside Tibet."

Setting up the "government in exile." In the early 1960s, the Dalai clique convened the "people's congress of Tibet" in Dharamsala, India, which established the so-called "Tibetan government in exile." A so-called "constitution" was promulgated, which states that "the Dalai Lama is the head of state," "the ministers shall be appointed by the Dalai Lama" and "all work of the government shall not be approved without the consent of the Dalai Lama." The 1991 revised "constitution" of the Dalai clique still stipulates that the Dalai is "the head of the state." The Dalai Lama and his so-called "government in exile" kept levying an "independence tax" on Tibetans residing abroad, established "offices" in some countries, published magazines and books advocating "Tibetan independence" and engaged in political activities for "Tibetan independence."

Reorganizing the armed rebel forces. In September 1960, the Dalai clique re-organized the "religion guards of the four rivers and six ranges" in Mustang, Nepal, which carried on military harassment activities along the Chinese border for ten years.

Its first commander-in-chief Anzhugcang Goinbo Zhaxi wrote in his memoirs *Four Rivers and Six Ranges* that "a series of attacks were organized on Chinese outposts" and "sometimes, 100 or 200 Tibetan guerrillas went as far as 100 miles into the area occupied by the Chinese." The Dalai Lama wrote articles praising Goinbo Zhaxi.

Spreading rumors and calumnies and plotting riots. Ignoring facts, the Dalai Lama fabricated numerous lies to sow dissension among the various nationalities and incite the Tibetan people to oppose the central government during his 30-year self-exile abroad. He said that "the 17-Article Agreement was imposed on Tibet under armed force"; "the Hans have massacred 1.2 million Tibetans"; "owing to Han immigration, the Tibetans have become a minority in Tibet"; "the Communists in Tibet force women to practice birth control and abortion"; the government opposes religious freedom and persecutes religious people; traditional Tibetan culture and art are in danger of extinction; the natural resources in Tibet have been seriously depleted; there is severe environmental pollution in Tibet, etc. The riots in Lhasa from September 1987 to March 1989 were incited by the Dalai clique and plotted by rebels who were sent back to Tibet. The riots incurred severe losses to the lives and property of Tibetans.

The Dalai's words and deeds have showed that he is no longer only a religious leader as he claims. On the contrary, he has become the political leader engaged in long-term divisive activities abroad.

FRIEDRICH-NAUMANN-STIFTUNG AND THE TIBETAN PARLIAMENTARY AND POLICY RESEARCH CENTRE

The Friedrich-Naumann-Stiftung (FNSt) established in 1958 is a non-profit organization for public benefit. It promotes the liberal principle of Freedom in Human Dignity in all sectors of society, both nationally as well as internationally, in developed as well as developing countries.

The Foundation is active in more than 75 countries. In the South Asian Region comprising the SAARC countries the Foundation's work encompasses projects concerned with support for economic liberalisation; fostering regional economic cooperation in South Asia; promotion of civic rights; and environmental protection. All these activities are carried out in co-operation with local, national and international NGOs, the emphasis being on self-reliance and the setting up of democratic institutions. Friedrich-Naumann-Stiftung in partnership with the Assembly of Tibetan People's Deputies has set up the Tibetan Parliamentary and Policy Research Centre (TPPRC) with the purpose of strengthening the Tibetan diaspora in building up a healthy democratic working ethos.

The objective is to prepare the Tibetans in exile for the assumption of responsibilities that would respond to their hopes and aspirations through a framework of legislative, executive and judicial institutions based on the concept of the Tibetan polity guided by *Saddharma* and with a view to generating human values and considerations based on man's free will, equality, justice and non-violence.

There is also the standing need to constantly remind the Tibetan diaspora of their national identity, culture and heritage and the global community of Tibet's unique contribution to the world of thought and culture. Extablished in 1994, the Centre has already reached a very representative section of Tibetans residing in India and Nepal, encouraging them to get actively involved in their new democratic institutions and helping their leadership to formulate a vision for the future. Moreover, the Centre has a sound back-up programme of publications to disseminate information to build up national and international public opinion for the fulfillment of a just cause.

POLITICAL STATUS OF TIBET : AN INDIAN VIEWS

For centuries long-ago Tibet had flourished as storehouse of an ancient culture flourishing under the silence and solitude of a vast firmament, away from the tumult and turmoil of the world. Tibet was known to mankind not for its wealth and weaponry but for the heights of its spiritual glory and depth of its philosophical thought. Religion had been the keynote of this culture. Here, man was not the measure of all things but an humble creature with his share of *Karman* in the *Samsara* of activity and fruits thereof in the inexorable vortex of life. What was titanic in him was not vanity but the effort to emerge out of it, through suffering and sacrifice, meditation and prayer, compassion and congregation. Life continued in its spiritual endeavour in the mountain fastnesses, the glens and the plateau of Tibet until recently when the force of circumstances changed the shape of things.

ANTIQUITY OF INDO-TIBET ASSOCIATES

Generally, we think of India's contacts with Tibet with result from the advent of Buddhism there. According to the Tibetan tradition, however, these contacts go farther back in history. Tibetan chronicles and scholars like

Bu-ston suggest that the Tibetan race stems from the descendants of a military general named Rupati belonging to the Kaurava army. According to the Tibetan legend, Rupati fled to Tibet after the defeat of the Kauravas at the hands of the Pandavas in the epic battle of Mahabharata, and was followed by a large number of his followers. T.W.D. Shakabpa in his work 'Tibet: A Political History' states that a large number of learned Tibetans claim their race to have descended from Rupati and his followers. The claim is based on a letter written by the Indian pundit.Sankarapati, (Deje-dakpo in Tibetan) about a hundred years after the death of the Buddha. The latter described the migration of Rupati's followers to Tibet

Esteemed Ground of Noble Master

Buddhism went to Tibet directly from India. Being the land of the Noble Master, the Buddha, India represents to the Tibetan mind the birthplace of all that is noble in thought and deed. Tibet's religion, philosophy, art, poetry all show a deep Indian influence.

Buddhism was introduce in Tibet by the memorable efforts of two Tibetan kings, Sron-btasn-sgam-po and Khri-sron-lde-btsan, whose names are written in the golden pages of Tibetan history. One flourished in the first half of the 7th Century A.D. and the other in the second half of the 8th century. Before Buddhism reached Tibet through Bhiksu Santaraksita, Kamalasila and Padmasambhava, it had undergone a profound evolution in it doctrine and practice in India itself. The three *Pitkas* viz. *Vinaya,* Sutra and *Abhidharma* were brought into Tibetan language and constituted the foundation of Tibetan culture with oral transmission and uninterrupted lineage of tradition.

The core of the entire Tibetan attitude to life, is *Karuna* or Compassion. Their religious leader, the Dalai Lama is Karuna's incarnation par excellence. As an incarnation of *Avalokitesvara,* he dominates by the power of love through the conquest of the heart. The next important incarnation is Panchen Lama representing Hod-dpag-med or Amitabha-Infinite Light - the Dhyahi-Buddha of the existing Kalpa. Apart from these two Grand Lamas, there are numerous incarnate Lamas called Tulkus. They are believed to be incarnations of accomplished saints. In Tibetan Buddhism, the Indian concept of *Avatara* has been taken to its logical conclusion so that it ensures the presence of several saviours at the same time in the midst of the vast suffering humanity.

The system of reincarnation, originally Indian, and familiar to the Tibetan since the advent of Buddhism in Tibet, came into popular vogue in their country largely from the time of Gendun-dubpa, the first Dalai Lama. The transmission of the title is not automatic from father to son. Instead of being hereditary it is based on a very discreet process of selection of the true reincarnation of the deceased Dalai Lama, Rinpoche or Tulku. The process of selection is so rigorous that it might take years before the 'right' choice is made. The reincarnation may be found thousands of miles away from the place where the previous incarnation departed from his body. The basis of this belief and practice is the age old Indian philosophy of rebirth, which does not see death as an end, but as an occasion for the soul to assume a new cloak after the previous one no more remains fit to serve it. However, the word Dalai Lama is not an Indian word. Dalai is the Mongol translation of the Tibetan word 'rgyamtsho' which means Great Ocean.

THE MONASTIC TRADITION

Tibet imbibed its monastic tradition, too, from India. Buddhism was the first monastic religion of the world. Monasteries are sprinkled throughout the length and breadth of Tibet as a monument to its Indian connection. The atmosphere inside them transports the visitor into a realm of inner experience and makes him look within for atma-paryavekshana, self-scrutiny. The presiding divinity installed in the shrine at the back of the prayer hall dominates the cosmos around, of which the temple is the very symbol and the devotee a part. Scenes from the life of the Buddha taken from the Jatakas painted in frescoes are reminiscent of Ajanta paintings of India. However, the direct inspiration to the Tibetan painter came not from Ajanta, but from the are of the Pala kings of Bengal.

Literary Affinity

Sanskrit and Pali works from India contain been translated into Tibetan by a very successful and scientific method employing two experts, one of each language. The translations are so perfect, if one translates them back, the original is restored almost in its entirety. It is probably true that the Mahayana literature from India was properly catalogued and preserved for the first time in the Tibetan language. It is also true that many works no more extant in their original Sanskrit form are available only in the Tibetan language. Through their libraries, frescoes, and images the Tibetan monasteries preserved and transmitted the Indian mystic tradition in all its glory in a superb manner.

TIBET: THE STRENGTH OF INDIA

Thus the culture of Tibet, is a glowing example of how the stream of Indian consciousness crossed the Himalayan frontiers and flowed into far-off lands, transforming them body, mind and soul into an eternity of love, peace and compassion through a community of ideals and institutions.

Lime Om Mani Padme Hum, like the jewel in the lotus, these ideals inspired Tibetans into a life of virtue, devotion and sacrifice. The grandeur of man's material advances in the world outside were matched by the glory of spiritual heights on the 'Roof of the world' where millions of people tuned themselves to the gospel of the Arya, the Noble one, the Buddha from India and sought salvation through it. While India is fast forgetting these ancient links with Tibet, Tibetans everywhere adore India as the root of all that is noble and good and worthy of emulation in the history of human civilization.

REACTIONS IN INDIA TO THE CHINESE INVASION

Consequent upon the entry of 40,000 troops from Eastern Tibet's provincial capital of Chamdo from eight directions, the smashing of the small Tibetan resistance force resulting in the death of some 4000 Tibetans and the capture of Ngapo Ngawang Jigme, the regional Tibetan Governor, India's Ministry of External Affairs sent a note to the Government of the People's Republic of China on October 26, 1950 which *Inter alia* stated as follows:

- "Now that the invasion of Tibet has been ordered by Chinese Government, peaceful negotiations can hardly be synchronised with it and there naturally will be fear on the part of Tibetans that negotiations will be under duress. In the present context of world events, invasion by Chinese troops of Tibet cannot but be regarded as deplorable and in the considered judgement of the Government of India, not in the interest of China on peace".

In India's view, thus, the entry of Chinese forces into Tibet was an act of invasion. Clearly India did not regard that as an internal matter of China. Sardar Patel reacted to the situation very sharply in a letter to Prime Minister Nehru less than two weeks later on 7th November, 1950. In the letter he not only charged the Chinese of perfidy but analysed the strategic implications of the Chinese invasion of Tibet with a great deal of foresight and clairvoyance.

Inter alia, the then Deputy Prime Minister made the following points:

- 'The Chinese Government has tried to delude us by professions of peaceful intention'.
- 'The final action of the Chinese, in my judgement is little short of perfidy. The tragedy of it is that the Tibetans put faith in us; they chose to be guided by us; and we have been unable to get them out of the meshes of Chinese diplomacy or Chinese malevolence'.

- 'Even though we regard ourselves as friends of China, the Chinese do not regard us as their friends'.
- 'We have to consider what new situation now faces us as a result of the disappearance of Tibet, as we knew it, and the expansion of China almost upto our gates'.
- 'We can therefore, safely assume that very soon they will disown all the stipulations which Tibet had entered into with us in the past'.
- 'That throws into a melting pot all frontier and commercial settlements with Tibet on which we have been functioning and acting during the last half a century'.
- 'While our Western and North-Western threat to security is still as prominent as before, a new threat has developed from the North and the North-East. Thus, for the first time, after centuries, India's defence has to concentrate itself on two fronts simultaneously'.

Sardar Patel could not have been more clinically precise and more right. Quite by coincidence, the same day as Sardar Patel wrote to Prime Minister Nehru on Tibet, the Tibetan Government appealed to the United Nations for its intervention through a letter to the Secretary General on November 7, 1950 as follows:

- "Though there is a little hope that a national dedicated to peace will be able to resist the brutal effort of men trained to war, we understand that the United Nations has decided to stop aggression wherever it happens".

However, ten days later when El Salvador formally asked the General Assembly to include the Chinese aggression against Tibet on its agenda, the matter was not taken up by the august body for discussion at the suggestion of the Indian delegation. The Indian delegation asserted that a peaceful solution which is mutually advantageous to Tibet, India and China could be reached between the parties concerned. In the outcome Tibetan officials signed on Agreement with China on May 23, 1951 under duress and without the authority of the Tibetan Government in Lhasa on 'Measures for the Peaceful Liberation of Tibet'.

Known as the 17-Point Agreement between the Chinese Peoples Government and the local Government of Tibet, it was, quite contrary to Indian assurances, neither advantageous to Tibet nor to India. The latter was simply ignored. The peaceful Liberation of Tibet was achieved by 23000 Chinese troops entering Lhasa on 9th September, 1951 from all sides! The 17-point Agreement was not an Agreement but a dictate. The Dalai Lama and his Government came to know of it four days after it was 'signed' when

Radio Beijing broadcast it on 27th May, 1951. They did not even know its contents until then. A shocked and stunned Tibet 'heard' the news.

The Agreement empowered the Chinese Government to enter its forces into Tibet and to handle its external affairs. Tibet was deprived of the symbols of its Sovereignty in one assault. The occupation of Lhasa in September that year was followed by the occupation of other principal cities of Tibet as far as Rudok and Gartok in the far west and Gyantse and Shigatse in Central Tibet. Then Tibet was cut into pieces and parts of it incorporated in China's neighbouring provinces. A large part of Tibet's Kham province was incorporated into China's Sichuan province and its another portion into Yunnan. A new Chinese province called Qinghai was also created with the bulk of Tibet's Amdo province and part of Kham.

The remaining part of Amdo was incorporated into the Gansu Province. With only a little part of Kham and the Central Province of U-Tsang left, Tibet was reduced to a shadow of its former self. The People's Liberation Army had come to liberate Tibet of its serfdom. It reduced it to servitude. As early as on 6th April, 1952, MaoTse Tung himself admitted in the "Directive of the Central Committee of CPC on the Policies For Our Work in Tibet":-

- "Not only the two Silons (Prime Ministers) but also the Dalai and most of his clique were reluctant to accept the Agreement and are unwilling to carry it out – And yet we do not have a material base for fully implementing the agreement, nor do we have a base for this purpose in terms of support among the masses or in the upper stratum".

While that was the situation on the ground, India sanctified the Chinese military occupation of Tibet by accepting it as a region of China in the 1954 Sino-Indian Agreement on trade with Tibet. As that Agreement enunciated the principles of Peaceful Co-existence, the panchashila, Dr. Bhimrao Ambedkar, said the following in the Rajya Sabha: "Our Prime Minister is depending on the Panchsheel which has been adopted by Comrade Mao and the Panchsheel which is one of the clauses in the No-Aggression treaty on Tibet. I am indeed surprised that our Hon'ble Prime Minister is taking this Panchsheel seriously. Hon'ble Members of the House, you must be knowing that Panchsheel is one of the significant parts of the Buddha Dharma. If Shri Mao had even an iota of faith in Panchsheel, he would have treated the Buddhists in his country in a different manner". Dr. Ambedkar then warned the Prime Minister in no uncertain terms:

- "…. Prime Minister will realise the truth in my words when the situation matures further. I don't really what is going to happen. By letting China take control over Lhasa (Tibetan Capital) the Prime Minister has in a way helped the Chinese to bring their armies on the Indian borders. Any victor who annexes Kashmir can directly reach Pathankot, and I know it for sure that he can reach the Prime Minister's House also".

Eight years later the Chinese annexed Aksai Chin in North eastern Kashmir. Prime Minister Nehru had his share of warnings but apart from his genuine desire to have close and friendly relations with China, he knew it was not possible for the Indian Armed forces to take on both Pakistan and China, a spectre to which Sardar Patel had drawn his attention.

Nehru's effort was to avoid a direct military confrontation with the Chinese throughout the fifties. He had no power to halt the Chinese avalanche through Tibet. In December, 1950 he had stated that the last voice in regard to Tibet should be the voice of the people of Tibet and of no one else. The Chinese guns had effectively silenced that voice and the men behind them crossed the Himalaya into India equally effectively in the late fifties and early 60s. Our armies could not stop them even at our frontier. Reacting to the Chinese betrayal and belligerence, Dr. Rajendra Prasad said at the Gandhi Maidan in Patna on October 24, 1962:

- "Freedom is the most sacred boon. It has to be protected by all means — violent or non-violent. Therefore Tibet has to be liberated, from the iron grip of China and handed over to Tibetans".

Even before the Chinese invasion of India, there had been voices galore in India to protect Tibet's freedom and the Tibetan right to self-determination. Acharya Kriplani who in the Lok Sabha debate in 1954 had openly charged China of having committed an act of aggression and in 1958 had talked about Panchshila having been born in sin because it was enunciated to put the seal of our approval upon the destruction of an ancient nation associated with us spiritually and culturally, said of Tibet in the Lok Sabha on May 8, 1959L:

- "It was a nation which wanted to live its own life and it sought to have been allowed to live it own life. A good government is no substitute for self-government".

The same year at the all India convention on Tibet on 30 May, 1959, Lok Nayak Jaya Prakash Narayan, in his Presidential address, pleaded for a United World opinion to be created 'against Chinese aggression and for Tibet's independence'. He emphatically called it a fight for the Rights of Man'. He, however, predicted that Tibet was not lost forever. 'Tibet will not die' he said, because there is no death for the human spirit. Jaya Prakash Narayan concluded:

- "Tyrannies have come and gone and Caesars and Czars and dictators. But the spirit of man goes on forever. Tibet will be resurrected".

It is a tribute to Nehru's character as an ardent lover of peace and international harmony that even after the Chinese branded India as running dogs of imperialism, nay even after they launched their pincer movement against India in 1962 a concerted attack in all the three sectors of the Indo-Tibetan border in the Himalayas, and inflicted a crushing defeat on the Indian Armed forces, he stuck to his advocacy of PRC's entry into the U.N. A large section of India's public opinion failed to interpret India's Tibet policy in terms of the Prime Minister's lofty idealism or the constraints on him in terms of India's actual military capabilities, faced as it was now with aggression from two quarters.

It was seen throughout the fifties as a policy of yielding too much ground to the Chinese in regard to Tibet. Said Acharya Kriplani in the Lok Sabha repeatedly: (1954, 1958, 1959). 'In international politics when a buffer state is destroyed by a powerful nation, that nation is considered to have committed aggression against its neighbours'. 'England went to war with Germany not because Germany had invaded England, but because it had invaded Poland and Belgium'. 'I do not say that because China conquered Tibet we should have gone to war with it. But this does not mean that we should recognise the claim of China on Tibet.

We must know that it is an act of aggression against a foreign nation'. 'A small buffer state on our borders was deprived of its freedom. When we made a protest, we were told we were the stooges of western powers (If I remember it right, we were called running dogs of imperialism)". The criticism in the Indian Press, that watchdog of the people, in regard to India's Tibet policy was even more blatant and gallic. After the Peoples Liberation Army crushed the Peoples rebellion in Tibet, the Indian Express wrote in an editorial entitled "India and Tibet" on March 20, 1959:

- 'The Government of India's silence in the face of this situation is difficult to decipher and even more difficult to condone. Discretion and restraint are too often alibis for moral and political poverty'.

Above all, the Tibetans as a brutally oppressed people are entitled, as fellow human beings, to the goodwill of the civilized world, not least of India which in its long history has also known bondage and suffering'. On March 30, The Times of India in its editorial on Repression in Tibet commented: 'The news from Peking has killed the last lingering hope that, faced with a popular revolt in Tibet, the Chinese would try to come to terms with the people rather than seek to coerce them into surrender' 'All the levers of power are in fact in the hands of the commanders of the Chinese forces in the region'.

'But the military victory of the Chinese is in fact a political defeat'. 'The Chinese, determined to exploit the rich mineral wealth of the region, will now do everything they can to quicken the pace of change, break the power of monasteries, settle large number of their own people in the region and integrate it completely with the rest of China'. 'In the face of a military fait accompli, the Indian government can do little to restore Tibetan autonomy, but even so there is no reason for it to stretch the concept of non-interference to the point where it has to maintain an uneasy silence in the matter'. In its editorial 'The Rape of Tibet', the Hindustan Times said the same day: (March 30, 1959):

- 'Let us hold our heads low to-day. A small country on our border has paid the ultimate penalty for its temerity to aspire for independence. Tibet is dead'.
- 'Tibet was dying a long time before death came. It was eight years ago that the Chinese communist moved in to assert a theoretical suzerainty over a people with a long history as a distinct entity, geographical, ethical, linguistic, cultural and religious'.
- 'But if the Chinese did at times establish effective rule over Tibet, let it also be remembered by those who are now willing enough to help Peking rewrite history that there was a Tibetan king who once extracted tribute from the celestial empire'.
- 'Tibet is dead. Much else could die with Tibet if we do not even now heed the warning'.

The Indian Press was adequately voicing the mood of the people of India and India's leadership had to pay heed. Prime Minister Nehru broke his silence on the troubling question of Tibet in the Parliament of India on March 30, 1959, the same day as the above editorials appeared. He spoke of the relationship of India with Tibet being something deeper than the changing political scene, that he wanted to have friendly relations with the people of Tibet and he wanted them to progress in freedom. At the same time, it was important, he said, for us to have friendly relations with China. The next morning, the Indian Express retorted that he could not equate the aggressor with the aggressed and reminded him of his own statements in 1949 to the US House of Representatives:

- 'Where freedom is menaced or justice threatened, or where aggression takes place India would not be neutral'.

Meanwhile, things moved in Tibet at a dramatic speed — faster than anticipated. The Dalai lama had gone back to Tibet in 1956 at the instance of Nehru after participating in the 2500th Buddha Jayanti Celebrations. Chou-en- Lai had assured Nehru at that time that 'Tibet was not China but an autonomous region which had been part of the Chinese state'. In his March 30, 1959 statement to the Lok Sabha, Nehru quoted Chou-en-Lai as having said that 'China practice the Chinese intensified the socialist purges against Tibetans, parcelled out its territories to become part of Chinese provinces, considerably reinforced the Chinese army, denied the Tibetan monasteries of their spiritual and material wealth, and wee making plans, so the Tibetans believed, for abducting the Dalai Lama to Peking. Their worst suspicions were confirmed when their religious and temporal head was invited to come to a theatrical show at the Chinese military barracks on March 10, 1959 without any bodyguards. In a massive demonstration of their will to protect their leader, the people of Lhasa surrounded Norbulingka, Dalai lama's Summer Palace, to prevent him from attending the Chinese show. Within days the episode turned into a national uprising touching every part of Tibet. Open fighting broke out in Lhasa and several places outside the capital with Tibetan blood littered everywhere as a consequence of Chinese repression. With no help available from any quarter, the Dalai Lama left his hearth and home and his kingdom to seek refuge in India and appealed for international help from outside. On 28th March, Chou-en-Lai 'dissolved' the Government of Tibet by an order of the State Council. Even the fiction of Tibetan autonomy was scrapped. Prime Minister Nehru interpreted the gory march of events in Tibet to the Parliament of India on March 30, 1959 how the Khampa region of Tibet was incorporated into China and how their reforms had brought the Chinese into trouble with the Khampas whom he described as 'mountain people, rather tough people, not liking anybody ruling them; how this conflict had 'come out into the monasteries and valued manuscripts.

Right when as the Prime Minister was telling the Parliament, 'our sympathies go out very much to the Tibetans', the ruler of Tibet, the Dalai Lama was already at the portals of India. He actually crossed into our territory on the evening of March 31, 1959, after seeking political refuge two days earlier before entering India. As he walked into freedom, he denounced the 17-Point Agreement with China and declared it null and void. On 5th April in his Press Conference in Delhi, Prime Minister Nehru agreed that the 1951 Agreement between China and Tibet had broken down and confessed that there was no autonomy in Tibet. He said that rather emphatically:

- 'Now what has happened in Tibet is related to the Agreement between China and the authorities in Tibet, in 1950, I think. You will see that on both sides there, it is stated that agreement has ended or broken up. There is no doubt about it, and events also indicate that. Now, that is an important fact that it has broken down,'. The agreement was based on two factors — (I) on the recognition of the suzerainty of China over Tibet and (ii) the autonomy of Tibet. These are two major factors. The breakdown of the Sino-Tibetan agreement, which in any case had been a one-way affair and hardly an agreement, meant that both major factors comprising it, *i.e.* (I) the recognition of the Chinese suzerainty over Tibet by the people and the government of Tibet and (ii) the autonomy of Tibet had collapsed. Tibet was without a Tibetan government, even it and it was a land with millions of Tibetan people under the occupation of an alien force exercising rights which it did not have under any law temporal or moral. Tibet, which in Nehru's own view expressed at the Press Conference on April 5, 1959, culturally speaking, was "an offshoot of India" had been shamelessly annexed by China and swallowed up.

At his Press Conference India's Prime Minister admitted: 'it is obvious that at present, since this uprising, there is no autonomy in Tibet'. The Indian Press and leading public figures in India, therefore, grilled Nehru on his Tibet policy even further. On April 8, 1959, in a forceful editorial titled "Second Thoughts", the Leader commented:

- 'When the World allowed Japan to work her will upon Manchuria, it did not promote the cause of peace... When Britain and France committed aggression in Egypt, President Eisenhower did not uphold their action even though the United States is more akin ideologically to Britain and France than India is to China....... Pt. Nehru can do no better than emulate the example of President Eisenhower and ask China to retrace here steps."

"THOUGHT" reminded Nehru in a pungent editorial on April 11, 1959, of what he knew already, that the 1951 Agreement stood on the twin pillars of Tibet's autonomy and China's suzerainty. Without the first the latter would be a grotesque imposition. On April 20, 1959, the Times of India seriously questioned Prime Minister Nehru's conviction that 'Tibet's autonomy and Chinese suzerainty' could coexist. There was thus a strong demand that since the situation on the ground in Tibet had changed materially, India too alter the course of its policy in the matter.

Prime Minister Nehru however continued to explain that India's policy kept three factors in view, "the major factor being, of course our own security; the second factor, 'our desire to have and continue to have friendly relations with China' and the third factor, our strong feelings about developments in Tibet". Prime Minister Nehru was soon in for rude shocks. While he continued in his quest for continued friendly relations with China, the Chinese openly charged India of keeping the Dalai Lama in India under duress. Nehru met the charge by declaring in the Indian Parliament on April 27, 1959 that the Dalai Lama was free to go anywhere he chose and anyone including the Chinese Ambassador was fee to meet him. Moreover, while the Chinese were fuming and fretting at their embarrassment to see 'the Dalai Lama and his clique' successfully cross into India despite their attempts by air and on the ground to track him down before he did so, they shamelessly called India expansionist — inheritor of the British tradition of imperialism and expansion. That was typical of the behaviour of the Chinese government of the time.

Before the world could call them imperialist and expansionist, for what they had done in Tibet and to Tibet, they started levying these charges against India which had done nothing but acquiesce in their colonial occupation of Tibet and was hoping to sustain a friendly relationship with them despite the loss of Tibet as a buffer.

Nehru called the Chinese charges strange and use of the cold war language. He told the Lok Sabha on April 27, 1959. "It would be a tragedy if the two great countries of Asia, India and China, which have been peaceful neighbours for ages past, should develop feelings of hostility against each other. We for our part will follow this policy, but we hope that China also will do likewise and that nothing will be said or done which endangers the friendly relations of the two countries which are so important from the wider point of view of the peace of Asia and the world. The Five Principles have laid down, *Inter alia*, mutual respect for each other. Such mutual respect is gravely impaired if unfounded charges are made and the language of cold war used". However, these pleas made no sense to China's rulers. Their plans to complete their work in Tibet went apace and as they consolidated their hold, they moved further South. Peace in Asia and the world must come under their own terms. Meanwhile their territorial claims stemming from their own imperial borders must be made a reality, by peace if possible, by war if necessary. When India saw the writing on the wall and placed a few pickets on the border, ill manned, ill equipped and ill connected, they came down like a hurricane in one clean sweep destroyed them.

And in their defence, they charged India of a forward policy which invited quite naturally their wrath, while a full scale military occupation of Tibet in the decade of the 50s was no part of a 'forward Policy' to which India had any right to react. The 19th century was one of colonial expansion. The first half of the twentieth century was marked by two world wars as a legacy of those colonial powers. In the second half of our century, mankind has taken pride in liquidating much of the abominable legacy of the colonial and the imperial times. Even the Soviet empire has collapsed. But the torch of colonialism is still burning strong in Tibet. All his life Nehru had fought and fought successfully against the forces of colonialism and imperialism and fascism.

He could not have been oblivious to what the Chinese were doing in Tibet but he had been hoping that the Chinese would heed the verdict of history against such forces, listen to reason and fulfil their own promises about respecting the autonomy of Tibet. By the year 1962 this great statesman of Asia and the world was a thoroughly disillusioned person. All the pillars of his Tibetan policy and policy towards China had fallen one by one. The Chinese had successfully breached the sovereignty and the territorial integrity of India. Tibet's autonomy was a matter of the past which India had bartered for the independence that country had enjoyed till 1950 and the friendship with China had turned into a nightmare of bitter hostility. The Sino-Indian Agreement of 1954 enshrining Panchshila now lay in shreds. It died a natural death in 1962 with neither side willing to revive it and China stood as the undisputed monarch of all it surveyed in Tibet and beyond upto the territories of India now under its occupation. In the wake of their mastery over the Roof of the World, the Chinese turned Nehru's dream of Sino-Indian friendship, so elegantly proclaimed in the slogan Hindi-China Bhai Bhai, into a nightmare that ultimately sapped life out of that most precious jewel of India.

CHINA IS WRONG ON SIKKIM-TIBET BOUNDARY

The standoff between Chinese and Indian troops in the Doklam area, at the tri-junction with Bhutan, is accompanied by competing narratives: attempts to clarify, justify or rationalize their positions. These are aimed at multiple audiences, especially third countries that know little about the details of the problem. The Chinese have been far more active with a series of official statements, which have been getting progressively tougher towards India.

The nub of the Chinese position, set out at length in their latest statement, is that Indian troops have crossed a settled international boundary and entered Chinese territory. This needs some historical perspective. Is the Doklam area assuredly Chinese territory? Hardly. China claims the area, but it is disputed by Bhutan. And the two sides have had 24 rounds of talks.

The Chinese are right in stating that the boundary between Sikkim and Tibet was defined by the Anglo-Chinese convention of 1890. This is the basis of their claim that India has violated a settled international boundary with China. There are two aspects to this issue. First, since Bhutan was not a signatory to this treaty, is the tri-junction between Tibet, Sikkim and Bhutan—which is also the eastern extremity of the boundary between Tibet and Sikkim—binding on Bhutan? Second, how solid is the Chinese claim about their preferred tri-junction?

In 1890, the British government could not presume to speak for Bhutan in the same way that it could for Sikkim. Following the Treaty of Titalia signed between the ruler of Sikkim and the East India Company in 1817, the British government of India assumed the power of paramountcy vis-à-vis Sikkim—a relationship akin to that with other "princely states" of India. Hence, Britain's ability to negotiate the Sikkim and Tibet boundary with China.

By contrast, the Treaty of Sinchula signed between Britain and Bhutan in 1865 did not lead to a similar relationship. In fact, the Treaty of Punakha concluded in 1910 modified the provisions of the Sinchula Treaty and added the following: "The British Government undertakes to exercise no interference in the internal administration of Bhutan. On its part, the Bhutanese Government agrees to be guided by the advice of the British Government in regard to its external relations." So, the 1890 Anglo-Chinese convention is not at all binding on Bhutan. The tri-junction remains to be fixed after tripartite negotiations.

The Chinese claim that Gipmochi (Gymochen)—mentioned in Article I of the 1890 Convention as the eastern extremity of the Sikkim-Tibet boundary—should automatically be the tri-junction is problematic for yet another reason. Article I states upfront: "The boundary of the Sikkim and Tibet shall be the crest of the mountain range separating the Waters flowing into Sikkim Teesta and its affluents from the waters flowing into the Tibetan Mochu and northwards into other rivers of Tibet." Only then does it identify Gipmochi as the starting point. The principle of defining the boundary therefore was the highest watershed: the highest line of mountains separating the rivers flowing on either side. This is the most logical way of drawing a boundary in mountainous regions.

However, subsequent surveys showed that Mount Gipmochi is not on the highest watershed in the area. The latter is the line running from Batangla to Merugla to Sinchela and then down to the Amo Chu river (known as Mochu in Tibet and Torsa in West Bengal). A glance at survey maps will confirm this. The Gipmochi peak is at 14,518ft above the mean sea level, while Merugla and Sinchela (both passes) are respectively at 15,266ft and 14,531ft. The Batangla-Merugla-Sinchela line is undeniably the highest watershed in the region. Hence Bhutan claims it as the boundary line with Tibet and regards Doklam area as its territory. Hence too, India's claim that Batangla should be the tri-junction.

Again, if these issues were not in contention, why should the Chinese have entered into negotiations with India on the Sikkim boundary as well as with Bhutan? In May 2006, India stated in a non-paper that "both sides agree on the boundary alignment in the Sikkim Sector," that is, on the principle of the highest watershed. The following month, the Chinese replied in their non-paper that based on the 1890 Convention, both sides may "verify and determine the specific alignment of the Sikkim sector and produce a common record." As the external affairs minister told Parliament, the Chinese subsequently made a proposal to finalize the Sikkim boundary, calling it an "early harvest". After follow-on negotiations, the two sides agreed in 2012 both on the "basis of the alignment" and on the need to fix the tri-junction in consultation with Bhutan. In short, the Chinese claim that the Sikkim border is already settled is disingenuous. Equally untenable is the claim by the Chinese deputy chief of mission in India that the 2012 understanding is immaterial to the current situation.

There are only three facts that matter to the current situation. First, China's construction of a road in violation of an understanding with Bhutan to maintain status quo. Second, China's attempt to create facts on the ground about the location of the tri-junction. Third, the presence of Indian troops on territory disputed between Bhutan and China. Restoration of status quo ante will require all sides to undo their actions.

All said, it is in India's interest to press for an early resolution. The assumption that this could be a prolonged standoff like the one in Sumdorong Chu in 1987 may be dangerous whistling in the dark.

ENDLESS ROUND OF BORDER DISPUTE NEGOTIATIONS BY CHINA

Endless rounds of border dispute negotiations have taken place between China and India. These have taken place at two levels, namely:

Joint Working Group (JWG) discussions which commenced in 1988

Special Representatives talks at the level of India's National Security Advisers and Chinese Vice Minister level since June 2003. The JWG has already completed over fifteen rounds of discussions. The Special Representatives held Seventh Round of talks in March 2006.

The standard responses after each round have been of the type that was stated in March 2006: "The two Special Representative continued their discussions for an agreed framework for the resolution of the boundary question in a constructive and friendly atmosphere". Chinese leaders on visits to India come out with the oft-repeated statement that the boundary dispute should be left to future generations to resolve and meanwhile China-India relations in other fields should move forward. This is just an excuse to keep alive the border dispute as a strategic pressure point against India.

This leads to the question whether China is really serious about resolution of the China-India border dispute?

The endless round of negotiations does not suggest so. It is best exemplified by an Indian media news report that no meetings have been scheduled between Indian and Chinese Special Representatives for talks on the boundary dispute before the visit of Chinese President Hu Jintao on November 20 "as India doesn't expect any substantive progress on the border issue in the near future." Symbolically, China's reluctance can be read as dissatisfaction with growing US-India strategic relationship and keeping alive the border dispute as a strategic pressure point against India. Obviously China is actively involved in delays and prolonging the resolution of the boundary disputes for strategic reasons.

Strategic Reluctance on Boundary Settlement with India by China

Veiled references in the past were made by Indian official spokesmen that progress could not be made as China was constantly pressurizing India to accept a swap by India of Tawang in lieu of Aksai-Chin. China has now come out in the open to demand and advocate this proposal. An Indian news-report covering the closed door meeting organized between Chinese distinguished experts and Indian academics by China's Institute of Asia-Pacific Studies, which is part of the giant official Chinese Academy of Social Sciences had this to report:

Chinese experts said that China would be magnanimous on the issue of Aksai Chin area if India agreed to give up Tawang. The high-level Chinese experts which included former Chinese Ambassador to India Chen Rui

Sheng made it clear that the border dispute could be solved if India handed over Tawang to China.

The Strategic Significance of Tawang for India

At the outset it must be made clear that for the Chinese, Tawang is not just the Tawang Monastery region. For them Tawang implies the whole of India's Arunachal Pradesh. So as not to dilute their claim, they officially will not call it that Arunachal Pradesh should be returned to them. Coming to the strategic importance of Arunachal Pradesh or Tawang in Chinese parlance the following need to be recognized: Arunachal Pradesh provides strategic depth to India's Brahmaputra Valley and India's other North Eastern states. Arunachal Pradesh provides security to Bhutan on it entire Eastern flank by geographical contiguity.

Bhutan would be then be in a pincer group of China on both it flanks if Tawang is given away. This would be detrimental to India's security. China's borders would then rest on the plains of Assam; India might as well write off its other North Eastern states. The Chinese obsession with the Tawang Region is totally strategic in its aims. In any future conflict with China and if India singly or in coalition with some other power develops offensive capabilities against China, this region offers the shortest cut to China proper and to Tibet. India's communications infrastructure in this region developed in World War II for US military aid to China is existent and can be further improved.

Arunachal Pradesh offers all-wealthier lines of communication to India for military needs to the Tibet border as compared to Aksai-Chin. In terms of any air operations by China in this region, Arunachal Pradesh would provide multilayered air defence deployments on the ground as deterrence. The region is rich in terms of mineral and natural resources prospects. There are many more reasons that one can state but the major ones should be enough. Arunachal Pradesh is of vital strategic importance for the territorial integrity and defence of India's North East states and should be non-negotiable.

China would be politically naive of it perceives that in the 21st Century, a powerfully rising India would accept the bait of a Chinese strategic barter of Aksai-Chin in lieu of Tawang India would be more politically naive than China if it thinks that China would concede the area of Aksai-Chin through which passes its lifelines to keep Xinjiang under Chinese control. Both in Aksai Chin and in the Arunachal Pradesh area, the strategic interests of China and India clash in the most intense manner. It would be a magical wonder if China can turn around to be strategically accommodative of India's strategic sensitivities. China's strategic reluctances to solve the border dispute with India can therefore be expected to bedevil China-India relations for a long time to come.

INDIA-CHINA STAND-OFF IN SIKKIM: CHINA FOR VIOLATING BILATERAL AGREEMENT

The tiny Himalayan nation of Bhutan has raised its voice against the mighty China asking it to not violate their bilateral agreement along the India-China-Bhutan tri-junction border in Sikkim, which has led to a stand-off between Indian and Chinese armies.

In a statement, Bhutan's foreign ministry said they have conveyed to the Chinese side, both on the ground and through the diplomatic channel, that the construction of the road inside Bhutanese territory is a direct violation of an agreement between them.

Bhutan said the move by China affects the process demarcating the boundary between the two countries. On June 16, the Chinese Army started construction of a motorable road from Dokola in the Doklam area towards the Bhutan Army camp at Zompelri.

"Boundary talks are ongoing between Bhutan and China and we have written agreements of 1988 and 1998 stating that the two sides agree to maintain peace and tranquillity in their border areas pending a final settlement on the boundary question, and to maintain status quo on the boundary as before March 1959," Bhutan said.

The agreements also state that the two sides will refrain from taking unilateral action, or use of force, to change the status quo of the boundary, it said. Bhutan hopes that the status quo in the Doklam area will be maintained as before June 16.

SIKKIM AS A BRITISH PROTECTORATE

In 1890, the Anglo-Chinese Convention, an agreement signed between the British and Chinese monarchies, Sikkim was declared as a "protectorate" of the British Empire. Over the next few decades, Sikkim became a full-fledged Princely State in British Colonial India.

Post-1947: Indian Protectorate

When the British left India, all Princely States, including Sikkim, became independent nations. A popular vote was conducted, over whether Sikkim should become a part of the Indian Union, and the people rejected the proposition. Sikkim continued to be an independent nation but in 1950,

Prime Minister Jawaharlal Nehru facilitated the signing of the Indo-Sikkim Treaty, under which Sikkim became an Indian protectorate. Sikkim would continue to be a sovereign nation but in matters of external affairs, defense and communications, it would defer to India.

Merger with India and Chinese Reaction

While Sikkim became a Constitutional monarchy under Indian suzerainty, anti-royal protests continued to break out in the Himalayan state. The Sikkim National Congress, a pro-India group, led the protests against the Chogyal of Sikkim. In 1975, the Prime Minister of Sikkim urged the Indian Parliament to merge Sikkim into the Union. In April, the Indian Army marched into Gangtok and disarmed the palace guards. A referendum was held and the people of Sikkim voted overwhelmingly, with a 97.5% majority, to join the Indian Union. In May 1975, the Kingdom of Sikkim became the 22nd state in the Union of India.

China, however, refused to acknowledge the democratic referendum as legitimate. Beijing continued to regard Sikkim as an independent nation, which it regarded as being occupied by India. China claimed that the referendum was conducted by India under military occupation.

Long-standing Issue

After Sikkim's accession to India, several high-level meetings were held between New Delhi and Beijing. Despite visits from then External Affairs Minister Atal Bihari Vajpayee, Prime Ministers Rajiv Gandhi and PV Narsimha Rao and Chinese premiers Li Peng and Jiang Zemin, Sikkim continued to be a thorn in Sino-Indian relations. It was finally in 2003 that a compromise between the two nations led to a thaw. China agreed to officially recognize Sikkim as an Indian state on the condition that India declared Tibet as a part of China. However, the biggest development on the India-China freeze over Sikkim came with the opening of the ancient Himalayan pass Nathu La in 2006 as a border crossing. The two nations agreed to allow trade through the route, which laid to rest the dispute over whether Sikkim was a part of Indian territory.

Sikkim

Sikkim is a state in Northeast India. It borders the Tibet Autonomous Region in the north and northeast, Bhutan in the east, Nepal in the west and the Indian state of West Bengal in the south. Sikkim is also located close to India's Siliguri Corridor near Bangladesh. Sikkim is the least populous and second smallest among the Indian states. A part of the Eastern Himalaya,

Sikkim is notable for its biodiversity, including alpine and subtropical climates, as well as being a host to Kanchenjunga, the highest peak in India and third highest on Earth. Sikkim's capital and largest city is Gangtok. Almost 35% of the state is covered by the Khangchendzonga National Park.

The Kingdom of Sikkim was founded on the Silk Road by the Namgyal dynasty in the 17th century. It was ruled by a Buddhist priest-king known as the Chogyal. It became a princely state of British India in 1890. After 1947, Sikkim continued its protectorate status with the republic of India. It enjoyed the highest literacy rate and per capita income among Himalayan states. In 1975, the Indian military deposed the Sikkimese monarchy. A referendum in 1975 led to Sikkim joining India as its 22nd state.

Modern Sikkim is a multiethnic and multilingual Indian state. Sikkim has 11 official languages: Nepali, Sikkimese, Lepcha, Tamang, Limbu, Newari, Rai, Gurung, Magar, Sunwar and English. English is taught in schools and used in government documents. The predominant religions are Hinduism and Vajrayana Buddhism. Sikkim's economy is largely dependent on agriculture and tourism, and as of 2014 the state had the third-smallest GDP among Indian states, although it is also among the fastest-growing.

Sikkim accounts for the largest share of cardamom production in India, and is the world's second largest producer of the spice after Guatemala. Sikkim achieved its ambition to convert its agriculture to fully organic over the interval 2003 to 2016, the first state in India to achieve this distinction. It is also among India's most environmentally conscious states, having banned plastic water bottles and styrofoam products.

Toponymy

The origin theory of the name *Sikkim* is that it is a combination of two Limbu words: *su*, which means "new", and *khyim*, which means "palace" or "house". The Tibetan name for Sikkim is *Drenjong* (Wylie-transliteration: *'bras ljongs*), which means "valley of rice",while the Bhutias call it *Beyul Demazong*, which means '"the hidden valley of rice". According to the folklore, after establishing Rabdentse as his new capital Bhutia king Tensung Namgyal built a palace and asked his Limbu Queen to name it. The Lepcha people, the original inhabitants of Sikkim, called it *Nye-mae-el*, meaning "paradise". In historical Indian literature, Sikkim is known as *Indrakil*, the garden of the war god Indra.

History

The Lepchas are considered to be the earliest inhabitants of Sikkim. However the Limbus and the Magars also lived in the inaccessible parts of

West and South districts as early as the Lepchas perhaps lived in the East and North districts. The Buddhist saint Padmasambhava, also known as Guru Rinpoche, is said to have passed through the land in the 8th century. The Guru is reported to have blessed the land, introduced Buddhism, and foretold the era of monarchy that would arrive in Sikkim centuries later.

Foundation of the monarchy

According to legend, Khye Bumsa, a 14th-century prince from the Minyak House in Kham in eastern Tibet, received a divine revelation instructing him to travel south to seek his fortunes. A fifth-generation descendant of Khye Bumsa, Phuntsog Namgyal, became the founder of Sikkim's monarchy in 1642, when he was consecrated as the first Chogyal, or priest-king, of Sikkim by the three venerated lamas at Yuksom. Phuntsog Namgyal was succeeded in 1670 by his son, Tensung Namgyal, who moved the capital from Yuksom to Rabdentse (near modern Pelling). In 1700, Sikkim was invaded by the Bhutanese with the help of the half-sister of the Chogyal, who had been denied the throne. The Bhutanese were driven away by the Tibetans, who restored the throne to the Chogyal ten years later. Between 1717 and 1733, the kingdom faced many raids by the Nepalese in the west and Bhutanese in the east, culminating with the destruction of the capital Rabdentse by the Nepalese. In 1791, China sent troops to support Sikkim and defend Tibet against the Gorkha Kingdom. Following the subsequent defeat of Gorkha, the Chinese Qing dynastyestablished control over Sikkim.

During the British Raj

Following the beginning of British rule in neighbouring India, Sikkim allied with Britain against their common adversary, Nepal. The Nepalese attacked Sikkim, overrunning most of the region including the Terai. This prompted the British East India Company to attack Nepal, resulting in the Gurkha Warof 1814. Treaties signed between Sikkim and Nepal resulted in the return of the territory annexed by the Nepalese in 1817. However, ties between Sikkim and the British weakened when the latter began taxation of the Morang region. In 1849, two British physicians, Sir Joseph Dalton Hooker and Dr. Archibald Campbell, the latter being in charge of relations between the British and Sikkimese governments, ventured into the mountains of Sikkim unannounced and unauthorised. The doctors were detained by the Sikkimese government, leading to a punitive British expedition against the kingdom, after which the Darjeeling district and Morang were annexed to British India in 1853. The invasion led to the Chogyal of Sikkim becoming a titular ruler under the directive of the British governor.

Sikkim became a British protectorate in the later decades of the 19th century, formalised by a convention signed with China in 1890. Sikkim was gradually granted more sovereignty over the next three decades, and became a member of the Chamber of Princes, the assembly representing the rulers of the Indian princely states, in 1922.

Indian protectorate and statehood

Prior to the Indian independence, Jawaharlal Nehru, as the Vice President of the Executive Council, pushed through a resolution in the Indian Constituent Assembly to the effect that Sikkim and Bhutan, as Himilayan states, were not 'Indian states' and their future should be negotiated separately. A standstill agreement was signed in February 1948.

Meanwhile, the Indian independence and its move to democracy spurred a fledgling political movement in Sikkim, giving rise to the formation of Sikkim State Congress (SSC). The party sent a plate of demands to the palace, including a demand for accession to India. The palace attempted to defuse the movement by appointing three secretaries from the SSC to the government and sponsoring a counter-movement in the name of Sikkim National Party, which opposed accession to India.

The demand for responsible government continued and the SSC launched a civil disobedience movement. The Chogyal Palden Thondup Namgyal asked India for help in quelling the movement, which was offered in the form of a small military police force and an Indian Dewan. In 1950, a treaty was agreed between India and Sikkim which gave Sikkim the status of an Indian protectorate. Sikkim came under the suzerainty of India, which controlled its external affairs, defence, diplomacy and communications. In other respects, Sikkim retained administrative autonomy.

A state council was established in 1953 to allow for constitutional government under the Chogyal. Despite pressures from an India "bent on annexation", Chogyal Palden Thondup Namgyal was able to preserve autonomy and shape a "model Asian state" where the literacy rate and per capita income were twice as high as neighbouring Nepal, Bhutan and India. Meanwhile, the India-backed Sikkim National Congress demanded fresh elections and greater representation for Nepalis in Sikkim. People marched on the palace against the monarchy. In 1973, antiroyalist riots took place in front of the Chogyal's palace.

In 1975, the Prime Minister of Sikkim appealed to the Indian Parliament for Sikkim to become a state of India. In April of that year, the Indian Army took over the city of Gangtok and disarmed the Chogyal's palace guards.

Thereafter, a referendum was held in which 97.5 per cent of voters supported abolishing the monarchy, effectively approving union with India. India is said to have stationed 20,000–40,000 troops in a country of only 200,000 during the referendum. On 16 May 1975, Sikkim became the 22nd state of the Indian Union, and the monarchy was abolished. To enable the incorporation of the new state, the Indian Parliament amended the Indian Constitution. First, the 35th Amendment laid down a set of conditions that made Sikkim an "Associate State", a special designation not used by any other state. A month later, the 36th Amendment repealed the 35th Amendment, and made Sikkim a full state, adding its name to the First Schedule of the Constitution.

Recent history

In 2000, the seventeenth Karmapa, Urgyen Trinley Dorje, who had been confirmed by the Dalai Lama and accepted as a tulku by the Chinese government, escaped from Tibet, seeking to return to the Rumtek Monastery in Sikkim. Chinese officials were in a quandary on this issue, as any protests to India would mean an explicit endorsement of India's governance of Sikkim, which China still recognised as an independent state occupied by India. The Chinese government eventually recognised Sikkim as an Indian state in 2003, on the condition that India officially recognise Tibet as a part of China; New Delhi had originally accepted Tibet as a part of China in 1953 during the government of Jawaharlal Nehru. The 2003 agreement led to a thaw in Sino-Indian relations, and on 6 July 2006, the Sikkimese Himalayan pass of Nathu La was opened to cross-border trade, becoming the first open border between India and China. The pass, which had previously been closed since the 1962 Sino-Indian War, was an offshoot of the ancient Silk Road.

On 18 September 2011, a magnitude 6.9M_w earthquake struck Sikkim, killing at least 116 people in the state and in Nepal, Bhutan, Bangladesh and Tibet. More than 60 people died in Sikkim alone, and the city of Gangtok suffered significant damage.

Geography

Nestling in the Himalayan mountains, the state of Sikkim is characterised by mountainous terrain. Almost the entire state is hilly, with an elevation ranging from 280 metres (920 ft) to 8,586 metres (28,169 ft). The summit of Kangchenjunga—the world's third-highest peak—is the state's highest point, situated on the border between Sikkim and Nepal. For the most part, the land is unfit for agriculture because of the rocky, precipitous slopes. However, some hill slopes have been converted into terrace farms.

Numerous snow-fed streams have carved out river valleys in the west and south of the state. These streams combine into the major Teesta River and its tributary, the Rangeet, which flow through the state from north to south. About a third of the state is heavily forested. The Himalayan mountains surround the northern, eastern and western borders of Sikkim. The Lower Himalayas, lying in the southern reaches of the state, are the most densely populated.

The state has 28 mountain peaks, more than 80 glaciers, 227 high-altitude lakes (including the Tsongmo, Gurudongmar and Khecheopalri Lakes), five major hot springs, and more than 100 rivers and streams. Eight mountain passes connect the state to Tibet, Bhutan and Nepal.

Sikkim's hot springs are renowned for their medicinal and therapeutic values. Among the state's most notable hot springs are those at Phurchachu, Yumthang, Borang, Ralang, Taram-chu and Yumey Samdong. The springs, which have a high sulphur content, are located near river banks; some are known to emit hydrogen. The average temperature of the water in these hot springs is 50 °C (122 °F).

Geology

The hills of Sikkim mainly consist of gneiss and schist which weather to produce generally poor and shallow brown clay soils. The soil is coarse, with large concentrations of iron oxide; it ranges from neutral to acidic and is lacking in organic and mineral nutrients. This type of soil tends to support evergreen and deciduous forests.

The rock consists of phyllites and schists, and is highly susceptible to weathering and erosion. This, combined with the state's heavy rainfall, causes extensive soil erosion and the loss of soil nutrients through leaching. As a result, landslides are frequent, often isolating rural towns and villages from the major urban centres.

Climate

The state has five seasons: winter, summer, spring, autumn, and a monsoon season between June and September. Sikkim's climate ranges from sub-tropical in the south to tundra in the north. Most of the inhabited regions of Sikkim experience a temperate climate, with temperatures seldom exceeding 28 °C (82 °F) in summer. The average annual temperature for most of Sikkim is around 18 °C (64 °F).

Sikkim is one of the few states in India to receive regular snowfall. The snow line ranges from 6,100 metres (20,000 ft) in the south of the state to

4,900 metres (16,100 ft) in the north. The tundra-type region in the north is snowbound for four months every year, and the temperature drops below 0 °C (32 °F) almost every night. In north-western Sikkim, the peaks are frozen year-round; because of the high altitude, temperatures in the mountains can drop to as low as "40 °C ("40 °F) in winter.

During the monsoon, heavy rains increase the risk of landslides. The record for the longest period of continuous rain in Sikkim is 11 days. Fog affects many parts of the state during winter and the monsoons, making transportation perilous.

Government and politics

According to the Constitution of India, Sikkim has a parliamentary system of representative democracy for its governance; universal suffrageis granted to state residents. The government structure is organised into three branches:

- Executive: As with all states of India, a governor stands at the head of the executive power of state, just as the president is the head of the executive power in the Union, and is appointed by the President of India. The governor's appointment is largely ceremonial, and his or her main role is to oversee the swearing-in of the Chief Minister. The Chief Minister, who holds the real executive powers, is the head of the party or coalition garnering the largest majority in the state elections. The governor also appoints cabinet ministers on the advice of the Chief Minister.
- Legislature: Sikkim has a unicameral legislature, the Sikkim Legislative Assembly, like most other Indian states. Its state assembly has 32 seats, including one reserved for the Sangha. Sikkim is allocated one seat in each of the two chambers of India's national bicamerallegislature, the Lok Sabha and the Rajya Sabha.
- Judiciary: The judiciary consists of the Sikkim High Court and a system of lower courts. The High Court, located at Gangtok, has a Chief Justice along with two permanent justices. The Sikkim High Court is the smallest state high court in the country.

In 1975, after the abrogation of Sikkim's monarchy, the Indian National Congress gained a majority in the 1977 elections. In 1979, after a period of instability, a popular ministry headed by Nar Bahadur Bhandari, leader of the Sikkim Sangram Parishad Party, was sworn in. Bhandari held on to power in the 1984 and 1989 elections. In the 1994 elections, Pawan Kumar Chamling of the Sikkim Democratic Front became the Chief Minister of the state.

Chamling and his party have since held on to power by winning the 1999, 2004, 2009 and 2014 elections. Currently, the Governor of Sikkim is Shriniwas Dadasaheb Patil.

Subdivisions

Sikkim has four districts – East Sikkim, North Sikkim, South Sikkim and West Sikkim. The district capitals are Gangtok, Mangan, Namchi and Gyalshingrespectively. These four districts are further divided into subdivisions; Pakyong and Rongli are the subdivisions of the East district, Soreng is the subdivision of the West district, Chungthang is the subdivision of the North district and Ravongla is the subdivision of the South district.

Each of Sikkim's districts is overseen by a Central Government appointee, the district collector, who is in charge of the administration of the civilian areas of the district. The Indian Army has control over a large part of the state, as Sikkim forms part of a sensitive border area with China. Many areas are restricted to foreigners, and official permits are needed to visit them.

Flora and fauna

Sikkim is situated in an ecological hotspot of the lower Himalayas, one of only three among the ecoregions of India. The forested regions of the state exhibit a diverse range of fauna and flora. Owing to its altitudinal gradation, the state has a wide variety of plants, from tropical species to temperate, alpine and tundra ones, and is perhaps one of the few regions to exhibit such a diversity within such a small area. Nearly 81 per cent of the area of Sikkim comes under the administration of its forest department.

Sikkim is home to around 5,000 species of flowering plants, 515 rare orchids, 60 primula species, 36 rhododendron species, 11 oak varieties, 23 bamboo varieties, 16 conifer species, 362 types of ferns and ferns allies, 8 tree ferns, and over 900 medicinal plants. A variant of the Poinsettia, locally known as "Christmas Flower", can be found in abundance in the mountainous state. The Noble Dendrobium is the official flower of Sikkim, while the rhododendron is the state tree.

Orchids, figs, laurel, bananas, sal trees and bamboo grow in the Himalayan subtropical broadleaf forests of the lower altitudes of Sikkim. In the temperate elevations above 1,500 metres (4,900 ft) there are Eastern Himalayan broadleaf forests, where oaks, chestnuts, maples, birches, alders, and magnolias grow in large numbers, as well as Himalayan subtropical pine forests, dominated by Chir pine. Alpine-typevegetation is typically found between an altitude of 3,500 to 5,000 metres (11,500 to 16,400 ft). In lower elevations are found juniper, pine, firs, cypresses and rhododendrons from the Eastern Himalayan subalpine conifer forests. Higher up are Eastern Himalayan alpine shrub and meadows, home to a broad variety of rhododendrons and wildflowers.

The fauna of Sikkim include the snow leopard, musk deer, Himalayan tahr, red panda, Himalayan marmot, Himalayan serow, Himalayan goral, muntjac, common langur, Asian black bear, clouded leopard, marbled cat, leopard cat, dhole, Tibetan wolf, hog badger, binturong, and Himalayan jungle cat. Among the animals more commonly found in the alpine zone are yaks, mainly reared for their milk, meat, and as a beast of burden.

The avifauna of Sikkim include the impeyan pheasant, crimson horned pheasant, snow partridge, Tibetan snowcock, bearded vulture and griffon vulture, as well as golden eagles, quails, plovers, woodcocks, sandpipers, pigeons, Old World flycatchers, babblers and robins. Sikkim has more than 550 species of birds, some of which have been declared endangered.

Sikkim also has a rich diversity of arthropods, many of which remain unstudied; the most studied Sikkimese arthropods are butterflies. Of the approximately 1,438 butterfly species found in the Indian subcontinent, 695 have been recorded in Sikkim. These include the endangered Kaiser-i-hind, the Yellow Gorgon and the Bhutan Glory.

Economy

Sikkim's nominal state gross domestic product (GDP) was estimated at US$1.57 billion in 2014, constituting the third-smallest GDP among India's 28 states. The state's economy is largely agrarian, based on the terraced farming of rice and the cultivation of crops such as maize, millet, wheat, barley, oranges, tea and cardamom. Sikkim produces more cardamom than any other Indian state, and is home to the largest cultivated area of cardamom.

Because of its hilly terrain and poor transport infrastructure, Sikkim lacks a large-scale industrial base. Brewing, distilling, tanning and watchmaking are the main industries, and are mainly located in the southern regions of the state, primarily in the towns of Melli and Jorethang. In addition, a small mining industry exists in Sikkim, extracting minerals such as copper, dolomite, talc, graphite, quartzite, coal, zinc and lead. Despite the state's minimal industrial infrastructure, Sikkim's economy has been among the fastest-growing in India since 2000; the state's GDP expanded by 89.93 per cent in 2010 alone. In 2003, Sikkim decided to convert fully to organic farming statewide, and achieved this goal in 2015, becoming India's first "organic state".

In recent years, the government of Sikkim has extensively promoted tourism. As a result, state revenue has increased 14 times since the mid-1990s. Sikkim has furthermore invested in a fledgling gambling industry, promoting both casinos and online gambling. The state's first casino, the Casino Sikkim, opened in March 2009, and the government subsequently issued a number of additional casino licences and online sports betting licenses. The Playwin lottery has been a notable success in the state.

The opening of the Nathu La pass on 6 July 2006, connecting Lhasa, Tibet, to India, was billed as a boon for Sikkim's economy. Trade through the pass remains hampered by Sikkim's limited infrastructure and government restrictions in both India and China, though the volume of traded goods has been steadily increasing.

SIMMERING BORDER TENSIONS

Long-standing border disputes between China and India continue to cause friction between the two countries despite ongoing border talks that started in the 1980s. India claims that China occupies more than 14,000 square miles of Indian territory in the Aksai Chin along its northern border in Kashmir (commonly referred to as the western sector), while China lays claim to more than 34,000 square miles of India's northeastern state of Arunachal Pradesh (commonly referred to as the eastern sector). The two sides fought a brief border war in 1962 after China invaded the eastern and western sectors of their shared borders and ended up annexing the area of Aksai Chin, a barren plateau that had been part of the pre-partition princely state of Jammu and Kashmir. India also is a long-term host to the Dalai Lama and about 100,000 Tibetan refugees that fled after China annexed Tibet in 1950.

Meanwhile, according to Beijing, India is occupying territory unfairly claimed during the era of "unequal treaties." The Chinese Communist Party (CCP) has never accepted the validity of the McMahon Line as the demarcation of the Sino-Indian border in Tibet, viewing it as forced upon weak imperial and republican governments by the British Raj.

In 2003, each side appointed "special representatives" – national security adviser for India and vice foreign minister for China—to upgrade and regularise their border discussions. Since then, the two sides have clarified the mapping of the middle sector of their disputed frontiers (the border that demarcates the Indian state of Sikkim). However, there has been no exchange of maps of the eastern and western sectors under dispute.

China's interest in consolidating its hold on Tibet and its perceptions of India's expanding global influence and closer ties to the U.S. have led Beijing to harden its position on its border disputes with New Delhi over the past five years. China has increasingly questioned Indian sovereignty over the states of Arunachal Pradesh and Jammu and Kashmir and has stepped up probing operations along different parts of their shared frontier. The Chinese are also building up military infrastructure and expanding a network of road, rail, and air links in the border areas.

The hardening Chinese position can be traced back to comments made by the Chinese ambassador to India, referring to the entire state of Arunachal Pradesh as part of China, in the run-up to President Hu Jintao's November 2006 visit.

Moreover, in recent years, Chinese commentators have begun to refer to Arunachal Pradesh commonly as "Southern Tibet." Prior to 2005, there were no Chinese references to "Southern Tibet" in China's official media. In 2009, China opposed an Asian Development Bank loan, part of which was earmarked for a watershed project in Arunachal Pradesh – another demonstration that China is questioning Indian sovereignty over the state more openly.

These moves have signalled to New Delhi that the Chinese may be backing away from a 2005 border agreement, referred to as the "Agreement on Political Parameters and Guiding Principles for Settlement of the Boundary Question." More specifically, since the 2005 accord stipulated that "settled populations will not be disturbed," India argues that China has violated the 2005 agreement by laying claim to Tawang in Arunachal Pradesh. Chinese interlocutors claim Tawang is part of Tibet because one of the Dalai Lamas was born there. The Chinese have objected to recent visits to Tawang by the Indian Prime Minister and the Dalai Lama.

In addition to raising questions about the status of Arunachal Pradesh, China has called into question Indian sovereignty over the state of Jammu and Kashmir. In 2009, Beijing began stapling visas to Indian passport holders from Jammu and Kashmir. Furthermore, in July of last year, China denied a visa to Indian Lieutenant General B. S. Jaswal, chief of Northern Command, which includes parts of Kashmir. General Jaswal had intended to travel to Beijing to participate in a high-level China-India defence exchange. In response to China's refusal to grant General Jaswal a visa, India suspended further bilateral defence exchanges.

The visa issue appears to have been resolved, as India resumed defence contacts with China last month by sending an eight-member Indian military delegation to China. The visit followed media reports that China had begun issuing regular visas to Indian residents of Jammu and Kashmir.

Since the 1999 Kargil border conflict between India and Pakistan, Beijing's position on Kashmir seemed to be evolving toward a more neutral position. During that conflict, Beijing helped convince Pakistan to withdraw forces from the Indian side of the Line of Control following its incursion into the heights of Kargil in Kashmir. Beijing made clear its position that the two sides should resolve the Kashmir conflict through bilateral negotiations, not military force, but the stapled visas issue and Beijing's refusal to grant a visa to the Indian army official from Kashmir have raised concern in New Delhi that China is reverting to a policy of favouring Pakistan's position on Kashmir.

Indian commentators have noted that China's backtracking from its neutral position on Kashmir would likely be met with subtle moves by India that increasingly question Chinese sovereignty over Tibet.

Increasing Military Activities

Meanwhile, Chinese military activities in the region have expanded. In July 2010, the official newspaper of the PLA, People's Liberation Army Daily, reported that units of the People's Liberation Army Air Force (PLAAF) were engaging in armed combat air patrols. These are believed to have been advanced Su-27 or J-11 (domestically produced versions of the Su-27) fighter aircraft.

The combat air patrols were followed by an August 2010 logistics exercise involving the newly constructed Qinghai-Tibet railway. This exercise marked the first PLAAF use of the railway for military purposes, with the Military Transportation Department of the PLAAF Logistics Department overseeing the movement of "combat readiness materials" to Tibet. This would seem to reflect a growing PLAAF role in maintaining security along the Sino-Indian border in the Tibetan area.

In October 2010, there were reports that the PLA had conducted joint (inter-services) live-fire exercises in Tibet for the first time. These reportedly involved armour, artillery, air, and electronic warfare units and a variety of new equipment. Given the emphasis placed on joint operations in PLA doctrine, such exercises are not surprising, but instead reflect the extent to which they are being applied across the military, not just opposite Taiwan.

Indian expert observers do not interpret China's new-found assertiveness as preparation for imminent conflict, and they continue to calculate that the overall probability of another Sino-Indian war is low. However, they believe China may be trying to enhance its bargaining position in the ongoing border negotiations. The Indian observers note that incursions across the disputed borders are likely aimed at gaining tactical advantage to bolster Chinese territorial claims.

India has somewhat belatedly sought to match the Chinese moves and to reinforce its own claims in the disputed border areas by augmenting forces and constructing roads along the shared frontiers. These measures include the deployment of two squadrons of Su-30 MKI fighter jets in Assam and the raising of two mountain divisions for deployment in Arunachal Pradesh. India also has redeployed elements of its 27th Mountain Division from Jammu and Kashmir to the patch of land that intersects India, Tibet, and Bhutan and links India with the rest of its northeastern states.

India is reviving air fields along the border with China, including one in the Ladakh region.

India must increasingly factor the potential threat of conflict over its disputed borders with China into its security planning and projections. While Indian strategists assess that Pakistan poses the most immediate threat to India, they increasingly view China as the more important long-term strategic threat.

In order to deter Chinese aggression along India's border, Indian strategists believe they must develop the capability to inflict severe damage on Chinese forces in Tibet. China has an edge over India with regard to overall air power. Given infrastructure constraints in Tibet, however, China's ability to deploy significant air power on the border with India remains in question.

THE TIBETAN QUESTION AND THE CAUSE OF THE DISPUTE

The fact is that a large part of the border dispute hinges on the uncomfortable question of Tibet's sovereignty. If Tibet was sovereign at the time of the Simla conference, then the treaty is legal and it serves India's cause. If Tibet was not sovereign at that time, then the treaty is illegal and serves China's cause. Some activists campaigning for a free Tibet often bring up the Simla conference as proof of Tibet's independence. Their arguments are mainly two fold -

a) The Tibetan representative signed the treaty even though he was instructed by the Chinese representative not to sign, a clear indication undermining (Tibetan acceptance of) Chinese suzerainty over Tibet.
b) More importantly, since Tibet concluded a treaty with a foreign power on its own,*it was an independent country on that day.*

At the time of the Simla conference, although the Tibetan government had driven out all Chinese officials from Tibet after the collapse of the Qing dynasty and declared independence, the Nationalist government did not accept this and neither has the PRC nor any other government.

India had enjoyed certain privileges with regard to Tibet under the Simla Agreement, including those regarding trade and commerce. However, when China 'annexed' Tibet in 1951, India under Nehru recognized it as Chinese territory, thus giving up those privileges and undermining Tibet's sovereignty (which it may have momentarily enjoyed during the time of the Simla agreement). Thus in a sense the Indian government tacitly admitted that the Simla agreement was effectively illegal, which to this day remains China's official position. In doing so, India weakened its own position with respect to the border dispute. The Simla agreement was signed between Britain, Tibet and China. Now, from this information, two questions present themselves -

1) If Tibet *was* sovereign, why was China invited at the conference at all? Why didn't the British negotiate directly with Tibet?
2) If Tibet was *not* sovereign, why was *it* invited at the conference? Why didn't the British negotiate directly with China? (In other words, why did China accept to attend a conference where Tibet was represented as a separate party?)

The answer to (1) is that, as stated above, Britain recognised Tibet to be under Chinese suzerainty. Hence, any *bilateral* agreement that Britain signed with Tibet (without Chinese agreement) would be illegal. (But ironically, that is exactly what the British did)

(2) is a bit more complicated. There are indications that the British had blackmailed the Chinese into attending by threatening to -

a) withdraw their recognition of the new nationalist government, and,
b) sign the treaty with Tibet alone if China didn't participate, thus acknowledging that Tibet was in fact sovereign. (But later the British did exactly the same thing when China didn't agree to its terms during the conference).

Hence, it is clear that Britain's imperial designs and its policy of 'divide and rule' and double crossing everyone was in effect the cause of the entire dispute.

DOKLAM STANDOFF: TERSE VERSES

On June 30, the People's Liberation Army (PLA) spokesperson Col Wu Qian warned Army chief General Bipin Rawat to "stop clamouring for war", dismissing the latter's remarks that India was ready for a "two-and-a-half front war" as "extremely irresponsible". PLA spokesperson Col Wu Qian told reporters: "We hope that the particular person in the Indian Army could learn from historical lessons and stop such clamouring for war." In response to this, Union Defence Minister Arun Jaitley hit back at Beijing and asserted that the India of 2017 is different from what it used to be 55 years ago. "If they are trying to remind us, the situation in 1962 was different and India of 2017 is different," Jaitley said. Asking India to withdraw, China said the "trespassing" of Indian troops in Doklam was a "betrayal" of a treaty signed in 1890, and India had used Bhutan as an "excuse" to violate the international border between the two countries. A day before the G20 summit was supposed to begin in Hamburg, Germany, China dismissed the prospect of a meeting between Chinese president Xi Jinping and PM Narendra Modi, saying the "atmosphere is not right for a bilateral meeting". China once again demanded the withdrawal of Indian troops, citing it as a "pre-condition" for any talks to take place between the two countries.

With the stand-off continuing for over a month, Minister for External affairs Sushma Swaraj said in Parliament that India has the support of "all countries". Swaraj also demanded both countries to withdraw their troops in order to have a conversation on the issue. In response to Swaraj's comment, Chinese media mouthpiece Global Times said she had "lied" in the Parliament. It also warned of China resolving the "conflict through non-diplomatic means", highlighting the military strength of the Chinese forces. "The China-India border area may become a stage where China showcases the achievement of its long-term military development and reforms," it said.

Doklam standoff: NSAs meet

On the sidelines of the BRICS summit, National Security Advisor Ajit Doval met Chinese State Councillor Yang Jiechi and held talks which Beijing said included "major problems" and "regional issues". The two sides have remained tight-lipped about what was discussed in the meeting. After meeting National Security Advisors (NSAs) of BRICS countries, Chinese President Xi Jinping praised their efforts in enhancing mutual trust and cooperation. Doval said "vital" issues discussed at the meeting of the NSAs and its outcome will have an "impact" on the main summit in September. At an event marking the 90th anniversary of People's Liberation Army, Chinese President Xi Jinping said China has the "confidence to defeat all invasions". "No one should expect us to swallow the bitter fruit that is harmful to our sovereignty, security or development interests," he added. Though his comments did not point to anyone in particular, their timing seemed to them being directed at India.

Last week, reports emerged of Chinese soldiers making a brief transgression into Indian territory at the Barahoti area in Chamoli district in Uttarakhand on July 25. According to sources, this was the second such incident in the region this month — the first was on July 15. Sources said 15-20 soldiers came in at each time.

BHUTAN-CHINA BORDER NEGOTIATIONS

470 out of Bhutan's 1,075-kilometer border are adhered to China and the rest 605 to India. Bhutan was once the bridge between Tibet and the east part of South Asia, and shares intimate religious, political, economic, and cultural bonds with Tibet. The Tibetan people cross the Himalayas along the Manas Chhu in east Bhutan and Paro Valley in west Bhutan to Assam, Bangladesh, and Bihar for religious, cultural, and trade activities. The twice-per-year bazaar fair in Bumthang, east Bhutan is a huge attraction for many Tibetan people. The Tibetan caravans offer wool, brick tea, edible salt, and musk in exchange for Bhutan's rice, paper, and dried pepper. Local governments of Tibet deploy officials in areas near Bhutan to purchase rice. It has been a ritual for Tibetans to travel a long distance along the Manas Chhu to embark on pilgrimage at monasteries near Guwahati, Assam. The influx of Tibetan refuges forced Bhutan to close its border with China in 1959, shutting down all cross-border trade activities. No formal trade or commercial relations has been established between Bhutan and China since then.

As a large part of Bhutan-China border is unclear, the focus on China-Bhutan relationship is to resolve border dispute. Border issues between Bhutan and China used to be incorporated into China-India border discussions. In 1959, then PRC Premier Zhou Enlai issued a letter to India Prime Minister Jawaharlal Nehru expressing China's wish to stage direct bilateral talk with Bhutan. The letter suggests Zhou's intention to separate China-Bhutan border issue from China-India border negotiations. Yet direct border negotiations between China and Bhutan did not begin until 1984. Since then, the capital cities of Beijing and Thimphu have been taking turns hosting the annual border negotiations. By 2004, 17 rounds of talk had been conducted, with the 17th round being held in Bhutan.

Core issues in China-Bhutan border disputes are as follows:

In the 10th round of border talk held in 1996, China proposed to exchange 495 sq km area of Pasamlung and Jakarlung valleys in the northern borders of Bhutan for Sinchulumpa, Dramana and Shakhtoe with an area of 269 sq km in the northwest Bhutan, which share borders with Sikkim, India, but no final decision was taken.

The 12th round held in Beijing in December 1998 centered on establishment of diplomatic and trade relations and ended with the signing of the Agreement between PRC and Kingdom of Bhutan on Peace and Stability in China-Bhutan Border Areas. The five-article agreement demands mutual respect and equal status regardless of the territory and power of a nation. In the agreement, China states its complete respect for Bhutan's independent status, sovereignty, and territorial integrity. The first article provides basis for friendly and good neighbourly cooperation between the two under the five principles of peaceful coexistence. It is understood between the two that differences in border issues had been alleviated and guiding principles for border issue settlement had been established through friendly negotiations in the previous 11 rounds based on the spirit of mutual understanding, mutual trust, and cooperation. The talks have deepened mutual understanding and strengthened traditional friendship between the two, and China and Bhutan are willing to strive together toward the shared objective of settling border disputes in fair and reasonable ways as soon as possible under the principles above. China and Bhutan hereby agree to maintain the status quo of the border as prior to March 1959 and ensure peace and stability of border region before a final solution is reached, and oppose unilateral efforts by either side to change the status quo. As for the progress in the last 11 rounds of border talk, as both sides have made clear their stance, both hereby agree to resolve the issue through friendly negotiations.

While both sides agreed on the need to maintain peace and stability in border region, no final decision was taken on territory exchange. The King of Bhutan once nodded his head on territory exchange in 1997. China again offered the above-mentioned 495 sq km area in the northern border of Bhutan in exchange for the 269 sq km in the northwest Bhutan. The talks came to a halt when the subject of territory exchange was raised. However, following the signing of agreement, Beijing immediately responded to the issues of mule routes and lumber exploration in Pasamlung, and assisted the Tibetan after they were harshly punished by Bhutanese border security troops in Pasamlung for entering Bhutan to collect Tibetan medical herbs. At that time, China was a little bit displeased with Bhutan's mentioning of new issues following years of border negotiations, and therefore agreed to let Bhutan's specialists determine the territory boundary and draw the map of both countries' territories, and also agreed to the use of standard names for areas under dispute to avoid confusion. The King of Bhutan once told the National Assembly that there are 4 areas under dispute, starting from Doklam in the west, along Gamochen at the border, to the river divide at Batangla and Sinchela, and down to the Amo Chhu River.

(1) Up to 89 sq km in Doklam are under dispute.

(2) Approximately 180 sq km in Sinchulumpa and Gieu are under dispute. The border line stretches from Langmarpo Zam along the river up to Docherimchang, through the river divide to Gomla, along the river divide to Pangkala, and finally down to the Dramana River.

(3) Starting from Dramana, along the border line up to Zingula, and along the line of river divide down to Gieu Chhu River, and finally to Lungkala

(4) Starting from the middle of Pasamlum, along the border line and the river divide to Dompala and Neula, going from Neula along the border line and the river divide to Kurichhu Tshozam, along the river divide to Genla then to Mela, and go all the way to the east.

By 1999 China and Bhutan had yet to resolve their border disputes. China sent delegation to Bhutan to carry on with border talks and managed to settle most of the major border disputes. The talks ended satisfactorily for both sides and China, for the first time, expressed their wish to provide financial assistance to Bhutan.

The 14th round of negotiation held in December 2000 saw Bhutan extending their border line further on the one provided by the China government. Bhutan also suggested that technical discussions between experts from both sides be held using maps. In July of the following year (2001), the King of Bhutan said to the National Assembly that border between Bhutan and China should stretch further along Doklam, Sinchulumpa and Dramana. The King also expressed faith that the border dispute between a small nation of Bhutan and a powerful, friendly nation of China would come to a successful settlement in the near future.

Several official interactions between China and Bhutan took place in 2001. The Bhutanese cultural delegation visited China in April, in July the Bhutanese delegation visited Beijing to conduct border talks, and in November the 15th round of border talk was held in Thimphu, capital of Bhutan. However, no final decision was reached with regard to the 3 places (Doklam, Sinchulumpa and Dramana) in question.

In July 2002, the Bhutanese Minister of Foreign Affairs revealed to the National Assembly that China had claimed to be in possession of the license of ownership of the 3 places. Bhutan asked China to extend the generosity of a superpower to a small country like Bhutan, but China replied that it cannot afford to be generous to every single neighbor considering that it has 25 other neighbours. Both sides agreed in the 16th round held in Beijing in October of the same year to create a mechanism in which the border would be examined by map experts from both sides.

No border talk was held in 2003. The 17th round, held in Thimphu in April 2004, saw both sides agreeing to assemble a team of specialists as soon as possible to examine the border. Both sides expressed wish to determine the border as soon as possible and decided to assemble a team of experts to examine the border as proposed by each.

Mutual visits continued, though not on a regular basis. During his visit to Bhutan in April 2003, Hua Junduo, PRC Ambassador to India, reiterated China's friendly, good neighbourly stance toward Bhutan. While there is no formal diplomatic ties between Bhutan and China, said Hua, the relationship is developing in a positive way, and actual relationship is more important than formal diplomatic ties.

Of all countries in Asia and China's neighbouring countries, Bhutan is the only one that has yet to establish formal diplomatic ties with China, preferring to keep a cautious distance from this powerful neighbor. The lack of formal ties has never affected Bhutan's support for China on the international scene. Examples of support include casting a vote in 1971 to keep China's place in the United Nations, inviting the PRC Ambassador to India to the coronation ceremony of King Wangchuck in 1974, speaking repeatedly in favour of China in the United Nations Human Rights Council meetings since 1995, and speaking against Taiwan's bid to host the 2002 Asian Games and the bid to join United Nations. Since 1979, leaders of both sides have been exchanging congratulatory messages on each side's National Day. In the 17th round of border talk held in 2004, King Wangchuck, during his meeting with head of Chinese delegation Wang Yi, reiterated Bhutan's friendly stance toward China, complimented China on its successful reform and opening up, and thanked China for its friendly and good neighbourly stance toward Bhutan. The King also pledged Bhutan's support for China in issues related to China's sovereignty such as Taiwan, human rights, and Tibet.

THE BORDER BETWEEN CHINA AND TIBET

China took advantage of this period of instability in Tibet to seize the regions of Amdo and Kham, making them into the Chinese province of Qinghai in 1724. Three years later, the Chinese and Tibetans signed a treaty that laid out the boundary line between the two nations. It would remain in force until 1910. Qing China had its hands full trying to control Tibet. The Emperor sent a commissioner to Lhasa, but he was killed in 1750. The Imperial Army then defeated the rebels, but the Emperor recognized that he would have to rule through the Dalai Lama rather than directly. Day-to-day decisions would be made on the local level.

Era of Turmoil Begins

In 1788, the Regent of Nepal sent Gurkha forces to invade Tibet. The Qing Emperor responded in strength, and the Nepalese retreated. The Gurkhas returned three years later, plundering and destroying some famous Tibetan monasteries. The Chinese sent a force of 17,000 which, along with Tibetan troops, drove the Gurkhas out of Tibet and south to within 20 miles of Kathmandu.

Despite this sort of assistance from the Chinese Empire, the people of Tibet chafed under increasingly meddlesome Qing rule. Between 1804, when the Eighth Dalai Lama died, and 1895, when the Thirteenth Dalai Lama assumed the throne, none of the incumbent incarnations of the Dalai Lama lived to see their nineteenth birthdays.

If the Chinese found a certain incarnation too hard to control, they would poison him. If the Tibetans thought an incarnation was controlled by the Chinese, then they would poison him themselves.

Tibet and the Great Game

Throughout this period, Russia and Britain were engaged in the "Great Game," a struggle for influence and control in Central Asia. Russia pushed south of its borders, seeking access to warm-water sea ports and a buffer zone between Russia proper and the advancing British. The British pushed northward from India, trying to expand their empire and protect the Raj, the "Crown Jewel of the British Empire," from the expansionist Russians.

Tibet was an important playing piece in this game. Qing Chinese power waned throughout the eighteenth century, as evidenced by its defeat in the Opium Wars with Britain (1839-1842 and 1856-1860), as well as the Taiping Rebellion (1850-1864) and the Boxer Rebellion (1899-1901).

The actual relationship between China and Tibet had been unclear since the early days of the Qing Dynasty, and China's losses at home made the status of Tibet even more uncertain. The ambiguity of control over Tibet lead to problems. In 1893, the British in India concluded a trade and border treaty with Beijing concerning the boundary between Sikkim and Tibet.

However, the Tibetans flatly rejected the treaty terms. The British invaded Tibet in 1903 with 10,000 men, and took Lhasa the following year. Thereupon, they concluded another treaty with the Tibetans, as well as Chinese, Nepalese and Bhutanese representatives, which gave the British themselves some control over Tibet's affairs.

Thubten Gyatso's Balancing Act

The 13th Dalai Lama, Thubten Gyatso, fled the country in 1904 at the urging of his Russian disciple, Agvan Dorzhiev. He went first to Mongolia, then made his way to Beijing. The Chinese declared that the Dalai Lama had been deposed as soon as he left Tibet, and claimed full sovereignty over not only Tibet but also Nepal and Bhutan. The Dalai Lama went to Beijing to discuss the situation with the Emperor Guangxu, but he flatly refused to kowtow to the Emperor.

Thubten Gyatso stayed in the Chinese capital from 1906 to 1908. He returned to Lhasa in 1909, disappointed by Chinese policies towards Tibet. China sent a force of 6,000 troops into Tibet, and the Dalai Lama fled to Darjeeling, India later that same year.

The Chinese Revolution swept away the Qing Dynasty in 1911, and the Tibetans promptly expelled all Chinese troops from Lhasa. The Dalai Lama returned home to Tibet in 1912.

Tibetan Independence

China's new revolutionary government issued a formal apology to the Dalai Lama for the Qing Dynasty's insults, and offered to reinstate him. Thubten Gyatso refused, stating that he had no interest in the Chinese offer. He then issued a proclamation that was distributed across Tibet, rejecting Chinese control and stating that "We are a small, religious, and independent nation." The Dalai Lama took control of Tibet's internal and external governance in 1913, negotiating directly with foreign powers, and reforming Tibet's judicial, penal, and educational systems.

The Simla Convention (1914)

Representatives of Great Britain, China, and Tibet met in 1914 to negotiate a treaty marking out the boundary lines between India and its northern neighbors. The Simla Convention granted China secular control over "Inner Tibet," (also known as Qinghai Province) while recognizing the autonomy of "Outer Tibet" under the Dalai Lama's rule. Both China and Britain promised to "respect the territorial integrity of [Tibet], and abstain from interference in the administration of Outer Tibet."

China walked out of the conference without signing the treaty after Britain laid claim to the Tawang area of southern Tibet, which is now part of the Indian state of Arunachal Pradesh. Tibet and Britain both signed the treaty. As a result, China has never agreed to India's rights in northern Arunachal Pradesh (Tawang), and the two nations went to war over the area in 1962. The boundary dispute still has not been resolved.

China also claims sovereignty over all of Tibet, while the Tibetan government-in-exile points to the Chinese failure to sign the Simla Convention as proof that both Inner and Outer Tibet legally remain under the Dalai Lama's jurisdiction.

The Issue Rests

Soon, China would be too distracted to concern itself with the issue of Tibet. Japan had invaded Manchuria in 1910, and would advance south and east across large swaths of Chinese territory through 1945.

The new government of the Republic of China would hold nominal power over the majority of Chinese territory for only four years before war broke out between numerous armed factions. Indeed, the span of Chinese history from 1916 to 1938 came to be called the "Warlord Era," as the different military factions sought to fill the power vacuum left by the collapse of the Qing Dynasty.

China would see near-continuous civil war up to the Communist victory in 1949, and this era of conflict was exacerbated by the Japanese Occupation and World War II. Under such circumstances, the Chinese showed little interest in Tibet. The 13th Dalai Lama ruled independent Tibet in peace until his death in 1933.

The 14th Dalai Lama

Following Thubten Gyatso's death, the new reincarnation of the Dalai Lama was born in Amdo in 1935. Tenzin Gyatso, the current Dalai Lama, was taken to Lhasa in 1937 to begin training for his duties as the leader of Tibet. He would remain there until 1959, when the Chinese forced him into exile in India.

THE DYNAMISM OF CHINESE FOREIGN POLICY

The essence of Nepal's long term China policy should be anchored in an assessment of the rapid politico-social transformations underway in this country and more importantly in how these transformations can be consistent with augmenting Nepal's own economic development and more generally Nepal's national interests. This old Chinese aphorism literally alludes to the ever changing nature of things-"Thirty years the East River, thirty years the West River" (the river is the same but its course changes). Its application runs in the realm of philosophy but equally in Chinese politics and foreign policy. Analyses of Chinese politics and international relations generated in the western media commonly make the mistake of straight-jacketing China in a "time bubble" situated in the past and not in the present and therefore focus too closely on a static interpretation of Communist ideology, on Tibet and Xianziang and human rights, on nationalism, Tianamen, on Chinese military modernization, and so on and so forth. But as a noted Chinese scholar points out, "China has been changing in a constantly changing world...Chinese society is being de-politicized. China is now enjoying sustained economic growth, its society is diversifying and the influence of ideology is reduced".

Countries like Nepal in the process of consolidating bilateral relations with China should appreciate the nature of this change and craft their policies accordingly. The essence of Nepal's long term China policy should be anchored in an assessment of the rapid politico-social transformations underway in this country and more importantly in how these transformations can be consistent with augmenting Nepal's own economic development and more generally Nepal's national interests.

Whether by coincidence or otherwise, China has appeared to witness profound changes during the course of every thirty years. From the May Forth Movement in 1919 to the founding of the New People's Republic of China in 1949, China was engaged in a struggle against imperialism and feudalism; from 1949 to 1978 which broadly marks the year of Opening Up and Reform, China expended considerable efforts towards modernization and the laying down of a groundwork for its future rise; and for 30 years from 1978 to the hosting of the Olympic Games in 2008, China actively participated in the international division of labour and worked hard for its resurgence.

Moreover, the number 9 which is considered auspicious in China has been used to present an extraordinary formulation that conveys the dynamism and flexibility of the Chinese state, namely that it was in 1949 when Socialism saved China; that in 1979, Capitalism which saved China; that in 1989 it was China which saved Socialism; and finally, that in 2009, it is China which is saving Capitalism! The point is that China has been changing rapidly and her foreign policy has also reflected this, yet routinely China is presented in much more static terms with repercussions in the policy sector. Nepal should make every effort therefore to understand the broad spectrum of the Chinese state and situate its policy accordingly so as to the lay the foundations of a bilateral relationship that has the potential to be one of the most pivotal in Asia in the years ahead.

As Yang Jiemian of The Shanghai Institute of International Studies and younger brother of the current Chinese Foreign Minister Mr. Yang Jiechi has pointed out, "in the past three decades China has abandoned the erroneous ideology-centric approach to developing relations with foreign countries according to their social systems and replaced it with a more balanced approach to energetically developing relations with countries with differing social systems, cultural values and heritages and at different development levels". Indeed, this is the reason why the number of countries with which China enjoys diplomatic relations has increased from 120 in 1979 to 171 by 2008, and furthermore why China and particularly the Chinese Communist Party as the ruling party has over time disregarded ideological differences in party to party contacts.

Marking a shift in the Communist Party of China's rather narrow focus on developing international relations solely with Communist parties in other countries, even as early as the mid-1950s, in a meeting with a delegation of the British Labour Party, Chairman Mao Zedong commented that "We believe that different social systems can coexist peacefully". Subsequently in a meeting in October 1954 with Indian Prime Minister Nehru, Chairman Mao stated that "two countries, or two parties, can cooperate in spite of different ideologies and social systems". It is therefore somewhat surprising when many analysts in Nepal and even abroad seem to naively assume that the People's Republic of China and the Maoist Party of Nepal enjoy special (exclusive) rapport, whereas in fact this would be a gross underestimation of the great flexibility and nuance that inheres in the Chinese system. What should be pointed out here is the broader framework which animates Chinese foreign policy itself, which is that "China has laid out well-structured and mutually reinforcing plans in its diplomatic strategy under the guideline of regarding relations with major powers as the linchpin, with neighbouring countries as of primary importance, with developing countries as the foundation and multilateral diplomacy as an important arena in its diplomatic activities". These three sets of relationships with major powers, neighbouring countries and the developing world which are perceived to be at the core of China's foreign relations are further perceived to be "mutually reinforcing, mutually supportive and mutually-impacting....,[with] multilateral institutions [serving] to link the three together, lumping bilateral, regional and global issues as part and parcel of an integral whole".

What does this mean in the context of Nepal-China relations? What it means is that if Nepal truly wishes to promote this bilateral relationship to a strategically important level, Nepal can no longer afford to bask in the 2000 year history between the two countries and dwell on the architects and princesses of yesteryear. Substantial efforts are required to first understand the significance of Nepal to China (and vice versa) at the bilateral level, then regional level and finally at the global level, and then set out to create a policy framework that cuts across ideological and party divisions.

The friendship at the people to people level has been enduring and solid between our two countries but at the level of policy many gaps and weakness are clearly visible; these must be eliminated gradually in order to elevate Nepal-China relations to a broader plane, to deliver tangible benefits to people on the ground, and finally to demonstrate that Panchasheel or the Five Principles of Peaceful Coexistence are very much relevant in the effective conduct of contemporary diplomacy.

The Deng Xiao-ping era in China witnessed the traditional concepts of struggle, war and rivalry being eclipsed by new concepts of international cooperation centered on reconciliation, peace and harmony in China's foreign policy, which explains why from a position of more or less "self-enclosure" in the 1960s and 1970s wherein China's contacts with the outside world were largely limited and wherein China stood on the edge of the international arena, China is now unequivocally at the centre of the world stage and an insider to the mainstream international system. China is now party to nearly 300 international treaties and more than 130 international organizations, and participates actively in almost all regional mechanisms in its periphery such as the Asia Pacific Economic Cooperation Organization, 10+1, 10+3, the Shanghai Cooperation Organization, besides playing a pivotal role in working towards the creation of a stable security regime in East Asia based on the Six-Party Talks on the North Korean nuclear issue.

In other words, China's foreign policy has undergone a process of modernization in the past 30 years which shows that it is becoming more scientific, professional, democratic and institutionalized. This is nowhere more apparent than in the fact that after 30 years of reform, "foreign policy decision-making in China has been transformed from a unitary approach to an integrated, multi-echelon one" whose most salient feature perhaps is reinforced inter agency coordination. In other words, "an integrated structure of diplomatic work is taking shape: diplomatic activities in China have been broadened to involve all institutions including government agencies, political parties, and civil society groups in all fields-political, economic, academic, cultural, scientific, technological and military."

This emerging inter agency coordination in China should allow Nepal ample opportunity to execute two important tasks: first to understand the landscape of contemporary China which is much more diverse and fluid than is commonly assumed, and then to utilize this inter agency channel to start creating interlocking mechanisms that will bolster and expand the range and nature of Nepal-China relations.

SIKKIM AMID STANDOFF BETWEEN INDIAN AND CHINESE ARMIES

Army Chief General Bipin Rawat reached Gangtok in Sikkim on Thursday morning amid a standoff between Indian troops and Chinese army along the Sino-India border in the sensitive sector which is threatening to further strain the bilateral ties. General Rawat's visit to Sikkim, which official sources describe as routine, comes amid mounting tension between the two armies along the border in Sikkim following a scuffle between Indian troops and the personnel of China's People's Liberation Army in a remote area earlier this month.

The genesis of the latest face-off is understood to have had a link to Donglang, a narrow but strategically important tri-junction of India, China and Bhutan.

Of the 3,488-km-long India-China border from Jammu and Kashmir to Arunachal Pradesh, a 220-km section falls in Sikkim. According to official sources, China removed an old bunker of the Indian Army located at the tri-junction in Sikkim by using a bulldozer after the Indian side refused to accede to its request.

Beijing is believed to have not taken kindly to India building many new bunkers and upgrading older ones along the border in Sikkim in the recent past to augment its defences against the People's Liberation Army (PLA).

Accusing Indian troops of "crossing the boundary" in the Sikkim section, China demanded their immediate withdrawal, while asserting that it has shut down the Nathu La pass entry for Indian pilgrims travelling to Kailash Mansarovar because of the border standoff.

The first batch of Kailash Mansarovar pilgrims comprising about 50 people returned from Nathu La border post as the stand-off between India and China continues. China virtually accused India of having a "hidden agenda" in the current military stand-off with it in the Sikkim sector where Beijing has a territorial dispute with Bhutan.

Taking a dig at India, Chinese Foreign Ministry spokesman Lu Kang said that Bhutan is a universally recognised sovereign country. Lu also hinted that India was objecting to China's efforts to build the road in Donglang area of the Sikkim sector on behalf of Bhutan which does not have diplomatic ties with Beijing.

"Hope countries can respect the sovereignty of the country. The China-Bhutan boundary is not delineated, no third party should interfere in this matter and make irresponsible remarks or actions," he said. Meanwhile, Bhutan has issued a demarche to China over the construction of a road towards its Army camp in Zomplri area of Doklam and asked Beijing to restore status quo by stopping the work immediately. "We have issued a demarche to China through its diplomatic mission here. Recently, the Chinese army (People's Liberation Army) started construction of a road towards Bhutanese Army camp at Zomphlri in Doklam area which is in violation of an agreement between the two countries," Ambassador of Bhutan to India Vetsop Namgyel told PTI.

"Doklam is a disputed territory and Bhutan has a written agreement with China that pending the final resolution of the boundary issue, peace and tranquillity should be maintained in the area," said Namgyel.

The Bhutanese envoy also asserted that under the agreement, both Bhutan and China should refrain from unilaterally changing the status quo. "We have asked China to stop the road construction," he added. As the standoff between Indian troops and Chinese army continues, General Rawat, will travel to a number of other formation headquarters in the Northeast, will take stock of the operational matters and interact with top commanders in the formation headquarters of the force in the border state.

8

Geopolitics: Chinese Doklam Policy, Dalai Lama, Bhutan and India

Concerning the Tibetan issue, the focus on Bhutan appears to be even more fundamental. Though Chinese policies inside Tibet have displayed little concern for Tibetan aspirations, it is entirely possible that by having Bhutan in good faith – a country that shares ethnic, religious, cultural and historic ties with Tibet – Beijing plans to assuage Tibetans' ill will against China. That Bhutan never invited the current Dalai Lama nor was his Gelugpa sect ever allowed to build any monastic institutions due to hierarchical feelings which subordinated Bhutan's Drukpa sect in Tibet only suits communist ideology to an extent.

Nevertheless, the most important geopolitical consideration for China in keeping Bhutan tagged remains India. The approach of Beijing over last five decades has been to minimise the role and importance of India in Bhutan. By consistently refusing to accept any Indian advocacy for Bhutan coupled with the "pressure tactics of border incursions," the Chinese have brought Bhutan to the negotiation table even though they been unsuccessful in making deep inroads in Bhutan.

China realises its limited leverage in Bhutan given critical Indian centrality in Bhutanese affairs and South Asia as well due to sheer geographic advantage that India enjoys. All that China wants from Bhutan is for it to follow an 'independent' policy which essentially means that Bhutan do away with its traditional policy tilt towards India. China blames India of dominating Bhutan unfairly in the name of 'hegemony' – calling it the Indian version of Monroe Doctrine. Thus, Beijing wants Bhutan to confer on Beijing a diplomatic status equal to that of New Delhi and accept a Chinese Ambassador (Ibid).

China's pragmatic foreign policy in contemporary times with the smaller South Asian countries – for example the studied non-interfering role it played when the Sri Lankan Tamil crisis required an Indian Peace Keeping Force – indicates that China fully takes into account the existing geographical and economic limitations of Bhutan. China realises the extent to which Bhutan can go against India, and definitely does not expect a lean to China's side. However, it aims at neutralising Bhutan in the wake of any political or military conflict with India and use it as a base to further trade and commerce in Tibet and rest of South Asia. On a hopeful note, it might expect Bhutan to look up to China as an effective and reliable counterbalance to contain the inevitable Indian domination, something like Nepal. Bhutan has asserted its acceptance of China's core foreign policy concern i.e. One China Policy (Firstpost.com, 14 August 2012). Bhutan's transition from monarchy to parliamentary democracy saw the revision of the 1949 treaty with India in 2007 to one on a "more equal footing with both sides agreeing to 'cooperate closely with each other on issues relating to their national interests (Jacob 2012)'." The next in line could be Indian military presence there. As recent developments suggest, it could be a matter of time that Bhutan moves to balance its tilt towards India. In a world under growing Chinese domination and reducing geographical barriers, one can always expect an upward revision of Chinese strategies and objectives.

BHUTAN AND THE 1962 SINO-INDIAN BORDER CONFLICT

The tension between India and China eventually erupted into a border war in October 1962. Although Bhutan did not take part in this war, its territory was adjacent to the battlefield. Decisive combats took place in the Kameng district in NEFA (North-East Frontier Agency), just on the east of Bhutan. The RGOB was fully aware that an extension of the conflict could easily involve its territory. A strategic pass formed by a trans-Himalayan tributary of the Manas river, located on the Tibet-Bhutan border in Kameng district, was essential to Chinese strategy, should Beijing decide to continue military operations in NEFA. Fortunately for Bhutan, the war was brief. Chinese offensives were decisive. Indian forces were rapidly overwhelmed and had to retreat through the Trashigang area on Bhutanese territory. Eventually, China decided a unilateral cease-fire and withdrew its forces north of the main Himalayan range. This decision came as a relief for Bhutan.

Although brief, this war had important consequences in the power balance in the Himalayas. Bhutan could have reassessed some aspects of its diplomacy in the region. It was clear since the 1950s that China had not renounced to have direct influence in the southern Himalayas. While India had implicitly recognised China's sovereignty over Tibet in 1954, China criticised the close-up between Sikkim and India and encouraged Nepal's dual diplomacy. After the Sino-Indian conflict, some in Bhutanese elite circles, especially in the National Assembly, seemed to be in favour of a balanced diplomacy between India and China. Such diplomacy was supposed to be based on an equal friendship with Delhi and Beijing forged on the Nepali model. The RGOB however did not even consider this option, at least for three reasons. Bhutan was more sensitive than Nepal regarding the fate of Tibet. Common socio-religious origins with Tibetans and historical factors made Bhutanese highly concerned with Chinese strategy in the Himalayas.

Bhutan and Nepal had different treaty relations with India. Bhutan was also very critical regarding the so-called Nepali model. "Nepal had succeeded in creating a more positive international image abroad. But much of this was a mirage, as later developments demonstrated, and the price paid both politically and economically was very high". Bhutan refused to become an arena of big-power competition. It "believed that it could attain as positive results in a more gradual and less dramatic approach. The Bhutanese foreign-policy strategy was based upon the assumption that New Delhi would not obstruct the gradual expansion of Bhutan's relations with the outside world if this could be accomplished without undermining India's regional and security interests". Later developments proved Bhutan's option to be valid. Bhutan joined several international organisations including the United Nations, with Indian support, and pursued a cautious but pragmatic and effective diplomacy. As far as relations with Beijing were concerned, Thimphu preferred the status quo and chose to await the improvement in Indo-China relations to reassess its China policy.

Linkage Politics and Perceptions of Security

Although risks of direct confrontation rapidly disappeared after the end of the Sino-Indian conflict, Bhutan remained cautious during the 1960s vis-à-vis China. There were reports of China building roads and setting up military installations in border areas. Traditional grazing, along the Chumbi valley, formerly a Sikkimese possession, where yak and cattle follow the pasture, created friction between Bhutanese and Tibetan herdsmen. Although unsubstantiated, rumours about an alleged involvement of pro-Chinese elements in the assassination of the Bhutanese Prime Minister Jigme Dorji also circulated in 1964.

The spirit of détente in the early 1970s influenced to some extent Bhutan's China policy. With India feeling responsible for the protection of the borders of Bhutan, the kingdom had better wait for the improvement in Sino-India relations. The RGOB had strong reservations concerning possible interactions with China. Yet pragmatism commended some form of normalisation between the two countries. Bhutan had to solve very practical issues. The first related to the formal delimitation of the 200-miles Sino-Bhutan border. The boundary had never been demarcated in the past. Officials and local people had a clear understanding of territory limits only for areas adjacent to major pass traditionally used by traders. The rest of the frontier was largely unknown and nobody has expressed any interest for the demarcation of territorial jurisdictions prior to 1959. It is precisely in these unknown areas where difficulties arose during the 1960s. High-altitude pasturelands located on the border were periodically the cause of disputes between Bhutanese and Tibetan herders. Such disputes were not only of a casual nature. Beijing's policy in the Himalayan frontier region was to claim disputed areas on the basis of usage by Tibetans. China periodically indicated that it was ready to reach a boundary settlement with Bhutan through direct bilateral negotiations. Although Bhutan could agree with this objective, its treaty commitments to India made the Chinese approach infeasible before a complete normalisation of Sino-Indian relations.

Bhutan and the Tibetan Question

Apart from the Indian factor, the Tibetan question is an important element to be considered in the perspective of an evolution of the relations between Bhutan and the PRC. In some respects, the complexity of the relations between Bhutan and ancient Tibet has survived through the ages. The Drukpa sect has remained totally independent from the Gelugpa establishment. The relations between Bhutan and the Tibetans in exile must be addressed in that context. Bhutan's policy towards Tibetan refugees has not been designed in order to fit Chinese interests. The Chinese authorities however have all reasons to be satisfied with the RGOB's policy that exclude all kind of official contacts with Dharamsala. Surprisingly enough, the Dalaï Lama, who travels a lot, has never visited Bhutan. As the only Mahayana Buddhist state in the world, with strong cultural, religious and historical links with ancient Tibet, Bhutan has sympathy for modern Tibet. However the RGOB has never advocated a pro-active policy on the international scene in favour of the Tibetan question.

Tibetan refugees, including a few with marital ties to prominent Bhutanese families, who started pouring into Bhutan from 1959, were first welcomed in the Kingdom. Cultural and religious relations facilitated their installation. The RGOB even distributed land. During the 1960s, the Tibetan community prospered in Bhutan. Several Tibetans started businesses and opened shops in Thimphu, Trongsa, Trashigang and Bumthang. In 1973 the Tibetan community in Bhutan represented approximately 6,300 refugees. There were eleven Tibetan monasteries in Bhutan. Difficulties began in the late 1960s. The situation became critical during the mid 1970s. Tibetans became a factor in domestic politics and were regularly suspected to have helped foment some of Bhutan's internal upheavals. Although they respected Bhutan's political and religious institutions, their primary allegiance was towards the Dalaï Lama. From the RGOB point of view, the risk was real to see Bhutan become a shelter for Tibetan political activists who could use the Bhutanese territory to back up actions against China. Suspicion was nurtured by the influence of Tibetans in business circles and in the entourage of the King that created resentment and jealousy. That situation coincided with an atmosphere of conspiracy that prevailed on the internal scene. The arrival of new refugees forced the RGOB to take action in order to clarify the situation of the Tibetans in Bhutan. Refugees were pouring into Bhutan in numbers quite beyond the capacity of the RGOB to handle. In 1979, the National Assembly decided that Tibetans who had arrived in Bhutan after 1959, had to choose between becoming Bhutanese citizens and leaving the country. About 2,300 people accepted to make allegiance to the Druk Gyalpo and therefore became Bhutanese citizens. The situation of the remaining 4,000 refugees proved to be a difficult question to be solved. In the early 1980s, the Dalaï Lama regularly touched this issue while visiting Western countries. Some members of the National Assembly proposed to expel refugees who refused to become Bhutanese. Such a drastic solution was not consistent with Bhutan's principles and tradition. Therefore, the RGOB preferred to negotiate their departure with India. Half of the refugees eventually settled in India, while the others scattered in the west, mainly in Europe and North America. Since that period, the Tibetan question did not surface in international politics.

DERIVATION AND EVENTS LEADING TO BORDER DISPUTE

The 1914 Simla Convention between Britain and Tibet established the McMahon Line as the official border between British India and China, denying the right of Chinese suzerainty over Tibet. However, the line's namesake McMahon, was ordered back to London in disgrace over the "chicanery" he exercised in border negotiations in which he presented a different map to the Chinese envoy, thus distancing Britain from the legitimacy of the negotiated border. Thirty years later British cartographers began drawing the McMahon Line as the border between British India and China, thus reviving the lines legal legitimacy.

When India gained its independence from Britain in 1947 it inherited all of the British territorial agreements, and as such inherited the McMahon Line as the border between it and China. Indian belief in the legitimacy of the McMahon line dated back to the Simla Convention of 1914, as well as to the numerous maps of British India with the line delineating its northern border.

As such Nehru shrugged off Chinese insistence in border negotiation during the 1954 agreement stating that "the McMahon line marked their border with China, where was the need" ? Despite India's view of the McMahon Line's legitimacy, China had not signed the Simla Convention and under no circumstances consented to any bilateral agreement between Tibet and Britain because it violated their sovereignty.

Indian intransigence on negotiating a border acceptable to both parties led the PRC to act independently in areas south of the McMahon line. The justification for this was that in the absence of mutually negotiated borders, the true national boundary was a line of actual control represented by the extent of either nation's ability to administrate the territory.

Practical assertion of this idea was first revealed to India in 1957 when an Indian patrol discovered an all-weather road which had been constructed in the Aksai-Chin Plain connecting Xinjiang and Tibet. The Indian government launched diplomatic protests asserting a violation of their territorial integrity; however the PRC "considered [Aksai-Chin] to have long been Chinese territory". This issue was not resolved as the Indian government refused to engage in territorial negotiations until Chinese forces completely withdrew from the Aksai-Chin Plain. The PRC refused to do so, and instead of a diplomatic solution India began to pursue a more confrontational approach to assert their territorial claims.

The rebellion in Tibet helped to drastically sour relations between the PRC and India, but the border dispute widened due to a change in Indian military strategy. This change in military strategy was to create forward-posts behind the Chinese claim line, and in strategic locations to flank Chinese military positions.

These posts were constructed to assert Indian territorial claims in the Ladakh region and to threaten the Xinjian-Tibet road in Aksai-Chin. By September, 1962 a similar series of forward posts had been built beyond the

Chinese claim line in Tibet, and four such posts were built even beyond the McMahon Line. This resulted in an inability to claim that these posts were simply to defend Indian territorial integrity. The territorial dispute from India's perspective, coupled with the building of forward military posts by the Indian military caused the 1954 Panchsheel Agreement to not be renewed in 1961. Crossing both the claim and McMahon lines, both nations were in violation of each other's territorial conception, and India was now physically challenging Chinese sovereignty in Tibet.

BHUTAN-CHINA RELATION : THE CHINESE FACTOR

While the Chinese State news agency Xinhua and others said that "a historic moment" at the sidelines of the United Nations Rio+20 Conference on Sustainable Development in Brazil was the first ever meeting between prime ministers of Bhutan and China, where expressions to establish diplomatic ties were discussed, the Bhutanese PM's media cell has said the Chinese local media has misreported that Bhutan and China will forge formal diplomatic ties.

Instead, PM Jigmi Y Thinley and officials from the Ministry of Foreign Affairs have been taking this opportunity on the sidelines of the meeting to meet people to campaign for the UN Security Council's seat.

Back at home, some quarters of the Bhutanese intelligentsia Bhutan TODAY spoke to have their own say. "That the news was splashed by China's State news agency is an embodiment of the fact that China wants to have diplomatic relations with Bhutan," an observer seeking anonymity said. According to him, if China engages with Bhutan it is in regards to its borders. "Given that Bhutan shares a long border with China, its interest in Bhutan might be 'strategic,'" he said.

Meanwhile, the Gangzur – Minjay member of the National Assembly (NA) Karma Rangdol and head of the Druk Phuensum Tshogpa's Foreign Relations Committee is for a relation with China in the "near future" but "not immediately". "We have to think about the relationship at a later stage but I am for it in the near future", he said, adding that relations should be built cautiously. However, Karma Rangdol said the decision depends on the next government as the present one's term is about to end. Underlining that Bhutan has diplomatic relations with over forty countries, he said relations with China could benefit Bhutan economically. "Because of geopolitical situation we can gain a lot," he said.

The Dewathang-Gomdar National Assembly member Ugyen Dorji says that establishment of diplomatic tie would facilitate settlement of the long standing border dispute between the two neighbours. "That's what Chinese are pressing for (diplomatic tie). They badly want us to establish diplomatic relations with them," he said, adding that he felt "positive" when the news first came. The two countries held the 19th round of border talks here in January 2010. Contrary to the "Indian angle," which people bring in whenever Bhutan-China relations are discussed, Ugyen Dorji said he does not think that a diplomatic tie with China will hurt the Indian government. He said the people and government of India are "broadminded as we are" and Bhutan would never hurt Indian sentiments. "The meeting of the two Premiers is nothing."

A political analyst said the dynamics of global politics has changed. "The relationship that India and China has evolved very positively in the last few years and the mutual respect and trust between India and Bhutan is unparalleled," he said. He added that along with time the "old order" should change. "As far as I know, New Delhi should be assured and Bhutan should move ahead." An observer said China would look for a formal tie with Bhutan if the former support the latter's bid for a seat in the Security Council. "If Bhutan wants to gain important seats in the United Nations, China's support would be important as China is empowered by veto right and its influence over other countries is strong," he said.

Trashiyangtsi MP Dupthob said the question is not about whether to build ties but about time. "It (to establish diplomatic tie) is inevitable as the three countries Bhutan, India and China have share common objectives," he said. As both the neighbours are strong, Bhutan will definitely benefit. "After all, we have a long standing border issue with China, which even India would like to see resolved," he said. In an earlier interview with Bhutan TODAY, Indian Ambassador to Bhutan, Pavan K Varma said Bhutan's decision with regard to China is a matter of its sovereign will. "Bhutan, as sovereign country can take its own decision with regard to diplomatic relationship with any country including China," he had said. Meanwhile, the officiating foreign minister, Khandu Wangchuk also did not comment if Bhutan has plans to establish diplomatic ties with the second largest economy in the world. Lyonpo Khandu Wangchuk, who has also served as foreign minister in the past said: "We want good relations with all the countries".

Bhutan's foreign policy states that the government strives to promote goodwill and cooperation with nations, foster respect for international law and treaty obligations, and encourage settlement of international disputes by peaceful means in order to promote international peace and security. A

1949 treaty which gave India a say in Thimphu's foreign policy was revised in 2007.

CHINA IS A REALITY FOR BHUTAN

That even after the 19th round of Bhutan-China boundary talks, the two countries have not been able to conclude the boundary demarcations, speaks volumes regarding the unsteady relations between them. But nevertheless, China has recently been projecting its image as a peaceful and responsible superpower and neighbour.

On the subject of expanding diplomatic ties with Bhutan, China has to some extent, agreed to keep aside the issue of the boundary dispute. Bhutan has always maintained its acceptance for the One China Policy. This has led to restrictions of any kind of political activities of Tibetan refugees living in Bhutan.

On its part, India has encouraged Bhutan to take independent decisions on foreign policy. In fact, following the recent visit of the Indian Foreign Secretary to Bhutan, Ranjan Mathai categorically said that how Bhutan establishes ties with other countries is an internal decision for the country, and that India has no right to interfere in its internal decision making policy. But this is easier said than done. Bhutan is facing unique challenges today, not only across its borders but also internally. The gradual shift of power from the Palace to the Parliament will see a paradigm shift in its foreign policy making. How would a new democratic Bhutan see China as opposed to the perceptions of the traditional absolute Monarchy? With many stakeholders involved, will democratic Bhutan be able to balance both powerful neighbours? And if so, will it favour one against another? Who would it trust the most, vis-a-vis its own stability?

INTERPRETING NEW REALITIES

No doubt, there was definitely an element of rhetoric and public relations in China's initial reactions to India's nuclear tests. However, with the passage of time, what has gradually come to the fore is the fact that the advent of two nuclear weapon states on its southern borders has perturbed China's leaders far more deeply than what has been either highlighted in China's official reactions or appreciated in most Indian commentaries. At the least, this new reality has completely upset Beijing's security paradigms for the 21st century world.

Thanks partly to the assessments and analysis of China's India experts, the challenge to China's uncontested rise had been least expected from its southern frontiers where the most powerful country—India—was being dealt with their time-tested double-edged policy of slow-moving confidence building measures (CBMs) while simultaneously China also continued aiding and abetting Pakistan's nuclear and missile capabilities. But this constantly increasing proximity with both India and Pakistan was a contradiction in terms.

And the nuclear tests in Pokhran and Chagai were perhaps the natural outcome of such contradiction. And now, with two of these South Asian powers going overtly nuclear, the new reality, unlike the past, does not seem to conform to Beijing's policy framework. This is simply because, despite its increasing engagements in the Near and Far East, greater resources and attention may have now be devoted for dealing with these new challenges from its southern frontiers.

Accordingly, with the passage of time, as China's leaders revalue their expert analysis on these post-Pokhran II realities of Sino-Indian ties, this weakening of rhetoric has been gradually replaced by relatively hardened attitudes as also by far too well thought out expressions of their India policy. To give one example, while China has lately toned down its international campaign on seeking reversal of India's nuclear policies, it has simply shifted the pressure on bilateral policies.1 At the core of the current bilateral stalemate, as of now, the "hurt" caused by India's nuclear tests and their explanations remains at the core of the Chinese critique. They have since continued to stress that it is India which has to "untie these knots" in Sino-Indian ties.

According to various official and non-official statements from China, Beijing perhaps expects India to demonstrate its sincerity in building rapprochement by taking what it calls some "concrete steps" in that direction. These "concrete steps", however, remain undefined, which has further complicated India's policy choices. Most interpretations, however, broadly hint that China perhaps wishes New Delhi to retreat from it position whereby it explained its decision to conduct nuclear tests in terms of China's nuclear weapons and their proliferation and described China as its potential threat number one. As a result, there are far too many important questions that have today come to the table. The problem, however, is that both sides have not yet been able to agree to sit across this table and take these issues one by one.

There is no doubt that India understands its responsibilities. Partly this is borne out of various initiatives that the Indian side has been taking at all possible levels and forums. However, all this does not seem to as yet assuage

China's feelings. But, for some, that perhaps has been the normal, well-known refrain in Sino-Indian ties since the early 1950s. Notwithstanding all this, one thing remains very clear that, even today, New Delhi is not likely to be found wanting in taking positive initiatives provided there is an appropriate place and time for this as also a more or less positive response from the Chinese side. This is because by doing so, India will only be carrying further its time-tested tradition of taking bold political initiatives for improving Sino-Indian ties. However, such a policy may have its own limitations in the entirely new context of Sino-Indian nuclear stalemate following India's decision to exercise its nuclear weapon option. This proposition has also to be qualified by the following two conditions. One, that India does not need any certification for its nuclear weapon status but sees its efforts at reviving Sino-Indian rapprochement as part of its efforts at further strengthening India's image as a peace-loving country and to demonstate its commitment towards its long-standing disarmament policies. Secondly, any such decision to make the first move towards rapprochement will not mean any deviation from India's past record and, in fact, it fully conforms to the ethos of India's China policy over the last five decades.

Also, considering that historically Indian leaders have always sought security-in-peace and not peace-in-security, it falls in line with India's ethos, the current strategic thinking and future security needs. Therefore, to provide them appropriate atmospherics and meaning, India's policy initiatives vis-à-vis China would have to be viewed as very much part of India's larger policy objectives for international peace. However, compared with India's fire-fighting approach in responding to China's initial critical statements, dealing with China may now need a far more planned, integrated and piecemeal approach that should stress on areas of agreement while, at the same time, provide this long-term process a kick-start in the form of bold political initiatives from the highest level. While the results of such initiatives, as also the time-frame for achieving such results, may be difficult to predict, such a bold policy decision to be the first is not likely to have any adverse impact in terms of India's domestic politics. In fact, if anything, the impact of such bold political initiatives in the past has only been positive.

India's Track Record

In fact, going by the track record of the last 50 years, or even earlier, India's leaders have never been found wanting in taking bold political initiatives regardless of the fact as to who had tied the so-called knots and for what purpose. In fact, Prime Minister Atal Bihari Vajpayee, himself had been the first Indian Foreign Minister ever to visit Beijing in 1979. To recall a few of the major examples, India was not only amongst the first to recognise the new Communist regime but also at the forefront of defending China's membership of the UN Security Council while the Americans were sending feelers to New Delhi that India could well replace China as the permanent member at the UN Security Council. Even the 1962 war did not change New Delhi's policy stance on this issue and China was finally inducted into the United Nations in 1971. Later, during the second phase of Sino-Indian rapprochement as well, India was the first to announce as well as exchange Ambassadors (July 1975), and again the first to send its Foreign Minister (February 1979), Prime Minister (December 1988) and President (May 1992) to Beijing. This, of course, is not to say that China did not make any contribution to the process of Sino-Indian friendship. Nevertheless, China's reactions had often been long-drawn, reluctant and from the periphery of China's leadership, though the tenor in the end was invariably positive.

Especially seen in the backdrop of Prime Minister Jawaharlal Nehru's decision to surrender India's historic "presence" in Tibet followed by the Dalai Lama's arrival in India in 1959 and the Sino-Indian border war of 1962, the visit by Prime Minister Rajiv Gandhi in December 1988, had marked the most critical historic initiative by New Delhi that was aimed at building Sino-Indian rapprochement. During this visit, New Delhi virtually took a U-turn and agreed to the Chinese position that asked both sides to concentrate on areas of agreement and put aside difficult issues until the two sides had generated the required level of mutual confidence to resolve those disputes. The strength of such bold political initiatives has also to be seen in the face of the fact that there was a historic November 1962 resolution of India's Parliament that bound successive ruling regimes in India to open relations with China only after taking back "every inch" of India's sacred territory that was either claimed by, or under the occupation of, the Chinese. Accordingly, this was perhaps the most important instance when India's leaders so clearly demonstrated its commitment to making all possible efforts towards improving ties with China.

To appreciate the fact that this strategic U-turn by India was not an aberration, one has to see this historic visit as the culmination of the log-term initiatives that were started during Mrs. Indira Gandhi's regime. This piecemeal approach that had already begun to improve Sino-Indian ties since the early 1970s, raised diplomatic ties to Ambassador level in 1975, and carried out border talks from 1981. It is in this backdrop that the November 1988 resolution of the All India Congress Committee was seen as technically enabling Rajiv Gandhi's government to open formal negotiations with China. This resolution briefly urged the Rajiv Gandhi government to seek a settlement with China through "peaceful negotiations" based on "mutual interests" and "acceptable to the people of both countries", even if it took time. Even the Chinese scholars have recognised the importance of India's initiatives in building Sino-Indian rapprochement. For example, when, following the Tiananmen Square incidents of June 1989, most Western powers had imposed sanctions and isolated China, the period between the second half of 1989 and 1990 witnessed 10 high-level visits exchanged between India and China. These included visits by Vice Premier Wu Xueguian in October 1989 and by Foreign Minister Qian Qichen in March 1990.4 Moreover, barely five weeks following the historic incidents at the Tiananmen Square, the annual meeting of the Sino-Indian Joint Working Group on the Boundary Question was held as scheduled for July 1, 1989. What more could have demonstrated India's sincerity in improving Sino-Indian ties?

China's Policy Options

While India has always been at the forefront of making initiatives, China, on the other hand, has been generally slow and reluctant, though its belated response was nevertheless always positive and made India's initiatives workable. However, this has not been necessarily the result of some ill will on the part of Beijing. Instead, it is partly the outcome of policy perceptions from both sides which, of course, continue to be varied. Due to their respective historical legacies, compulsions and priorities, while China has perhaps been relatively higher in India's list of foreign policy priorities, the same has not been true of India's place in the case of China's list of priorities. In line with China's so-called "Middle Kingdom" syndrome, China's leaders have always sought to compare themselves with big powers like the United States and the former Soviet Union (now Russia).

Accordingly, while China viewed itself in the larger global context, it has historically tried to deal with India in a smaller regional framework of either Asia or, lately, in the still smaller context of the South Asian subcontinent. And, in this case, Beijing's policy towards India simply aimed at the following two objectives: (i) propping up India's smaller neighbours to keep New Delhi tied down to the South Asian region; and (ii) continuing the rapprochement efforts by accepting an extremely slow-moving process of CBMs. But China's ever expanding indulgence, aimed at enabling Pakistan to be a counter-balance against New Delhi, was to gradually lead New Delhi to lose patience with China's slow pace in the process of CBMs. These contradictory policies were finally to result in India breaking out of China's traditional low-cost India policy by finally exercising its nuclear weapon option, and India's capabilities today can no longer be dealt with by China in that old framework of the Indian subcontinent.

China, as a result, is in a difficult position today to continue to pay lip service to its desire to solve problems with India, as it is now required to respond to the new hard realities of a nuclear India. Beijing is accordingly required to move from its traditional approach of abetting Pakistan towards a more substantive nuclear policy towards South Asia in general and India in particular. No doubt, China's best interests will be served by making sure that India gives up its resolve to develop the nuclear deterrent vis-à-vis China and that Pakistan remains subservient to Beijing's piecemeal transfers in these sensitive technologies. But since that status quo has already been challenged by the nuclear explosions by India and Pakistan, the second best option available to China is to make sure that India's nuclear weapons remain focused or even equated with those of Pakistan and, therefore, never visualised or actually deployed for dealing with China's nuclear capabilities. And here, assessing the inevitability of the new realities, China has already moved away from seeking their roll-back or total elimination to stressing more and more on containing their negative fallout for Beijing. What makes China's policy options all the more limited is that, even after its decision to go nuclear, India continued to swear by its commitment to general and comprehensive nuclear disarmament. New Delhi believes that it is in a non-nuclear environment that its national interests will be best served. Also, even after demonstrating the capability to design and develop fairly sophisticated nuclear weapons, New Delhi has already announced its commitment to the doctrine of no-first-use and minimum deterrence that has further weakened China's credentials in raising anti-India campaigns at various global and regional forums.

But this should, in no way, obtain India any more leeway, for continued failure to open a dialogue with the Chinese can only further increase New Delhi's difficulties in sustaining such pacific postures. This is because leaders in New Delhi have to constantly seek approval for their policy postures from the masses who, thanks to the television era, have become much more aware and vigilant. Accordingly, New Delhi may come under domestic pressures for persisting with the olive branch for far too long, especially if the attitude in Beijing remains one of apathy or negation. It is not understandable to most Indians as to why China has been so averse to holding talks at established forums like the Sino-Indian Joint Working Group on the Boundary Question. The very ideal behind creating such a forum was to sort out all such differences under difficult circumstances. Sitting across the table, the two sides are sure to be in a much better position to explain their policy postures. This will any day better be than holding negotiations through the media or through third country forums where India is not even present. This confidence that talks will do only better is borne out of the good working relationship that the two sides have so assiduously evolved during the last three decades of Sino-Indian rapprochement.

Enhancing Areas of Agreement

To recall their cooperation before India's nuclear explosions last year, both India and China had evolved, over the years, a fairly good working relationship at various bilateral, regional and international forums. So much so that their cooperation at forums like the UN Human Rights Commission annual session at Geneva had come to be a major irritant in the Western powers' campaign to censure China (and India) on the question of human rights. While there is no dearth of examples on India's initiatives and many of these have already been listed under the aforesaid section on "India's Track Record", the important fact is that the 1990s had witnessed even the reluctant Chinese making an eloquent contribution to the Sino-Indian rapprochement. To give some examples of China's major conciliatory initiatives, Kashmir perhaps forms one good example where China had become increasingly objective in its assessment even at the cost of its closest ally, Pakistan. Though it was from the early 1980s that China had gradually evolved a more neutral tone in its statements on the Kashmir question, it was the Narasimha Rao-Li Peng Joint Statement of 1991 that provided the most favoured expression from the highest level of China's leadership. The statement clearly described Kashmir as a bilateral dispute between India and Pakistan and urged both sides to resolve it under the framework of the Shimla Agreement. By doing this, China in fact had nearly endorsed India's own position with relation to Jammu & Kashmir province.

Later, in December 1996, President Jiang Zemin, in fact, went a step further and suggested in his address to Pakistan's Senate that both sides should set aside their pending problematic issues left over by history and build a stronger network of ties in areas of mutual agreement. Also, it was the persuasion by China (and Iran) that resulted in Pakistan withdrawing its resolution on Kashmir at the UN Human Rights Commission's annual session at Geneva in March 1996. Similarly, in January 1995, when the Western powers had withdrawn the promise of supplying fissile fuel for India's Tarapore nuclear power plant, it was China that had come forward and supplied one instalment of enriched uranium. Similarly, the two countries had evolved a strong working relationship at various regional forums, be it in the Indian Ocean or East Asia. Most scholars have seen this goodwill as a result of expanding interactions between these two countries. India, for example, hosted the the China Fair in 1991 and later China hosted the India Fair in 1993. The two sides in 1995 became Asia's first two countries to actually implement disarmament as both of them agreed to pull out four military posts in the Wangdong region in the Eastern Sector where troops had been deployed at alarming proximity to each other. But the most important factor expanding their mutual stakes had been perhaps their bilateral trade since the early 1990s. By 1994, India had actually become China's largest trading partner from South Asia, thus, crossing Beijing's closest ally, Pakistan. This boosted their mutual confidence in such a way that the Joint Sino-Indian Business Council, in fact, declared in the 1997 meeting at Beijing that their bilateral trade would increase by at least five times during the 1990s decade, thus, crossing the $ 4 billion figure by the year 2000. And especially the fact that the post-Pokhran II confusion in Sino-Indian ties has not really affected their bilateral trade all that much makes it the strongest as also the most reliable (and most agreeable) pillar of Sino-Indian rapprochement during the 1990s. And this is perhaps one area that promises to bear dividends for the future as well.

Bilateral Trade: Positive Trends

Going by the experience of the last two decades, Sino-Indian trade has been one aspect of their bilateral ties that has shown constant improvement. According to recently released statistics by the China State Statistical Bureau for the last 20 years—1978-1997—while China's total international trade has gone up by 14 times, the Sino-Indian trade has gone up by 16 times during the same period. Also, despite the apparent reluctance in India's business community to invest in China, both China and India have already established over 50 big and small joint ventures in various areas. Over two dozen Indian companies are today doing business with their Chinese counterparts with most of them being success stories. But the importance of Sino-Indian trade cannot be gauged from statistics alone. In fact, the value of Sino-Indian trade does not really lie in terms of its total volume, which, however remains limited. Instead, its value has to be seen in terms of its intangible benefits in resolving Sino-Indian ties and these have made an important contribution.

Viewed as a CBM, Sino-Indian trade has led to greater (a) mutual confidence; (b) mutual commitment; and (c) greater transparency (i) in the interactions of their border communities and (ii) in the willingness to collaborate on the part of their national elite from both sides.

Their border trade may have remained extremely low as a percentage of their total bilateral trade volume yet, considering the freedom and interaction that it has brought for the border communities from both sides, it has greatly improved mutual trust on both sides. The two sides have, for example, free trade in 15 local items which include yak-tail, salt, borax, China clay, China silk, etc. Obviously, transactions in these items are not capital intensive and are not going to be correctly reflected when seen in terms of their monetary value. Nevertheless, increased border trade during the 1990s has resulted in the revival of various related cottage industries. In Pithoragarh district of India, for example, this has resulted in the revival of the carpet-weaving industry which had been completely shut down as it depended entirely on Tibetan wool. And finally, this border trade has also to be seen in the backdrop of the poor road and communication infrastructure and generally backward conditions of these border communities. And, in that context, this increased activity has resulted in generating momentum leading to improvement in these remote regions which ensures peace and stability in these otherwise disputed borders between China and India. Apart from improving the interactions and living standards of the border communities, their border trade has also facilitated the border management activities by both countries' personnel deployed for maintaining peace and tranquillity in the Sino-Indian border regions.

What perhaps most clearly brings out the strength of positive trends in Sino-Indian trade is that nothing of the recent temporary political problems following the nuclear tests of May 1998 seems to have affected the normal pace of improvement throughout last year. For example, even in the post-Pokhran II context of nuclear stalemate between India and China, scholars from China have continued to advocate for concepts like sub-regional cooperation between China's south-western and India's north-eastern regions which have remained relatively neglected in terms of building infrastructure for development.

Though the symbolic cancellation of the China Commodity Fair in Mumbai and China's low-profile presence during last year's India International Trade Fair in New Delhi did create a flutter amongst businessmen on both sides, the projections for 1998—based on half yearly trade statistics compiled by the Confederation of Indian Industry (CII)—clearly project how Sino-Indian trade does not even seem to notice India's nuclear tests at all . Especially, compared to China's recent trade statistics vis-a-vis East Asian countries this, in fact, shows encouraging signs for the future of Sino-Indian ties. In the long term, therefore, making efforts towards expanding mutual trade and investments can be one sure way of enhancing mutual stakes for building peace and security between India and China. But, looking at the continued stalemate in Sino-Indian ties, this would perhaps require some sort of a kick-start by bold political initiatives.

Atmospherics for Political Initiatives

Apart from these positive trends in Sino-Indian trade and commerce in the post-Pokhran II period, the first indicator of positive atmospherics in terms of bilateral relations was witnessed in the month of October (1998) when the first delegation of Indian academics visiting Beijing at the invitation of the China Institute for Contemporary International Relations (CICIR) which organised a seminar on the future of Sino-Indian ties. In response, a 16-member Chinese delegation (academics from the provinces of Yunnan, Sichuan, and Beijing) travelled to the Indian cities of Calcutta, New Delhi, Mumbai, Bangalore and Chennai where it participated in seminars and meetings on Sino-Indian ties during November-December 1998. Besides, various other Sino-Indian businessmen and experts, continued to exchange visits at their normal, earlier pace. All this portends more positive interactions at the formal level as well, and indications are that Sino-Indian ties may gather greater momentum during 1999.

Equally important initiatives have also been taken at the highest level of India's leadership. Jaswant Singh (then as the Prime Minister's special emissary) held a meeting in September 1998 with China's Foreign Minister, Tang Jiaxuan, during the Asean Regional Forum's (ARF) annual meet at Manila. This had generated speculations that Jaswant Singh may be leading another high-level dialogue with China, just like the one he has been holding with Strobe Talbott of the United States. Such ideas have been further strengthened by the Prime Minister's statements in Parliament as also by repeated statements by the Prime Minister's Principal Secretary, Brijesh Mishra, echoing sentiments in favour of improving Sino-Indian ties. In fact, following Jaswant Singh's taking over as Foreign Minister during December 1998, the possibilities for an early Sino-Indian dialogue are understood to have increased manifold. This is partly because, according to Press reports, in his letter of congratulations to Jaswant Singh, China's Foreign Minister Tang Jiaxuan, expressed the hope that under his stewardship of India's Ministry of External Affairs, China and India should be able to further "consolidate and develop" the friendly and good neighbourly relations between their two nations.

An equally positive response was reportedly provided by Jaswant Singh's reply to Tang Jiaxuan's letter. Also, addressing his first formal Press conference after taking over as Foreign Minister, Jaswant Singh reiterated India's commitment to "further improving" ties with China and he urged China's leaders to help India "untie the knots" through frequent consultations and dialogue. And going by the current whispers-in-the-wind, the official Sino-Indian dialogue is now expected to begin some time early next year.

To conclude, therefore, it is only a matter of time for the Sino-India rapprochement to come back to its normal equilibrium. Looking at China's own example, India can perhaps afford to wait or even ignore China's criticism. In the face of China's own nuclear explosion in October 1964, the Kennedy Administration had even thought of physically eliminating China's nuclear facilities. In such adversity, Beijing had, however, continued to denounce American reactions to its nuclear weapons and Washington had to finally give up its policies and build détente with the Chinese. And going by their interactions during 1990, the two sides have since evolved into strategic partners. So much so that, in the case of the Indian tests, China seems to be speaking the language of the United States, and President Clinton seems to have given China a free hand in leading the anti-Indian campaign on behalf the Five Nuclear Weapon Powers. However, it is not the outcome but the time involved that is important. And here, New Delhi may not feel the need for a Chinese certification of India's nuclear weapon power status and also it may be in position to wait and watch until China decides to come around and recognise the new reality of India's nuclear weapons; yet, there are reasons why the two sides should hasten to open their official dialogue.

However, these comparisons from history have their own limitations. First of all, the non-proliferation lobby seems today far better organised and far more coercive in nature. Its leader, the United States, is also no longer either deterred by a parallel superpower (like the Soviet Union) or embroiled in any Vietnam War type protracted quagmire.

China, on the other hand, happens to be the most adversely affected party from India's decision to exercise its nuclear option, and its disaffection is clearly being used by the non-proliferation lobbies to wedge further distrust between India and China. But, at the same time, India's nuclear tests happen to be a reality which cannot be "dis-invented", and all parties involved have to come to terms with this basic fact. In such as a scenario, any hardened attitude by China (and other nuclear weapon powers) will only make India stick to its guns and become far more defensive and perhaps inflexible in any unduly delayed negotiations. The only way to evolve mutual understanding, therefore, is dialogue and deliberation at an early date.

Considering the fact that it is the evolution of Sino-Indian good neighbourly relations and not browbeating that happens to be India's objective, any indefinite delay will only further weaken the prospects for peace between India and China.

This will also further reduce their options in opening talks and make matters far more difficult for both sides. All this makes it imperative for both Beijing and New Delhi to put a premium on time and try to resolve their ties as early as possible.

However, opening a serious official dialogue may, once again, require, some bold political initiatives. As regards India, this should not deter New Delhi from taking initiatives like proposing a Foreign Minister's visit to Beijing for this would well conform to India's China policy of the last 50 years. But the Chinese side will also have to, once again make a contribution by positively responding to India's initiatives for opening a high-level official dialogue.

BHUTAN-CHINA BILATERAL RELATIONS

Bilateral relations between the Himalayan kingdom of Bhutan and the People's Republic of China have historically remained tense. Bhutan and the PRC do not maintain official diplomatic relations. The PRC shares a contiguous border of 470 kilometres (km) with Bhutan to the north and its territorial disputes with Bhutan have also been a source of potential conflict. Since the 1980s, the two governments have conducted regular talks on border and security issues aimed at reducing tensions.

Throughout history, Bhutan has had strong cultural, historical, religious and economic connections to Tibet. Relations with Tibet were strained when Bhutan sided with the British Empire in its war with Tibet. For a brief period, the Republic of China officially maintained a territorial claim on Bhutan. Unlike Tibet, Bhutan had no history of being under the suzerainty of China, instead being under British suzerainty during the British raj.

With the increase in soldiers on the Chinese side of the Sino-Bhutanese border after the 17-point agreement between the local Tibetan government and the central government of China, Bhutan withdrew its representative from Lhasa. Its border with China has never been officially recognised and demarcated and the 1959 Tibetan Rebellion and the 14th Dalai Lama's arrival in neighbouring ally India made the security of its border with China a necessity for Bhutan. An estimated 6,000 Tibetans fled to Bhutan and were granted asylum, although Bhutan subsequently closed its border to China, fearing more refugees.

Border Issues

Along with the occupation of Tibet, the Chinese People's Liberation Army occupied eight western Tibetan enclaves under Bhutanese administration. A Chinese map published in 1961 showed China claiming territories in Bhutan, Nepal and the kingdom of Sikkim (now a state of India).

Incursions by Chinese soldiers and Tibetan herdsmen also provoked tensions in Bhutan. Imposing a cross-border trade embargo and closing the border, Bhutan established extensive military ties with India. During the 1962 Sino-Indian War, Bhutanese authorities permitted Indian troop movements through Bhutanese territory. However, India's defeat in the war raised concerns about India's ability to defend Bhutan. Consequently, while building its ties with India, Bhutan officially established a policy of neutrality.

According to official statements by the King of Bhutan to theNational Assembly, there are four disputed areas between Bhutan and China. Starting from Doklam in the west, the border goes along the ridges from Gamochen to Batangla, Sinchela, and down to the Amo Chhu. The disputed area in Doklam covers 89 square kilometres (km^2) and the disputed areas in Sinchulumpa and Gieucover about 180 km^2.

Engagement

Until the 1970s, India represented Bhutan's concerns in talks with China over the broader Sino-Indian border conflicts. Obtaining membership in the United Nations in 1971, Bhutan began to take a different course in its foreign policy. In the U.N., Bhutan, incidentally alongside India, voted in favour of the PRC filling the seat occupied by the ROC and openly supported the "One China" policy.

In 1974 in a symbolic overture, Bhutan invited the Chinese ambassador to India to attend the coronation of Jigme Singye Wangchuk as the king of Bhutan. In 1983, the Chinese Foreign Minister Wu Xueqian and Bhutanese Foreign Minister Dawa Tseringheld talks on establishing bilateral relations in New York. In 1984, China and Bhutan began annual, direct talks over the border dispute.

In 1998, China and Bhutan signed a bilateral agreement for maintaining peace on the border. In the agreement, China affirmed its respect for Bhutan's sovereignty and territorial integrity and both sides sought to build ties based on the Five Principles of Peaceful Co-existence. However, China's building of roads on Bhutanese territory, allegedly in violation of the 1998 agreement, has provoked tensions. In 2002, however, China presented what it claimed to be 'evidence', asserting its ownership of disputed tracts of land; after negotiations, an interim agreement was reached.

APPARENT PARADOX IN BHUTAN-CHINA'S RELATIONSHIP

There is an apparent paradox in Bhutan-China's relationship. The geographical location of Bhutan gives it both political and strategic importance in the Himalayan region. Bhutan has a long tradition of cultural and religious interaction with Tibet and shares a common border with China. Yet, the kingdom is China's only neighbour which does not have diplomatic relations with the People's Republic of China (PRC). Even trade and economic contacts between the two countries are very small and their common border remains closed.

However, the status quo resulting from the turmoil that followed the integration of Tibet in the PRC and the Sino-Indian border conflict in 1962 is about to change. Political contacts have been resumed since the mid 1980s. The two governments have been using the annual border consultations to exchange views on a wide range of bilateral issues. Both countries have interest in the normalization of their relationship. Yet, their perspectives are different. While Bhutan prefers to remain cautious according to the approach it has always favoured on the diplomatic scene, China is considering its relation with Bhutan as part of its "Western development strategy", that could allow Tibet to regain a central position in the Himalayan region.

The present paper places Bhutan-China relations in an historical perspective that shows the importance of the Tibetan factor. Linkage politics and perceptions of security in the context of India-China relations are also described. Though a sign of further détente in the region, the perspectives of normalization of Bhutan-China relations open a new step in Himalayan politics.

The Chronological Standpoint

Historically, Chinese claims to Bhutan had been totally dependant upon Tibetan claims. For that reason, the Bhutan-Tibet relationship must be addressed in the first place. There are several cultural, social and religious similarities between Bhutanese and Tibetans, who have had many interactions for a long time. Tibetan influence had been a decisive factor in the evolution of Bhutan's social and political structures.

In the early 8th century, when Tibet was a military power, Tibetan armies invaded Bhutan. Tibetan lamas also arrived in the Southern Valleys where some Tibetans settled down and intermarried with local people.

People of Tibetan origin became predominant in the western part of Bhutan. During the 9th century, Tibetan armies withdrew from Bhutan, but lamas kept on coming intermittently to Bhutan where they exercised both spiritual and temporal authority. These migrations were decisive in the conversion of the local people to Buddhism. Since that period, Tibet has remained a sacred land for most Bhutanese.

However, the most significant interaction between Tibet and Bhutan dates back to the arrival in Bhutan in 1616 of Zhabdrung Ngawang Namgyal, the prince-abbot of Ralung monastery. At that time, Bhutan had already social, economic and religious structures imported from Tibet. Trade had helped organize relations between different valleys as shown by iron-chain suspension bridges built by Thangtong Gyalpo, a famous Tibetan saint, who visited Bhutan during the 15th century.

At that time Bhutan was not a unified country. Ngawang Namgyal, a refugee forced out from Tibet by the Tsangpa and Gelugpa rulers of Tibet, unified Bhutan. He secured his control over the western region and extended his power eastward. He successfully contended with local rulers, rival lamas and Tibetan troops that unsuccessfully kept on invading the Southern Valleys in the mid 17th century. Among his major achievements was the building of *dzong*, the fortified monasteries strategically located in the main valleys that serve both as centres of local government and administration and as state monasteries even today.

Despite the changes that occurred after the establishment of the Zhabdrung system, warfare remained the normal condition between Bhutan and Tibet during the 17th and 18th centuries. The Gelugpa (yellow-hat)-dominated political system in Tibet intended to establish its authority over the entire Buddhist world in the Himalayas, while Drukpa (red-hat) Bhutan sought to resist.

In 1731 the Tibetan ruler Polhane took the opportunity of Bhutan's internal turmoil to impose suzerainty on the Southern Valleys. Although Tibet occasionally claimed a legitimate right to interfere in local politics, there is no evidence of Tibet ever having practically implemented its rule in Bhutan.

The advent of the British East India Company on Bhutan's southern borders in the mid-18th century created a new situation. Bhutan and Tibet had similar concern that led to some degree of co-operation. After its defeat in the Anglo-Bhutan war over Kuch Bihar (1772-1773), Bhutan was forced to arrange the first British mission into Tibet.

Thanks to Bhutanese authorities, Lt. George Bogle, who led the mission, visited the Panchen Lama in Shigatse. Bhutan was clearly perceived by the British as a trade and political channel to Tibet. From the advent of the monarchy in Bhutan in 1907 and the signing of Punakha Treaty in 1910, under which the Kingdom accepted British guidance of its foreign relations, to the independence of India in 1947, relations between Bhutan and Tibet continued, but under British influence both in Lhasa and Punakha.

It is clear from the above that Bhutan had a close, although often conflicting, relation with Tibet, including in the political field. Yet, these relations were mainly of cultural and religious nature. Tibet's rulers certainly considered Bhutan as a vassal. Occasionally, Bhutan even pretended to accept that situation in order to play down British influence. In 1946 for instance, the King of Bhutan wrote to the Viceroy and Governor General of India that Bhutan was very close to Tibet and that it had "acknowledged Tibetan sovereignty" up to 1860. Some evidence could confirm such an interpretation.

An annual payment to Tibet was due in recognition of its alleged suzerainty over Bhutan, and a Bhutanese representative was posted in Lhasa up to 1959 as part of a tributary relation. However the traditional Tibet-Bhutan relationship should not be interpreted in terms of "a superior/inferior syndrome, supposedly involving some form of Bhutanese vassalage to Tibet. The political elite of Bhutan may have been largely Tibetan in origin, but all of their ancestors came to Bhutan as political refugees and not as feudatories. Tibetan migration to Bhutan did not constitute colonization nor did it constitute an extension of Tibetan political authority into new lands in south of the Himalayan range". While the formal political relationship between the two countries can be described as independent, their religious and cultural relationship is more ambiguous. They both had theocratic political systems, the coexistence of which was misleading. Yet the situation was quite clear. "As the most prestigious of Buddhist reincarnates, the Dalai Lama received the greatest degree of respect and deference, but the gifts made to him by the Zhabdrung were not tributes. The most conclusive evidence of the limitations of Tibetan government influence in Bhutan is that no monastic institutions of the Dalai Lama's Gelugpa sect were ever allowed in Bhutan. Somewhat more complicated were the relations between the dominant Drukpa sect in Bhutan and its mother monastery in Tibet – Ralung. There was an implicit superior/inferior status in their traditional relation, but because the Drukpa sect was a subordinate sect in a Gelugpa-dominated political system in Tibet, this situation never created any political tutelage over Bhutan".

DPT AND INDO-BHUTAN RELATIONS

DPT's foreign policy direction hinged consistently on the unquestionable and inextinguishable reality that India would always be the cornerstone of Bhutan's foreign policy matrix. The DPT government, therefore, did everything possible to expand, deepen, elevate and secure Bhutan-India relations in the past five years. This was evident from the fact that Jigmi Y Thinley visited India nine times in five years, more than any other Bhutanese leader before him, with the exception of Their Majesties. In fact, Jigmi Y Thinley's first overseas visit as prime minister of democratic Bhutan was to India, barely a month after assuming office. His last official overseas visit, when leaving office, was also to India, in February 2013.

Jigmi Y Thinley interacted with Indian leaders at all levels from a wide social and political spectrum during his tenure as prime minister. His visit to Bihar resulted in the granting of two acres of land by the Bihar government to Bhutan at Rajghir, Bodhgaya, to build a Bhutanese temple and guesthouse. He also met the chief minister of Andhra Pradesh, and was in Madhya Pradesh in the capacity of chief guest at a Buddhist University. He hosted the chief minister of Assam in Bhutan and met Mamata Banerjee, the West Bengal chief minister. Further, he was invited by the government of India to deliver the prestigious Hiren Mukherjee memorial address to the Lok Sabha. He was also the keynote speaker at PAN IIT congress of the prestigious IIT, besides meeting Indian corporate leaders twice in Mumbai and Kolkata. Similarly, other Bhutanese cabinet ministers met Indian leaders, including the prime minister, in India, as well as at every international fora outside of India.

The visit of Indian leaders to Bhutan was also unprecedented during the tenure of the DPT government. The Indian prime minister, Dr Manmohan Singh, came to Bhutan twice, first on a state visit and second for the 16th SAARC summit hosted for the first time in Bhutan. The opposition leader, Susma Swaraj, also visited Bhutan, besides parliamentarians and leaders from all political walks.

It looks highly implausible that, after such intense and friendly interactions between the two governments and nation states in the past five years, that India should harbour any doubt and suspicion at all of the royal government's commitment to Bhutan-India relations. If it is indeed true that India is still offended by the routine, harmless and friendly overture extended by Bhutan under the DPT government to China, as it did to so many other countries and heads of government at the Rio Earth summit, and is choosing to implicate DPT (and consequently Bhutan) with culpability at such a crucial point in the elections, I must confess that I am totally baffled and confounded.

DALAI LAMA VISIT IGNITES SINO-INDIAN BORDER DISPUTE

In early November, the Dalai Lama is going to visit the majestic Tawang Monastery, perched atop a ridge in the Indian province of Arunachal Pradesh. Surrounded by thick clouds and perennial mist, the monastery sometimes seems almost to be suspended from heaven. It is also at the very centre of thousands of square kilometres of terrain claimed by both China and India, although India currently possesses it. It now risks becoming a proxy battleground on which both India and China seek to proclaim their sovereignty. The religious leader's visit can be seen as a card played by both India and the Tibetan exile community to keep pressure on China.

Home to one of the most sacred Buddhist monasteries, Tawang is the birthplace of the sixth Dalai Lama, Tsayang Gyatso, in the 17th century. The current Dalai Lama passed through this region when he fled into exile in 1959. Chhime Chhoekyapa, the exiled Tibetan spiritual leader's aide, told the media that the Dalai Lama is "going there for teaching.

This has nothing to do with politics, there is nothing political about it." In Chinese eyes, however, and perhaps Indian eyes as well, everything the Dalai Lama does has something to do with politics. And this is a region that Beijing calls "Southern Tibet."

When asked about the Dalai Lama's upcoming visit, Beijing officials have fumed. "China expresses strong concern about this information," said Jiang Yu, the spokeswoman for China's Foreign Ministry. "The visit further reveals the Dalai clique's anti-China and separatist essence. China's stance on the so-called Arunachal Pradesh is consistent. We firmly oppose Dalai visiting the so-called Arunachal Pradesh." Tension has slowly been ratcheting up between the two Asian giants, with media commentators fanning the flames. "Is China itching to wage war on India?" asked Professor Brahma Chellaney in the September issue of the Far Eastern Economic Review. Reports have appeared in Chinese state media alleging that India was moving troops and fighter aircraft to the northeast, specifically into Sikkim and Arunachal Pradesh.

India, however, is acutely aware of its shortcomings in the territory it controls. The Chinese, with their extensive roads and railways, can actually come up to the Line of Actual Control, take a stroll and walk back. Two years ago, Chinese soldiers demolished a Buddhist statue that Indians had erected at Bumla, the main border pass above Tawang, according to a member of the Indian Parliament, Nabam Rebia. It takes several days for India's troops to get to the border. But slowly India is finding its voice as it struggles to speed up its own preparedness.

China claims around 90,000 square kilometres of territory, roughly the size of Arunachal Pradesh, regarding the area as "disputed." China lays claim to Tawang on behalf of the Tibetans. But in the exile community in Dharamsala, where the Dalai Lama and thousands of Tibetan refugees live, the community is not impressed. They do not claim Tawang as Tibetan, let alone Chinese territory. The Dalai Lama's travel plans were announced a week after his recent visit to Taiwan to visit victims of tropical storm Morakot. China denounced the Taiwan trip, although its complaints were remarkably muted. The visit to Arunachal Pradesh has now drawn further attention to China's treatment of Tibetan activists and the Dalai Lama's calls for cultural and religious freedom and autonomy.

Tawang became part of modern India when Tibetan leaders signed a treaty with British officials in 1914 that established the McMahon Line between Tibet and British-run India. Tawang fell south of the line. The treaty, the Simla Convention, is not recognized by China. "We recognize it because we agreed to it," said Samdhong Rinpoche, prime minister of the Tibetan government-in-exile. "If China agreed to it now, it would be a recognition of the power of the Tibetan government at that time."

Tawang's native population is almost entirely Buddhist. Its origin is obscure. It was a part of the kingdom of Tibet in medieval times although local tribal rulers have governed it from time to time. The British declared the area off-limits in 1873. India's independence from Britain severed it from Tibet. In 1962 Chinese troops conquered Tawang during the invasion of Tibet and for six months it was controlled by the Chinese. After their retreat, Tawang again came under Indian control.

India denied the Dalai Lama permission to visit Tawang the last time he requested to do so. This time it is playing the Dalai Lama card to the full. Officials in India's Ministry of External Affairs insist that "things are changing" and that India is getting more assertive. On Sept. 16, India's foreign minister, S.M. Krishna, rejected China's opposition to the visit.

In an interview on IBN7, the sister channel of India's CNN-IBN, Krishna said China's objections had no merit. While the government has not explicitly said the visit will be permitted, Krishna said: "Arunachal Pradesh is a part of India and the Dalai Lama is free to go anywhere in India. The only question is that he is not expected to comment on political developments." Analysts say the Tibetan leader's visit will reassert Arunachal's status as an Indian territory. "The timing of his trip [to Arunachal Pradesh] is significant. It comes while the debate over his visit to Taiwan is still hot," said Bhaskar Roy, a New Delhi-based China analyst. "Tibetans are as good at playing these games as the Chinese. They know such a visit will keep up the pressure on China."

In Dharamsala, Samdhong Rinpoche, Tibet's prime minister in exile, called Beijing's objections to the visit "absurd," adding that "Arunachal Pradesh and the Tawang region are an integral part of India. If the Dalai Lama, who has stayed in India for the last 50 years, is visiting any part of the country why does this bother China? If the Dalai Lama goes to Chinese territories it can raise objections but in this case has no business to interfere." The Arunachal Pradesh government is urging New Delhi to ignore the Chinese opposition. "Chinese claims over Arunachal Pradesh are simply baseless and not correct. Arunachal Pradesh is an integral part of India and would continue to be so," said Chief Minister Dorjee Khandu. "They [the Chinese] are opposed to everything that His Holiness does," said a spokesman for the Dalai Lama's private office in Dharamsala.

Tawang's strategic importance cannot be ruled out. The place provides the shortest route from Tibet into India. The Dalai Lama himself took this route to escape into India in 1959. Indian defence officials have already raised alarms declaring China and not Pakistan to be India's biggest threat.

They believe that control over Sikkim and Arunachal Pradesh would enable Chinese forces to overrun the entire northeast border region. Chinese troops repeatedly have attempted to gain control of Sikkim's evocatively named Finger Area, a tiny but key strategic location where Beijing does not dispute the frontier.

In June this year, General J J Singh, governor of Arunachal Pradesh and former chief of army staff, announced the deployment of two army divisions of around 25,000 to 30,000 soldiers each along the Arunachal Pradesh border with China.

The strength of India's Sukhoi fighter jet fleet in the Northeast is being increased. It remains to be seen if the Dalai Lama's visit will be the trigger that causes them to be used.

DOKLAM DEADLOCK: INDIA AND CHINA WILL CONSTANTLY CHALLENGE EACH OTHER, GET USED TO IT

The ongoing standoff between India and China in the Doklam area in Bhutan is the result of a disagreement over the terms of the 1890 convention relating to Sikkim and Tibet (pdf), signed by the colonial British government in India and the Qing empire in China.

Contrary to the Chinese stress today on "Mount Gipmochi on the Bhutan frontier" (Article I) as the beginning of the boundary between Tibet and Sikkim, India has pointed out that the specific trijunction point should be that point which adheres to the watershed as indicated in the same Article I of the Convention.

Under the 2005 Agreement between India and China, the two countries agreed that "the delineation of the boundary will be carried out utilising means such as modern cartographic and surveying practices and joint surveys" (Article VIII) and that "(p)ending an ultimate settlement ... the two sides should ... work together to maintain peace and tranquility in the border areas" (Article IX).

This clarifies several dimensions of this issue. Mt Gipmochi cannot be taken as the final trijunction point since the Indians and Bhutanese believe that the trijunction point, according to the watershed, lies further north at Batang La, and, therefore, this dispute will have to be settled through modern cartographic methods. This dispute will have to be settled through modern cartographic methods.

Secondly, the Chinese must be aware that their road-building through disputed territory threatened Indian security and thereby also violated the 2005 and earlier bilateral agreements to maintain peace and tranquillity in the India-China border areas.

Disputed territory between China and Bhutan surely has implications for the border areas of India and China. Also, the Chinese action violates a similar injunction in their agreements of 1988 and 1998 with the Bhutanese themselves, as per the June 29 official statement by Bhutan's ministry of foreign affairs.

Next, if the Sikkim-Tibet boundary was as settled as the Chinese claim it to be, then there should have been no reason for several clashes between the Indian and Chinese armies over the decades along the Sikkim-Tibet border, including the major confrontation in 1967. While there is agreement on the broad principle of the watershed as the basis of alignment of the boundary between between India and China, there are clearly differences on the alignment itself. Further, the Chinese action, and subsequent claims about Mt Gimpochi as the settled trijunction, run contrary to the 2012 understanding reached between then special representatives Shivshankar Menon on the Indian side and Dai Bingguo on the Chinese side "that tri-junctions will be finalised in consultation with the third country concerned." This understanding was part of a kind of progress report on the negotiations thus far between the two sides on the eve of Dai's retirement from his post of Special Representative, as revealed by Menon.

So what impact will the present situation in Doklam have on India-China relations? One border incident does not constitute the full picture of the bilateral relationship. And this is a relationship that is today increasingly multidimensional, going beyond the boundary dispute to ever-increasing economic exchanges, including between the states in India and provinces in China as well as regional and global cooperation on issues of mutual interest such as anti-piracy or climate change.

Indian observers should also look at the whole gamut of China's external preoccupations in the weeks of June and July. The Bhutan standoff is just one of the many security and foreign policy issues that preoccupied China: Xi Jinping's visit to Russia, his participation in the G-20 summit, and Chinese concerns over the US's THAAD anti-ballistic missile defense system in South Korea all took up attention. The point here is that for Indian observers to maintain a granular focus on what China says about India without paying attention to the overall context does not help reveal the true picture about China's actions or intentions.

Meanwhile, for those alarmed by the travel advisory that China put out for its citizens to be cautious while in India, this is part of standard Chinese practice and not nearly as strong as it could have been, or is with respect to the several Chinese travel advisories on Pakistan. Contrary to their own advisories, there have been continuing visits of Chinese political leaders to India. For instance, leaders from both Guizhou and Guangxi provinces were in India in late June and earlier in July, respectively, an important sign of the health of any bilateral relationship.

While the official Chinese rhetoric is cooling down, the cold vibes remaining will not evaporate easily. This is in the nature of international relations—India and China will constantly challenge each other as a way to validate their importance in their neighbourhood and in the global order.

In the meantime, it is important that both sides resist the temptation to take their cues from the current heated rhetoric in the media. The Indian side, especially, must desist from jeremiads based on the columns in English in China's Global Times. Any pullback of troops on both sides in the Doklam area is unlikely.

As for the military intrusion: Any pullback of troops on both sides in the Doklam area is unlikely, or, if it happens at all, will be temporary at best. In fact, it is more than likely that the Chinese will continue with their assertiveness in the India-China border areas at some later date, possibly right after the September 2017 BRICS summit in China, which the Chinese will want Indian prime minister Narendra Modi to attend and ensure that it is a success.

This will happen despite China entering a very sensitive period domestically, with the Communist Party's 19th Congress scheduled for sometime in October or November. The Congress is expected to confirm Xi Jinping for a second five-year term as general secretary, and see a large turnover of leaders at the highest echelons.

There is, in fact, precedent for such Chinese action. It was practically on the eve of the 18th party congress in 2012 that the Sino-Japanese spat over the Senkakus escalated with anti-Japanese violence in China—including protests in front of the Japanese embassy—and frequent intrusions into the waters of the Senkakus by Chinese civilian fishing vessels, with the latter continuing through the Congress.

It should not surprise Indian defense planners if the Chinese test and prod the Indian military by opening up road-building, patrolling, and other forms of activity in areas along the disputed boundary that have hitherto remained dormant or not seen any such activity at all. The most likely venue for such increased activity will be the Eastern Sector—given India's greater difficulties of access and in maintaining logistics supplies there.

Bibliography

Acharya Sanjay : *Bhutan: Kingdom in the Himalayas,* Lustre Press/Roli books, New-Delhi, 1999.

Ajey Lele: *Strategic Technologies for the Military : Breaking New Frontiers*, Sage, Delhi, 2009.

Allen Carlson, *Unifying China, Integrating with the World: Securing Chinese Sovereignty in the Reform Era,* Stanford: Stanford University Press, 2005.

Amitabh Sikdar: *India and China : Strategic Energy Management and Security*, Manas, Delhi, 2009.

Anderson, J.: *Transnational Democracy: Political Spaces and Border Crossings*, Routledge: London and New York, 2002.

Anderson, M. and Bort, E.: *Boundaries and Identities: The Eastern Frontier of the Asia*, Edinburgh: International Social Sciences Institute, University of Edinburgh, 1996.

Anil, K.C.: *Military and Democracy in South Asia : Challenges, Politics and Power*, Sumit Enterprises, Delhi, 2009.

Asha Gupta: *Military Rule and Democratization : Changing Perspectives*, Deep & Deep, Delhi, 2003.

Barbara, Adams : *Traditional Textiles of Bhutan*, White Orchid, Bangkok, 1984.

Bhat, T.P. : *Bhutan and China : Trade Complementarities and Competitiveness*, Bookwell, Delhi, 2008.

Blanche, Christin : *The Dragon Kingdom: Images of Bhutan*, Boston: Shambhala, 1988.

Cheek, Timothy: *Mao Zedong and China's Revolutions: A Brief History with Documents.* Boston: Bedford/St. Martin's, 2002.

Christian Schicklgruber : *Bhutan: Mountain Fortress of the Gods,* Serindia, London, 1997.

Coakley, J.: *The Territorial Management of Ethnic Conflict*, London: Frank Cass, 2003.

Conway, G. 1992. *Sustainable Rural Livelihoods: Practical Concepts for 21st Century.* Sussex: Institute of Development Studies.

David W., : *Buddhist and Taoist Practice in Medieval Chinese Society,* Honolulu, HI: University of Hawaii Press, 1987.

Debray, Regis. *Revolution in the Revolution*. New York: Grove Press, Inc., 1993.

Deepak, B R : *India and China : 1904-2004 : A Century of Peace and Conflict*, Manak, Delhi, 2005.

Digumarti Bhaskara Rao: *Military Conversion : Impact on Science and Technology*, Discovery, Delhi, 2003.

Dixit, A.K. : *Military Wars and Rescue Techniques*, Cyber Tech Pub, Delhi, 2010.

Donnan, H. and Wilson, T. M.: *Borders: Frontiers of Identity, Nation and State*, Oxford: Berg, 1999.

Dorji, Rigzin : *Forms of Address in Bhutan*, New Delhi: Royal Bhutan Mission, 1976.

Erik H.: *Gandhi's Truth: On the Origins of Militant Nonviolence*, W. W. Norton, New York, 1969.

Evelyn Goh, *Meeting the China Challenge: The U.S. in Southeast Asian Regional Security Strategies*, DC: East-West Center, 2005.

Faure, Bernard : *The Will to Orthodoxy: A Critical Genealogy of Northern Chan Buddhism*, Stanford, CA: Stanford University Press, 1997.

Gandhi, Sita : *In the Shadow of Mahatma : A Grand-Daughter Remembers*, New Delhi, Sampark, 2005.

Gao, Mobo: *The Battle for China's Past: Mao and the Cultural Revolution*, London, Pluto Press, 2008.

Gaur, Mahendra : *Indian Policy of Neighbour*, Delhi, Kalpaz Pub., 2006.

George Mathew: *Grass Roots Democracy in India and China : The Right to Participate*, Sage, Delhi, 2007.

Gupta, Asha: *Military Rule and Democratization : Changing Perspectives*, Deep & Deep, Delhi, 2003.

Heimanson, Rudolph: *Dictionary of Military*, N.Y.: Oceana Publications, 1967.

Huntington, S.P.: *The China Modernisation Military and the State*, N.Y., Vintage Books, 1964.

Ian Storey: *ASEAN and the South China Sea: Movement in Lieu of Progress*, Washington, D.C., Jamestown Foundation,2012.

Ikram, S. M.: *Indian Muslims and Partition of India*. Delhi: Atlantic, 1995.

Imtiaz, A.: *State and Foreign Policy: India's Role in South Asia*, New Delhi, Vikas, 1993.

Jagannath P. Panda: *China's Path to Power : Party, Military and the Politics of State Transition*, Pentagon, Delhi, 2010.

James R Blaker: *Transforming Military Force : The Legacy of Arthur Cebrowski and Network Centric Warfare*, Pentagon Press, Delhi, 2008.

John McRae: *The Northern School and the Formation of Early Ch'an Buddhism*, Honolulu, HI: University of Hawaii Press, 1984.

Jones, W.H.: *Politics of Military*, London, Hutchinson, 1971.

Juvale, R.P. : *Military Strategy and Diplomacy*, Cyber Tech Publications, Delhi, 2010.

Kansakar, V. B. S.: *"International Migration and Citizenship in Nepal"*. Kathmandu: Central Bureau of Statistics/UNFPA, 2003.

Kant, Adhikari, Krishna . *Nepal under Jang Bahadur, 1846-1877*. Kathmandu: Buku, 1984.

Kapur, C.K. : *Bhutanese Military Modernisation*, Manas, Delhi, 2003.

Keane J.: *Democracy and Civil Liberty*, London, Verso, 1988.

Kudaisya, Gyanesh: *The Aftermath of Partition in South Asia*. London: Routledge, 2000.

Kumar, Satish. *Rana Polity in Nepal: Origin and Growth*. New York: Asia, 1967.

Kunju, N. : *Indo-Pak : Nuclear Cold War*, Reliance, Delhi, 2002.

Lamrimpa, Gen : *Realizing Emptiness: Madhyamaka Insight Meditation*, Ithaca, NY: Snow Lion, 2002.

Lohia, Ram Manohar: *Guilty Men of India's Partition*. Allahabad: Navahind, 1960.

Major Donovan: *Air Defence Power*. Sampson Low. London, 1940.

Marie Lecomte : *Hindu Kingship, Ethnic Revival, and Maoist Rebellion in Nepal*, Oxford University Press, Delhi, 2009.

Menon, Manju and Kanchi Kohli: *Large Dams for Hydropower in Northeast India*. Delhi: Kalpavriksh, 2005.

Misra, H.N. : *Bhutan: Problems and Policies*, New Delhi: Heritage, 1988.

Namgyal Takpo : *Mahamudra: The Quintessence of Mind and Meditation*, Boston, MA: Shambhala, 1986.

Narendra K Dash : *Buddhism in Indian Literature*, Aryan Books International, 2007.

Nayyar, K K : *National Security : Military Aspects*, Rupa, Delhi, 2003.

Nevile, P.: *Lahore: A Sentimental Journey*. New Delhi: Penguin, 1993.

Nishioka Keiji : *Flowers of Bhutan*, Asahi Shimbum, Tokyo, 1984.

Olschak Blanche : *Ancient Bhutan: a Study on Early Buddhism in the Himalayas*, Swiss Foundation for Alpine Research 1979.

Parmanand. *The Nepali Congress since Its Inception: A Critical Assessment*. Delhi: B.R. Publishing, 1982.

Pemble, John. *The Invasion of Nepal: John Company at War*. Oxford: Oxford University Press, 1971.

Phuskele, Preeti : *India and China : Emerging Superpowers*, ICFAI University, Delhi, 2009.

Pommaret Francoise : *Tibetian Mountain Fortress of the Gods*, Serindia, London, 1997.

Posen, B.R.: *The Sources of Military Doctrine*, Ithaca, 1984, Cornell Univ. Press.

Prabir De: *India and China in an Era of Globalisation : Essays on Economic Cooperation*, Bookwell, Delhi, 2005.

Radhakrishna: *Military Ethics: Guidelines for Peace and War*, Sumit Enterprises, Delhi, 2009.

Rao Y Sudershan : *Buddhism and Modern Society*, Deep and Deep, Delhi, 2008.

Raza, Hashim S.: *Mountbatten and the Partition of India*. New Delhi: Atlantic, 1989.

Robert M Cassidy: *Counterinsurgency and the Global War on Terror : Military Culture and Irregular War*, Pentagon Press, Delhi, 2008.

Salim, Ahmad: *Lahore 1947*. New Delhi: India Research Press, 2001.

Samuel P. Huntington: *The Soldier and the State : The Theory and Politics of Civil-Military Relations*, Natraj Pub, Delhi, 2005.

Seshagiri, K. L. : *Mahatma Gandhi and Comparative Religion*, Motilal Banarsidass, New Delhi, 1978.

Sharma, P. 1989. *Urbanization in Nepal*. Hawaii: East-West Population Institute.

Simon, D. : *Public Administration and Policy of Indian Military*, New York, Knopf, 1950.

Singh, S: Taming *the Water: The Political Economy of Large Dams in India,* Delhi: Oxford University Press, 1997.

Snodgrass, Adrian : *The Symbolism of the Stupa,* Ithaca, NY: Southeast Asia Program, Cornell University, 1985.

Som, A.: *Lahore: Portrait of a Lost City*. Lahore: Vanguard Books, 1998.

Spector, Leonard S., *Going Nuclear*, Cambridge, MA: Ballinger Publishing Company, 1987.

Stuart R. Schram: *The Political Thought of Mao Tse-Tung*. New York: Praeger, 1969.

Suman Chaterjee : *Buddhism : The Way to Wisdom*, Cyber Tech Pub, Delhi, 2009.

Thampi, Madhavi : *India and China in the Colonial World*, Social Science Press, Delhi, 2010.

Theodore, William : T*he Buddhist Tradition in India, China and Japan,* New York: Vintage Books, 1972.

Tse-tung Mao: *Mao and the Nepali Revolution*. London: Oxford University Press, 1965.

Uddhab P : *Maoist Movement in Nepal: A Sociological Perspective*, Adroit, Delhi, 2007.

Upreti, B C : *Maoists in Nepal : From Insurgency to Political Mainstream*, Kalpaz Pub, Delhi, 2008.

Vas, E.A. : *The Dragon Kingdom: Journeys Through Bhutan*, New Delhi: Lancer International, 1986.

Verma, Ravi : *India's Role in the Emergence of Contemporary Bhutan*. Delhi: Capital, 1988.

Wakamiya Yoshibumi, *The Postwar Conservative View of Asia,* Tokyo: LTCB International Library Foundation, 1999.

Wapner, Paul : *Environmental Activism and World Civic Politics,* Albany, SUNY Press, 1996.

Weinstein, Stanley : *Buddhism under the T'ang,* Cambridge, UK: Cambridge University Press, 1987.

Wolpert, Stanley: *Shameful Flight: The Last Years of the British Empire in India*. Oxford and New York: Oxford University Press, 2006.

Wright, Arthur : *Studies in Chinese Buddhism,* New Haven, CT: Yale University Press, 1990.

Zaman, M.: *Students' Role in the Pakistan Movement*. Karachi, Quaid-iAzam Academy, 1978.

Zimmermann, Michael : *Buddhism and Violence,* Lumbini International Research Institute, 2006.

Index

I

M

N

P

S

T

❑❑❑